DIPLOMA IN F&B SERVICE, THE COMPLETE SYLLABUS

DR ANSHUMALI PANDEY

ISBN 979-888546154-2

"I dedicate my book to all the under privileged children who could not get better education due to lack of timely resources."

Contents

Contents

Foreword

Irrespective of whether you get a formal college education or not, books consisting of all the basic elements of Food and Beverage Service are always a great help in establishing and running a commercial food outlet.

The scale of investment and type of outlet may vary but the fundamentals of F&B Service and Management are always based on Hygiene, Nutrition, Food Cost, Customer satisfaction, and Honesty. These fundamentals do not change for a sustainable food business, or any business for that matter.

This book "Diploma in F&B Service, The Complete Syllabus" is written with an aim to help the Students, the Teachers, and all those would be chefs and managers who could not get a formal education in the field of Commercial Food, Service and Catering.

The Complete Syllabus indicates the Theory component of the Diploma in F&B Service course as prescribed in the syllabus of various AICTE, UGC approved Government Universities and the National Council for Hotel Management & Catering Technology.

There is always scope for further reading and the limit is endless. However in my experience if the readers could follow the concepts from this book and focus on more and more practical training and practice, it will give them an edge and will save time.

Best wishes...

Dr. Anshumali Pandey

Part A: FOOD SERVICE

"Food Service"

CHAPTER ONE

UNIT 1: Hospitality Industry and the Waiter

"A hotel is defined as a place where a valid traveller can receive food and shelter, provided he is in a position to pay for it, and is in a fit condition to be received."

Introduction:

India, a vast country, which has very good potential for the development of Food & Beverage service Industry. The number of people availing the services of food & beverage industry is steadily increasing due to their increased disposable income. Eating out in future will not be a luxury but an essential activity. The food & beverage service industry is different from other industries in satisfying the needs of customers. It satisfies one of the most important physiological needs of the consumer, that is, of hunger and thirst. From last decade food & beverage Industry is expanding very fast.

The F & B department is the send major revenue producing department of the hotel. The Activities of this department are highly complex, demanding varied skills level to perform the job. Waiting at table involves close contact with customers and their food and means that waiters are under constant observation. Food is not appetizing if served by a person who is slovenly and unclean. Uniforms must be clean and well-ironed. A well-trained, smart and helpful staff can sometimes make up for aspects which are lacking elsewhere in the operation. Food & beverage service staff must see that the guest have everything they require and are completely satisfied. It is of great importance to anticipate customers need. Establishment's success depends on effective Co-ordination of all staff; a waiter should aim to help his fellow worker. A co-operative waiter cultivates his ability to get on well with customers and colleagues alike and to further the policies of the Management.

1. History of catering

The food and beverage service industry in India traces its roots to the traditional community feasts and the movement of people on Pilgrimage thousands of years ago. Most people were on the move primarily for preaching religion and hunting. People took shelter under trees when they were away from their homes and depended on natural sources for their food. Their lives were endangered by wild animals and wayside robbers, which forced them to look for a place that assured them safety, accommodation and food. Dharamshalas and Chatrams came up to protect the lives of travellers from wild animals and robbers. These were buildings where travellers could stay free of cost. The travellers were also provided stables and sheds for horses and bullock carts, respectively, free of charge. They were given food and accommodation at no cost during the rule of kings. Kings entertained common people and merchants with feasts consisting of a variety of rich dishes, traditional dances, bravery arts, etc, during festivals.

The outsiders who came to India during the course of its history include the Greeks under Alexander the great, the Kushanas from Central Asia, the Mongols under Genghis Khan, Muslim traders and invaders from the Middle East and Central Asia, and finally the British and other Europeans. It was during the Mughal rule that Sarais were developed to provide accommodation to travellers which were later converted to inns and western style hotels during the British rule. The invasion by other dynasties brought in their cultures and cuisines to the land.

Europeans visited the country to trade for the finest cotton textiles as well as spices. Eventually the British colonized the region. They introduced their cuisines, the skills of making wines and distilled drinks and eating habits. Table etiquettes and the art of eating with continue to eat with. However, even today, people continue to eat with their fingers. In Tamil Nadu, people eat their meals from banana leaves and in the north, from a thali. Economic activities Paved the way for development of western-style hotels and restaurants, mainly to cater to the requirements of the British & European traders.

The development of catering in India is mainly attributed to the British, who introduced hotels and restaurants similar to the ones in Europe. The rapid development of transportation, especially the railways in the mid-nineteenth century, enabled people to move in large numbers. This led to the establishment of small lodges and restaurants in and around railway stations to cater to the needs of the travellers. Refreshment rooms at railway stations and Pantry cars in some of the trains were introduced. Reputed hotels such as Taj, The Oberoi and the ambassador were well established when India became independent.

After independence, the hospitality industry grew at a faster rate. Civil aviation developed rapidly soon after the Second World War. The introduction of international flight services in the year 1948 and additional services in the mid-1950s encouraged a lot of foreigners to visit India and also many international chains of hotel such as the Holiday Inn, the Sheraton, and the intercontinental and so on, started their operations in India. The Oberoi group establishment the first franchised hotel with the Inter continental hotels in Delhi in the early 1960s. The people of India, in general did not Prefer dining out till the early 1960s. They always carried with them home made food to the workplace, school a while travelling.

Even today, some people carry food whenever they go out. Perhaps this could be one of the reason for dabbawalas, who are food vendors engaged in distributing meals in dabbas (Boxes) to clients at their workplaces, doing so well in Mumbai. In South India, people used to packed food such as lime rice, tamrind rice and curd rice from vendors. In the north, bhojanalayas served local dishes, especially roti, sabji and salad. Indian Tourism development corporation (ITDC) was set up in 1966 with the developing & expanding tourism infrastructure in the country and thereby promoting India as a tourist destination. ITDC succeeded in achieving its objectives by promoting the largest hotel chain in India and providing all tourist services such as accommodation, catering, transport, in house travel agency and so on. For development of manpower to meet the growing needs of hotels, restaurants and other hospitality based industries.

For this purpose, Institute of Hotel Management (IHM) and Food craft Institute (FCI) were established. These programmes impart adequate knowledge and training in the core operational and managerial areas of the hospitality industry. This makes the students understand the environment and execute their job professionally. In 2002, Ministry of Tourism (MOT) launched a programme called **Capacity Building For service provider**

(CBSP) to train persons engaged in small hotels, dhabas, eating joints & and restaurants. Projects Priyadarshini was launched in 2005 to impart training to women in taxi driving/operation, entrepreneurship such as setting up souvenir kiosks and so on, to adopt tourism as their profession. People of different region in India have different style of food like Hyderabadi Cuisine, Avadhi Cuisine, Goan Cuisine, South Indian cuisine etc. A lot of foreign food service organization such as McDonald's, Pizza king, Dominos, subway and soon, have set up their operation in India, which has made local restaurant fine-tune their operations in order to compete with these outlets.

2. Catering establishments:

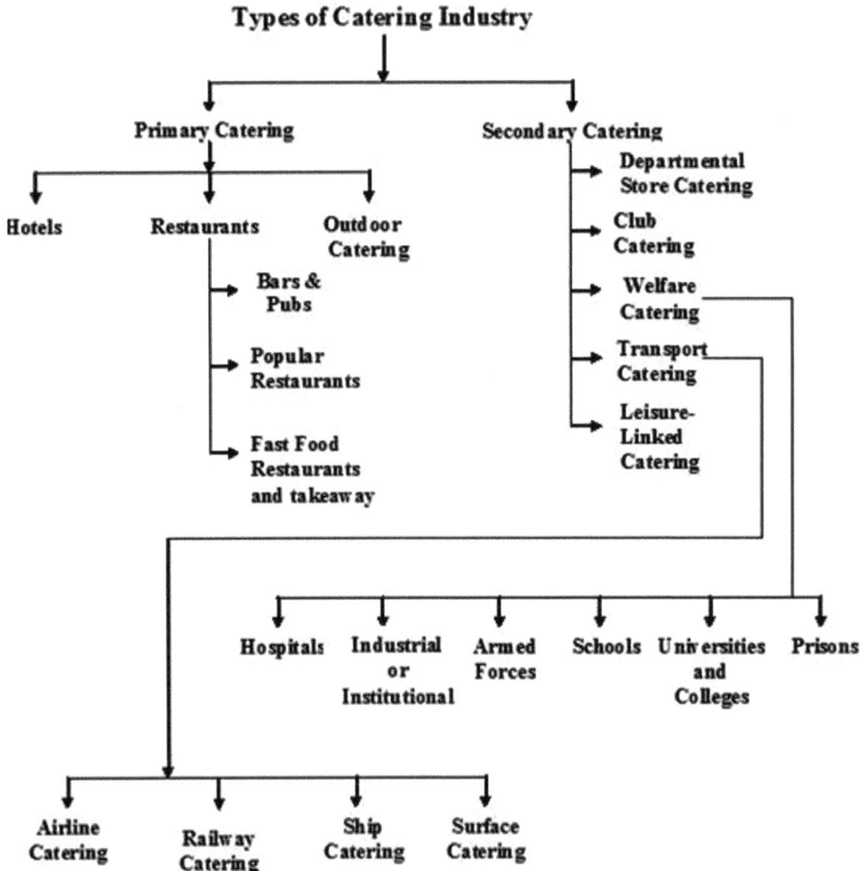

2.1 Primary Catering Establishments:

Establishments such as hotels, restaurants and fast food outlets which are primarily concerned with the provision of food and beverage are called primary catering establishments.

2.1.1 Hotels: The main purpose of hotels is to provide accommodation, which may or may not include the service of food & beverage. A hotel may be a small family-run unit providing a limited service in one restaurant, or a large luxury hotel providing service through a number of outlets such as the coffee shop, room service, banquets, specialty restaurant, grill room and cocktail bars. The service in these types of hotels is usually personalized and the tariff is very high, as they generally cater to persons of a high social standing. Medium class hotels are similar to luxury hotels, through their surroundings are less luxurious category. The prices in the various categories of hotels often depend upon the service and choice of food and beverage that they offer to their clientele.

2.1.2 Restaurant: The primary function of commercial restaurant is the provision of food & beverage. Restaurants are of different standards. The food service and prices are often comparable to those of similar restaurants in luxury hotels. They offer a wide choice for an elaborate menu and a very high quality of service.

2.1.3 Bar and Pubs: The bar serves different types of alcoholic beverages to residential and non-residential guest in the hotel. The idea of pubs is fairly new in India. It has been borrowed from the concept of public houses in English and adapted to Indian conditions. They are geared to provide service of all types of alcohol with an emphasis on draught beer and good music. Food may also be served from a limited menu.

2.1.4 Popular restaurants: The objectives of popular catering restaurants are to provide quick and economical meal, in a clean and standardized dining room. These restaurants are commonly used by the vast urban population of India. They are of various styles and categories. Some restaurants serve only vegetarian food while some specialize in the food of a particulars region such as the Punjab or Andhra. Some restaurants serve food from more than one region.

2.1.5 The entry of pizza parlours and westernized popular food into India provides the urban Indian a wider choice, in the types of popular restaurants to choose from. The numerous outlets that have sprung up all over the country in the last decade show a new trend in the urban citizen‘s eating habits. This has resulted in an increased awareness among the public about the availability of various types of cuisine and catering service.

2.1.6 Fast food restaurants & take away: There is a predominant American influence in fast food style of catering. The service of food and beverages in a fast food restaurant is at a faster pace, than at an a la carte restaurant as the menu is compiled with a special emphasis on the speed of preparation and service. To make this type of service financially viable, a large turnover of customers is necessary. The investment is rather large, due to the specialized and expensive equipment needed and high labour costs involved.

The take-away or take out service that exploits to the full the concept of —Fast Foods‖. The take away operation offers a limited basic menu to the customer, but within this menu there may be a number of variations on the basic items. The time between customer placing orders and receiving their meals, aims to be faster than any other method of food service. The customer may either take the food out of the take away to eat, or it may be consumed on the premises, a large number of —take-away‘outlets now provide seating areas.

2.1.7 Outdoor / Off-Premise Catering: This means catering to a large number of people at a venue of their choice. Hostels, restaurants and catering contractors meet this growing demand. The type of food and setup depends entirely on the price agreed upon. Outdoor catering includes catering for functions such as marriages, parties and conventions. Off-premise caterers meet the needs of all markets segments, from the low budget customer who looks for the most quantity and quality for the least amount of money, to the upscale client with an unlimited budget who wants the highest level of service, the ultimate in food quality, and the finest in appointments such as crystal stem ware, silver plated flatware and luxurious linens. Off-premise catering is an art and a science. The art is creating foods and moods, as the caterer and client together turn a vision into reality. The science is the business of measuring money, manpower and material.

2.2. Secondary Catering Establishments

In secondary catering industry, the provision of food and beverage is a part of another business such as **welfare catering** and transport catering. Catering establishments are usually classified on the basis of the demands being met by them. The main aim of any catering organization is to attract different sections of the public to use its facilities, keeping in view the price of food and service it offers in relation to the location of the property and the class of clientele it attracts.

2.2.1 Department store catering:-Some departmental stores, apart from carrying on their primary activity of retailing their own wares, provide catering as an additional facility. This type of catering evolved when large departmental stores wished to provide food and beverages to their customers as a part of their retailing concept. It is inconvenient and time consuming for customers to take a break from shopping, and have some refreshments at different location. Thus arose the need for some sort of a dining facility in the departmental store itself. This style of catering is becoming more popular and varied nowadays.

2.2.2 Club Catering: This refers to the provision of food and beverages and accommodation to a restricted clientele. The origin of this service can be traced back to England, where membership of a club was considered prestigious. Clubs for people with similar interest such as turf club, golf clubs and cricket clubs, to name a few, have sprung up. The service and food in these clubs tend to be of fairly good standards and are economically priced. Facilities provided by the club may include sports, both in-door and outdoor, libraries, swimming pools, social activities, social work, the pursuing a specific hobby etc.

2.2.3 Welfare catering: The provision of food and beverages to people to fulfill a social need, determined by a recognized authority, is known as welfare catering. This grew out of the welfare state concept, prevalent in western countries. It include catering in institute or industries, hospitals, schools, colleges, prisons and armed forces.

2.2.4 Hospital: Hospital catering facilities have improved considerably over the past years. Hospital catering is a specialized form of catering as the patient is normally unable to move elsewhere and choose alternative facilities and therefore special attention must be given to the food and beverage so that encouragement is given to eat the meal provided. The hospital meals may be considered for the patients, the staff and the general public & visitors. The type of diets required for hospital patients may be classified as full or normal diets, light diets, soft diets, therapeutic diets and special diets.

2.2.5 Industrial or institutional: The provision of food and beverage to people at work, in industries and factories at highly subsidized rates is called industrial or institutional catering. It is based on the assumption that **better**

fed employees are happy and more productive. Today, labour unions insist on provision of this facility to employees. Catering for a large workforce may be undertaken by the management itself, or may be contracted out to professional caterers. Depending on the choice of the menu suggested by the management, catering contractors undertake to feed the work force for a fixed period of time at a predetermined price.

2.2.6. Armed forces: Armed forces, Navy, Army and Air force, the police and fire service and some government departments. The armed forces often have their own specialist catering branches. The levels of food and beverage facilities within the services vary form the large self-service cafeterias for the majority of personnel, to high class traditional restaurants for more senior members of staff. A considerable number of functions are also held by the armed forces leading to both small and large scale banqueting arrangements.

2.2.7. Schools: The school meals catering service was formerly structured on a dietary basis with a daily or weekly per capita allowance to ensure that the children obtained edequate nutritional levels from their meals. The school meals service caters for staff and children; in primary schools, children‘s ages vary from approximately 5 to 11 years and may include some nursery children, and in secondary schools from 12 to 16 or 18 years, Most of the schools used to operate their dining rooms on a family type service or a self-service basis. Nutritional value is important for catering in schools.

2.2.8 Universities and colleges: All institutions of further and higher education provide some form of catering facilities for the academic, administrative, technical and secretarial staff as well as for full and part time students and visitors. The catering service in this sector of the industry suffers from an under-utilization of its facilities during the vacation periods and in many instances at the weekends. Universities and colleges are autonomous bodies and are responsible for their own catering services. Residential students pay in advance for their board and lodgings. Non-residential students are provided with an on-site catering provision that has to compete against all other forms of locally provided catering.

2.2.9 Prisons: Prisoners are to be catered in prisons. The catering within the prisons is the responsibility of the Jailer with delegated responsibility being given to a catering officer with much of the actual cooking and serving being done by the prisoners themselves. In Tihar Jail, Delhi more than 10,000 prisoners were catered daily three times a day in systematic manner.

2.2.10: Transport Catering:- It includes that sector of food and beverage establishment which makes provision of food and beverage of people who are on the move. The provision of food and beverage to passengers, before, during and after a journey on trains, aircrafts, ships and in buses or private vehicles is termed as transport catering. It involves the feeding of a large at a catering facility and who need to be catered for in a specific time, for example, on board a plane.

2.2.11: Airline Catering: - Catering to airlines passengers on flights, as well as at restaurants situated at airport is termed as airline catering. Airline catering falls in two main areas:-

2.2.11.1: Terminal Catering: The catering services provided at airport terminals through lounges, cafeterias and takes-away comes under terminal catering.

2.2.11.2:In-transit or In-flight catering: The technological development in the field of aviation has totally revolutionized the catering facilities in air catering. Airlines have to provide food and accommodation to passenger in transit. Whereas passengers are stopped over at the best hotels in the city when they are making a scheduled stop-over at the airlines expenses or when a flight is unduly delayed, thus automatically taking care of the guests comfort. The problems faced by the catering personnel are how to provide delicious and wholesome food to passengers in flight. This is done by preparing all food in flight kitchens on the ground, or getting the food cooked by hotels under contract, freezing it and reheating the food in flight. The reheating of food is now being done by most of the major airlines by the use of microwave ovens in which very high frequency waves heat the food in seconds by inducing very high frequency molecular motion within the food.

The menu for the first class and economy class passengers are different and first class passengers are also served wines free of any additional charge. The food and beverage portions are highly standardized with meal portioned into plastic tray which is presented to passengers and from which they eat their meals. Disposable cutlery, napkins etc are used which reduce the facilities for washing up and cut down on breakage and wastages. For first class passenger garnishing, slicing etc, added according to their request. The crockery used may be bone china with fine glasses and cutlery.

2.2.12 Railway catering: Travelling by train for long distances can be very tiring, hence a constant supply of a variety of refreshment choices help to make the Journey less tedious. Catering to railway passengers both during the Journey as well as during halts at different railway station is called railway catering.

Railway catering may be divided into two Major areas:-

2.2.12.1 Terminal Catering: Catering at railway terminals usually comprises self-service and waiters service restaurants, fast food and take away units, supplemented by vending machines dispensing hot and cold foods and beverages.

2.2.12.2 In-transit catering: In transit catering can feature three kinds of service:- The first is the traditional restaurant car service where breakfast, lunch and dinner are organized in sitting and passenger go to restaurant car for service where appropriate seating accommodation is provided, and then return to their seats on the train after their meal. The second type of service is the buffet car, which is a self-service operation in which passengers go to the car and buy light refreshments over the counter. The third is a trolley service where snacks and drinks are delivered to customer at their seats. Pantry car is attached with passenger trains for production of food.

2.2.13 Ship Catering: voyages by sea were once a very popular mode of travelling, but with the onset of air travel, sea voyages have declined sharply. However, recently, it has again become popular with a large number of people opting for pleasure cruises. Both cargo and passenger

ship have kitchens and restaurants on board. The quality of food, service and facilities offered depends on the class of the ship and the price the passengers are wiling to pay.

There are cruises to suit every pocket. There are cruises of two to five days duration which offer budget accommodation comparable to a limited service hotel, while luxury cruises of seven days to three months duration offer luxurious staterooms and various other facilities that are comparable a first class resort. Luxury cruises pamper travellers with deluxe accommodation and attentive and specialized service at a very high premium. All these ships provide a variety of food and beverage service outlets, to cater to the individual needs of the passengers. They range from room service and cocktail bars to specialty dining restaurants. The ships that cater to the cruise sector today, are virtually flouting palaces with every conceivable guest service available abroad them. This sector has been growing in popularity in recent times, and has become affordable to a large cross section of people. Cruise companies offer attractive packages to passenger.

2.2.14 Surface catering: surface catering has progressed from the inns and taverns of earlier days used by those travelling on foot and horse back to the present day motorway service areas and other roadside catering outlets. Catering to passengers travelling by surface transport such as buses and private vehicles is called surface catering. These eating establishments are normally located around a bus terminus or on highways catering service to the traveling public and their food and beverage facilities usually include self-service and waiter service restaurants, vending machines and take-away foods and beverages.

2.2.15 Leisure-linked catering: This type of catering refers to the provision of food and beverages to people engaged in leisure. The increase in leisure and a large disposable income for leisure activities has made it a very profitable form of catering. This includes the provision of food and beverage through different stalls and kiosks at exhibitions, theme parks, galleries and theatres.

3. *What professional waiters do differently?*

3.1 While Talking to a Guest

- Always smile while welcoming the guest in your restaurant.
- Always maintain an interested and helpful expression on your face.
- Maintain eye contact. Even if you are busy writing or serving, look up once in a while to maintain eye contact.
- Maintain a distance of at least two feel from the guest while taking an order.
- Speak softly and clearly, without artificial accent.
- Avoid unnecessary movements of hands and facial gestures while describing dishes, or while speaking to guests.

3.2 While standing

- While standing to take an order or standing at the restaurant door, stand erect at ease, but not in a casual manner.
- Weight balanced
- Shoulders straight
- Chest out
- Stomach in

- Keep your hands on the sides or behind your back.
- Do not keep your hands in the pockets or on the hips.
- Do not cross your arms across the chest.
- Do not lean against the sideboard, panels or the reservation desk/Maitre D's desk.
- Remember, you may be in view of a guest even when you are not directly interacting with him/her. Maintain your poise at all times.
- Do not huddle together in bunches inside the restaurant. There is always something to be done in your area, even when the guests are not there.

3.3 While walking

- Walk at an even pace inside the restaurant, avoiding any sound of the footsteps.
- Never run inside the restaurant
- While walking in guest area. If guest are approaching, get aside and give them
- First right of way.
- If near a door, open the door for the guests to pass through
- Walk on the left hand side
- If accompanying a guest, walk on his/her right hand side and open the door for thc guest.
- Walk erect and maintain the poise

3.4 While talking to colleagues

- While communicating with your colleagues, do not point your finger towards any guest. Use cover numbers to describe who has ordered for what.
- Do not use abusive language with your colleagues.
- Speak politely while ordering food. Calling for pick up etc.
- Be aware of your conversation over the phone. Guest may be watching, or hearing.
- Never shout in to the telephone
- Do not have long conversations on phone, while a guest is waiting.
- Do not entertain personal calls while at work.

3.5 Courteous Behaviour

- Anticipate guest needs and fulfil them without being asked. For example:
- Open the restaurant door and let the guest pass ahead.
- Hand him a pen as he reaches for his own.
- Light his cigarette, as he gets ready to light it.
- Reach out for the heavy bag he is carrying.
- Do not get familiar with the guest, even when he treats when he treats you like a
- Friend. Maintain professional relationship.
- Treating guest courteously and turning to a colleague and talking to him impolitely destroy the image. Maintain the same finesse and politeness.
- Treat non resident guest with as much respect as resident guest.
- They are potential guests too.
- Do not forget the power of _word of mouth publicity' that the guests do for your restaurant.

3.6 Physical Attributes:

The physical attributes contains the proper personal hygiene and appearance. Since waiting staff deals with food, utmost cleanliness and good grooming is necessary at all times. This applies not only in high class hotels, but in every branch of catering however humble it may be. Guest is not likely to return to an establishment where staff does not maintain proper hygiene and grooming. There are times when food & beverage professionals are required to work overtime. Lifting and carrying service equipment also requires staff to be physically fit.

3.6.1 Hair: Hair should be kept healthy, trimmed and avoid dandruff. Hair should never fall over the eyes. Waitresses may adopt neat hair styles and particularly ensure a hair length which does not fall on to or below the collar or lengthy hair should be combed and tied neatly and properly.

3.6.2 Bath: Bath every day, without fail, before coming to shift.

3.6.3 Face: - Males should shave every day, before coming to shift. Moustache, if kept must be neatly trimmed. Do not use strong aftershave. Ladies should wear only light make-up. Do not use heavy perfumes.

3.6.4 Teeth: Teeth and a clean mouth are vital, both for appearance and a wholesome breath. Brush your teeth immediately before coming to duty. Do not eat onion, garlic or smoke before your shift. If you smoke, use mouthwash.

3.6.5 Hands: Always wash hands with soap before coming on shift keep your nails short and clean. Hands must always be clean, free of any stains and skin breaks. Always wash hands with soap, immediately after using toilets, eating, smoking or handling refuse.

3.6.6 Uniform: Uniform should always be clean, laundered and ironed. Change uniform whenever it is visibly soiled. Change socks and undergarments everyday. Always carry a handkerchief and change it daily. Uniform must be worm only on duty and not for personal use.

3.6.7 Feet: Feet need care, both for comfort and cleanliness. Keep toe nails trim and feet well washed. Corns and other painful blemishes may require treatment by a chiropodist disease. For more severe foot weakness medical advice should be sought. Socks or stockings should be changed and washed daily.

3.6.8 Shoes: Wear comfortable closed toed shoes. Air your shoes. Waitresses should avoid excessively high and pointed heels and shoes should be daily polished.

3.6.9 Cuts and burns: cuts and burns must be covered with correct dressing.

3.6.10 Illness: Inform your supervisor, if you suffer from:-

§ Fever

§ Diarrhoea

§ Upset stomach, nausea or vomiting

§ Sore throat or sinus infection

§ Coughing or sneezing

§ Conjunctivitis

It is better to have regular hours of sleep under good conditions rather than long irregular hours of sleep. Exercise is very essential for normal growth and development of the body and the perfect maintenance of health.

3.7 Posture: Good stance is also important for the appearance comfort and efficiency of waiting staff. To stand upright and walk erect is to give a good impression to guests and also to avoid the bodily stresses that accompany slouching. Waitresses who require support garments are advised to choose sound quality and proper fitting ones to aid posture and health as well as comfort and appearance.

4. Inter and intra departmental co-operation:

The food and beverage service department is the selling point of the Hotel. In order to enable maximum and efficient selling, other departments in a hotel also play important roles. It requires a working knowledge of other departments and their functioning to achieve this.

4.1 Food Production: In a service outlet, the F& B production has the most important role to play. Items prepares here are the ones that the service person sell. In the planning has any Restaurant, the first thing that comes to mind is the menu.

4.2 Kitchen Stewarding: This department is involved in the general cleanliness and upkeep of the kitchen. It has a pot wash where large vessels are cleaned and a wash area where service equipment is cleaned, washed and stored .This department also deals with the shortage and issue all service and kitchen equipment and hence the controls are also part of this department. The kitchen stewarding departments is headed a chief executive steward or steward manager. The requisitions of the service equipment are done through a kitchen stewarding indent book with signature from the outlet manager, F&B Manager and chief Executive steward.

4.3 Accounts: The service department does not deal with the Accounts department directly but indirectly through various outlet cashiers. The cashiers receive the copy of the KOT and raise bill accordingly. They also have detailed information about credit card and discount policies, etc. The general account department deals with payments of the company like employee salaries, bill settlements, vouchers etc. On a day – to- day level, the dining room is in direct coordination with the cashiers, and on a weekly basis with the control of KOT books and discrepancies with regard to entries in the KOT, bill authorization of signature etc.

4.4 House Keeping: The House keeping department takes care of general upkeep of the Hotel. It undertakes periodic cleaning of all public areas including cleaning of carpet and polishing of fittings. Service personnel may call on housekeeping staff to take care of occasional spillage, accidents etc. In the event of a guest‘s clothes getting spoilt, the house keeping staff will assist in laundering them, thus helping retain the customer. This department also organizes to have flower arrangements placed in the hotel . The book used in connection with housekeeping is the linen book, which lists all service linen used and exchanged on a **"One to One basis"** of the more costly items in the overheads.

4.5 Engineering: This department takes care of the air- Conditioning, lighting, plumbing and general maintenance. Communication is done through the maintenance work order book and reminders are used if required. Good coordination with the department is vital for the upkeep of equipment and helps to prevent breakdown during service.

4.6 Front Office: This is a **"Front of the - house"** position and deals with the guest directly. The check –in, check-out, billing, information, reservation, bell desk, telephones etc. all come under this department. The front office department may also be in- charge of the health club, beauty parlour, business centre and travel desk. All communication relating to the status of a guest (VIP, HG), group staying, company guests etc can be obtained from the front office. The dining room and room service need to coordinate with the front office for guest lists, billing instructions, amenities placement in rooms, problem handling during the night shift and other allied service.

4.7 Stores: This may be one or divided into separate areas such as food, liquor, materials, perishables etc. It may get its supplies through the purchase department gives the stores department its requirements of food items like proprietary sauces and seasonings and materials like doilies, paper napkins, candles, office materials, etc. through the corresponding indent book.

4.8 Personnel Department: All areas of staff requirement and employment are dealt by the personnel department in collusion with the concerned heads of departments **(HODs).** Any action to be taken regarding discipline will also be dealt with in the same way. This department is also in charge of the staff cafeteria, lockers etc. The service personnel get their leave applications processed and leave cards updated by the personnel department. This department also handles discrepancies in the time card. Job descriptions and job specifications are drawn up by this department in accordance with requirements from the individual departments. Recruitment, induction, training, evaluation and personality development programmes are also conducted by this department in the absence of a separate training cell.

4.9 Security:-This department handles the safety aspect of the organization. It is required to conduct safety and first aid drills, and fire fighting exercises. Security personnel also look into vehicle parking and are in close contact with the local police to look out for known criminals and Anti-social elements. Service personnel may use security personnel in case of drunks and unpaid bills. They have to maintain law and order in the establishment it and when difficult situations occur.

CHAPTER TWO

Unit 2: Classification and use of F&B Equipment

2.1 Requirements of Service Tools and Equipments: The operating Equipment used in hotels plays an important role in attracting customers. Attractive service ware, colourful and clean dishes, plates and glassware add to the décor of a restaurant. The choice of service equipment usually reflects the standard and style of a Restaurant. However several factors have to be considered while selecting the equipment. A Hotel should be well stocked with appropriate equipment to provide Quality service, for multipurpose use and to cut down costs, most hotels standardize equipment in terms of size and colour.

<u>2.1.1 For laying a cover on the table, we need following items:</u>

- **Flatware**: Flatware refers to denotes all forms of Spoon and forks.
- **Glassware**: Glassware refers to all type of glasses being used in restaurant for various purposes.
- **Cutlery**: Cutlery refers to knives, and other cutting implements.
- **Hollow wares:** hollow wares refer to any items made from silver, or
- **Stainless steel:** examples Teapots, milk jugs, sugar basins. Oval flats etc.
- **Crockery**: these refer to all items and from china

<u>2.1.2 Criteria for selecting Service tools & Equipments:</u>

- Type of service offered and the category of guest entertained.
- The size of the outlet.
- The layout of the food & Beverage service Area.
- Durability of the Equipment, costs and ease of Maintenance.
- Availability of the stock, facility of its storage and flexibility of use.

- Price factors, availability of funds and standardization.
- Design, shape and colour and delivery time of equipment.

2.2 Crockery:

Crockery or chinaware is made of silica, soda ash and china clay and dry glazed to give it a fine finish. Chinaware is available in different designs and colour and is sometimes coated with patterns on top of the Glazed ware. Chinaware is more resistant to heat than Glassware. Many large hotels and Restaurant have their china custom-made with their own design and monogram printed on it.

2.2.1 Care of Crockery: All china should be handled with care as it is fragile and can break easily.

- It should be properly stacked.
- Crockery should be stored in a dust free environment.
- Crockery should be rinsed and dried after washing so that no residual washing Powder is left.

2.2.2 Other items of China: Sugar Basin, Butter Dishes, Ashtrays, Egg cups, Hot milk Jugs, consommé cup & Saucer extra.

2.3 Glassware:

Food and beverage service outlets use variety of glasses for different types of drinks which call for a huge investment in delicate and fragile equipment. The style, quality, and sparkle of glassware selected portray the profile of the restaurant. Glasses are named by the drinks served in them. Though there are many glasses for different drinks it is better to go for limited types of glasses that may be suitable for all kinds of drinks. This not only saves the investments but also reduces storage area and makes replacement easier in case of breakage.

Silver and soda ash are used for making Glassware. Lead is added to make the glass crystal clear. Glass also contributed of the appearance of the table and the overall attraction of the service area. Most hotels use plain clear glassware although some high class Restaurants use cut glassware.

There are basically two types of glassware. Plain and cut glass. Plain glassware is preferred over cut glass as one can appreciate colour and brilliance of the contents of the clear glassware.

2.3.1 Glasses have any or all of the followings parts:

- Bowl
- Base or Foot
- Stem

2.3.2 Care of glassware: While purchasing glassware, one should check that the glasses are not to be cracked or chipped, transparent and free from air bubbles and pit holes. Glasses should be carefully washed in warm water and rinsed in clean hot water. They should be wiped dry using a linen cloth. Glassware should be kept inverted and neatly arranged in a row, either with a paper under liner or on a tray to avoid dust, Special plastic glass racks can also be used to stack glasses. These racks allow fresh air to circulate even when the glasses are overturned. They also facilitate smoother operations, especially in banquets. In a restaurant, glasses should not be carried on a plain salver, but with a tray mat to avoid slipping. Glasses should be polished and checked against light for finger prints before use.

The Capacity of the glasses is either measured in —OZ or —ml. The glass ware capacities are commonly expresses in OZ (ounce) and fluid ounce (fl oz) = 28.4 ml, in practice, it is taken 30 ml.

2.3.3 Different Types of Glasses:

2.4 Cutlery:

Cutlery refers to all types of knives and cutting implements & flatware such forks & spoons. Cutlery is available in various designs in silver, plated silver and stainless steel material. The type of metal needed for a service operation depends on the profile of the restaurant and the capital available. Silver and plated silver are expensive, suitable for high- class dining operations that cater to elite customers but maintaining this type of cutlery is very expensive and consumes more labour for polishing. Burnishing machine, Polivit and plate Powder method are sued for retaining the shine and to remove stains. Stainless steel cutlery is available in many grades of quality and finish. The two best qualities are those marked 18/8 which means a composition of 18 percent chromium and 8 percent nickel, and 12/12 which is 12 percent chromium and 12 percent nickel. It is available in matt or shiny finish.

2.5 Hollowware:

This includes items made from silver or stainless steel. Some of the hollowware used in hotels/restaurants is:

- Ice cream bowls
- Entrée dishes
- Chafing Dishes
- Trays and Platters
- Water Jugs
- Oval flats
- Soup tureens

2.6 Silverware:

Items made of Electro Plated Nickel Silver (E.P.N.S.) or stainless steel is also used in Restaurants. Some of them are:

- Milk Creamers
- Egg Cups.
- Condiment Trays.
- Sugar bowls
- Cruet sets
- Chinese service bowls.
- Butter Dishes
- Sauce boat
- Ash Trays.
- Bud Vase
- Toast racks
- Coffee Pots and Tea Pots.

2.6.1 silver cleaning methods:

There are various methods of silver cleaning. The method used depends on the size and class of establishment. Some of them are as under:

- Plate Powder Method
- Polivit Method
- Silver Dip
- Burnishing Machine

Plate Powder Method: This is a Pink powder, mix with a little Methylated spirit to obtain a smooth paste. The smooth paste rubbed on the article and being cleaned with a clean piece of cloth. The paste must be rubbed well in to remove all tarnish. The article is then left until the paste has dried and the paste is then rubbed off with a clean cloth. The method is time consuming but produces good result.

Polivit Method: Polivit is an aluminium metal sheet containing holes, which is best used in an galvanized iron bowl. The Polivit is placed in the bowl together with some soda. The silver to be cleaned is then put in to the bowl, ensuring that at least one Piece of silver has contact with the Polivit. Sufficient boiling water is poured into the bowl to cover the silver being cleaned A Chemical reaction takes place between the Polivit, soda, boiling water and silver, which causes the tarnish to be lifted. After 3 to 4 minutes the silver should be removed from the bowl and placed into a second bowl of boiling water and rinsed. On removal from the second bowl the silver is allowed to drain and then polished with clean cloth.

Silver Dip: This is a Pink- coloured liquid, which must be used in a plastic bowl. The silver to be cleaned is placed into a wire basket and dipped into the plastic bowl containing silver dip for few minutes. Take it out placed in warm water, rinsed and then polished with a clean cloth.

Burnishing Machine: This is revolving drum with a safety shield. It may be plumbed into the mains are remain portable with the water being poured from a tap. It may be divided into compartments to hold specific sizes of silver. It may also be possible to insert a rod through the centre of the drum from one end to the other. This rod is removable and is passed through the handled of teapots, coffee pots, milk Jugs, Sugar basins etc. to hold them in position while the drum is revolving. The machine is switched on. As the drum revolve the mixture of water and soap powder acts as an lubricant between silver and the ball bearing. Thus any tarnish is removed but the silver is not scratched.

2.7 Disposables:

Disposable are extensively used in all type of catering operations, thought the degree of usage is varied. Flight catering, Industrial catering, fast food outlets, off premises catering, coffee shops, takeaway counters, and so on, use more disposable to reduce labour and laundry cost, initial investment and breakages. Wide range of disposable is available in different colours Sizes, quality and prices to suit the need of catering operators. Suitable for –Take aways , fast food, automatic vending, outdoor catering.

2.7.1 Types of disposables

- Storage & Cooking Purpose- Aluminium foil.
- Service of Food & Beverage (Plates, Knives, Fork & Cups)
- Décor- Napkins, Place mats, Table Cloths
- Hygine
- Clothing- Chef hats, gloves, aprons

2.7.2 Advantages of Disposables

- Equipment and labour (reduces the need of equipment & Labour)
- Hygiene
- Time (fast food)
- Marketing (Promotion)
- Capital (Less investment)
- Easy transportation
- Economical

2.7.3 Disadvantages of disposables

- Disposables can be more expensive than some conventional equipment
- Customer acceptability may be poor.

2.8. Side Station:

This is a very important piece of furniture in a restaurant. It is used by the service staff for keeping all the service equipment at one place. It is also known as dummy water or sideboard. It is also used as a landing table for the dishes picked up from the kitchen en-route to the table and the dirty dishes from the guests table to the wash up area. For the convenience of the service staff, the side station should be strategically located in a restaurant. The side station should be kept clean and presentable as it can be seen by the guests.

The following service equipment can be stored in a side station:

- Coffee pots.
- Cruet sets.
- Tea Pots.
- Butter dishes
- Salvers
- Bread baskets
- Finger bowls
- Wine cradle
- Soup ladles
- Cigar cutters
- ICE buckets and tongs
- Candle holders
- Bottle and wine openers
- Toothpick stand
- But vases
- Creamers
- Tea Strainers and drip bowls.
- Straw stand.

2.9 Trolley:

The various trolleys used in the food and beverage service outlets are:

- Hors D‘ Oeuvre Trolley
- Gueridon Or Flambe Trolley
- Carving Trolley
- Dessert Trolley
- Room Service Trolley
- Wine Trolley

- Salad Trolley
- Cheese Trolley
- Liqueur Trolley
- Fruit Trolley

Hors D' Oeuvre Trolley: This trolley is probably the least popular in India, as a majority of guests are not too keen on Hors d‘ oeuvre as a starter. Hors d‘ oeuvre is the first course of a menu usually consisting of selection of small items of egg, Fish, meat, fruits, and vegetables in pungent (sharp) dressings. This trolley can be used to popularize the special dished that are introduced from time to time.

Gueridon Or Flambe Trolley: A gueridon or flambe trolley is a small mobile trolley that can be placed alongside the guest‘s table, It consists of one or two burners, a gas cylinder and a work and storage, space for plates and cooking equipments. Using this trolley, the food is flambéed at the guest‘s table. To flambé food means to cook it at the guest‘s table. The food is flambéd with the addition of spirit, before it is presented to the guest. Almost any food can be flambed but the more popular; items that are flambéd are fish, meat, fruit and desserts. Only skilled and well trained waiters are allowed to handle this service as there is there is the risk of spoiling food by overcooking it, and of the flame causing a fire on the premises.

Carving Trolley: It is used for carving Joints of meat of guest‘s table. The function of carving trolley is to act as an aid to selling. The Tranchuer (Carver) laid up the trolley with two methylated spirit lamp & in lower shelf carry the service plate, Joint plate & carving Knife.

Dessert Trolley: This trolley serves as a visual aid to selling desserts. Guests are more likely order a dessert it they can see what is available, Particularly if it is well presented. Some dessert trolleys are refrigerated. Gateaux, Pastries, and soufflés can be served from a Dessert Trolley. This trolley has several shelves and the bottom shelf is reserved for plates, Cutlery, linen and other service equipment. A glass or Transparent trolley top makes it easy for guest to select a dessert of their choice.

Room Service Trolley: This trolley is known for its versatility. It is used for the service of large order to guests in their rooms. The waiter sets up the meal and covers on the trolley and wheels it into the guest‘s room. This trolley may also be used as a dining table in the Privacy of the guest‘s room.

Wine Trolley: Wine service is important for its revenue potential. The wine trolley stocks and displays wines and spirits and is wheeled to the guest table to stimulate liquor sales. The trolley service is provided in gourmet restaurants and the person who provides this service is a qualified wine butler or sommelier.

Salad Trolley: Salads have become an important course nowadays because of an ever-increasing health-conscious have exclusive salad public. This change in guest preferences has prompted many restaurants bars dedicated to this public. Most would like to mix and match their salads to their taste. They would also like to have options of sauces.

Cheese Trolley: Cheese in European countries is an important part of a meal in the classical tradition. Gourmet restaurants still offer this as a cutting edge in their service.

Liqueur Trolley: A liqueur trolley is one that is an additional attraction in a gourmet restaurant that follows the classical menu preparations. The sommelier

would be in charge of this trolley as well.

Fruit Trolley: Guests may like to round off their meals with fresh fruits. This applies especially to diet-conscious guests who may opt to eat only salads and fruits. Restaurants recognize the health conscious and have a trolley for this niche public. The server will volunteer to cut the fruits into manageable portions and serve in the respective service ware.

CHAPTER THREE

Unit 3: The F&B Service Department

3.1 Staff Organisation of F&B Department:

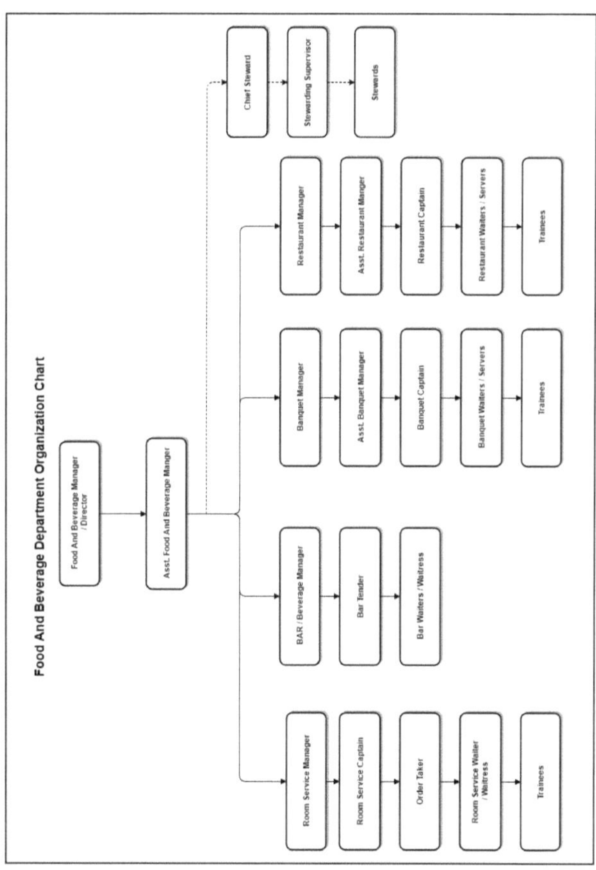

3.2. Duties and Responsibility of the waiter:

3.2.1 Job description of waiter (Commis de rang):

1. The waiters serve the food & Beverage ordered by a guest and are part of a team under a station captain.

2. They should be able to perform the duties of a captain to a certain extent and replace the captain if he is busy or not on duty.

3. They should also be knowledgeable about all types of Food and Beverages, so that they can effectively take an order from a guest, execute the order and serve the correct dish with its appropriate garnish and accompaniment.

4. He should be able to efficiently co- ordinate with the other staff in the outlet.

3.2.2. Job description of wine waiter (Sommelier)

1. His job is to take orders for the service of wine and alcoholic beverages and serve them during the meal.

2. They should have a good knowledge about wines that accompany a particular dish and the manner in which they should be served.

3. They should also be aware of Licensing Laws.

4. He should be efficient salespersons.

3.2.3. Job description of room service waiter (Chef d' etage)

1. Room service waiters work in the Room service outlet, serving both Food & Beverage to guests in their rooms.

2. The orders is placed by the guest on telephone, and is recorded on a kitchen order Ticket (K.O.T)

3. The Room Service waiter, who has been assigned that order, sets the tray according to the Food or Beverage ordered, picks up the orders when it is ready and serve it to the Guest along with the check, either for payment or signature.

4. The service should be prompt and efficient as one lapse means a complaint about service and a dis-satisfied Guest.

3.3. The Butler – (Role, Special Skills, Duties):

This post provides exhaustive information on the job description of a butler, to help you learn the kind of work that they do. It highlights the various duties, tasks, and responsibilities that typically make up the butler work description in most organizations. It also presents the major requirements most employers/recruiters will expect you to meet if you are seeking the butler role in their organizations.

3.3.1. Role of a Butler:

- A butler performs a wide range of functions like greeting and checking in guests, and making dining and entertainment arrangement.
- They provide some sort of personalized services to guests.
- They make tables ready for guest and ensure they are at the beck and call of the guests if they need anything.
- They are always around to attend to the needs of the guests.
- Butlers can work in hotels, restaurants, and individual homes wherever their services are needed.
- They could also work in functions like birthday and house warming parties, and wedding receptions, and any other function where their services are needed.
- Butlers play a key role in organizing, arranging, and ensuring guests are made comfortable in the venue.
- They greet guests, prepare dining, and make entertainment ready for guests.
- Simply put, the butler job description entails making guests happy and comfortable either in the hotel or anywhere else they are employed.
- They ensure that guests are giving a good experience during their stay.

3.3.2. Butler Job Description:

Here is a summary of the duties, tasks, and responsibilities that typically make up the butler job description:

- Meet guests on arrival and escort them to their rooms and ensure that they are settled in their rooms
- Take note of the needs of guests by learning about their likes, dislikes, allergies, etc.
- Have adequate knowledge of various drinks and foods in stock
- Serve drinks and foods to guests
- Assess and restock wine and all drink types when necessary

- Keep up with hotel policies on safety and hygiene
- Escort guests out of their rooms or tables when they are checking out of the hotel
- Appear presentable before guests at all times
- Recommend and arrange amenities for each guest in the hotel
- On hand to serve the guests when necessary
- Maintain communication with housekeepers to ensure rooms are kept clean for guests at their convenience
- Ensure that rooms meant for guests are kept clean always
- Carry luggage for guests on arrival to the room or the door of the room
- Ensure that guest deliveries are done on time
- Manage welfare of guests like shoe shining and cloth pressing, and other relevant services
- Carry out formal table service as well as service of drinks
- Maintain quality of fine antiques and art
- Arrange tables with flowers and other necessary decorations
- Work with kitchen staff to ensure timely service of food to guests
- Answer questions from guests in regards to hotel amenities and food & drinks menu
- Inform other departments in the hotel about the preference of individual guests
- Create updates in hotel software on preferences of various guests
- Perform basic check in and checkout functions as well as room reservation
- Handle requests, apply payment, verify and adjust bills, activate room keys, etc.
- Update company management on guest feedback or experience on their stay
- Maintain professional relationship with guests, applying caution and respect
- Serve as middleman between other departments and guests, relaying information both ways
- Clear table when guests are done with the food or drinks for maintenance of clean environment
- Could also give a farewell greeting to guests at the end of their stay.

3.3.3. Butler Skills:

The butler job requires high degree of discipline and positive attitude always. Also, flexibility is a must. An intending butler should be ready to handle different requests simultaneously with little or no mistakes whatever. If you are applying for the butler role in a company, here are major requirements you may be expected to meet by recruiters/employers to be hired:

Education: To qualify for this job, the candidate may need a diploma or Associate degree in Hotel Management, or in a related field.

Experience: Minimum of 2 years of experience is needed at a similar level or in a credible or well-known hotel.

More years of experience on the job will be an added advantage.

Computer skills: Candidates should be able to perform basic computer operations with sufficient knowledge of database.

Skills: Here are basic skills needed for success on this job:

- Excellent communication skills will be needed to maintain good conversation with both guests and colleagues in other departments
- Multitasking skills needed to handle more than one task simultaneously
- Good customer service skills which will be needed to ensure the comfort of guests during their stay
- Empathy needed to understand the feelings of guests when there is a complaint about a bad service
- People management needed to manage guests and other colleagues in the hotel
- Time management skills needed to attend to requests from guests in little or no time
- Good attitude needed to give customers a sense of belonging in the environment
- Attention to details
- Problem solving skills to help guests get the best solution to any challenge they could be facing while still around.

Professionalism: As a butler, professionalism is a norm and a rule which must be obeyed.

Keeping guests comfortable should be the first desire of the butler.

Care should be taken not to give guests a reason to be unhappy because of any unprofessional attitude or action.

3.4 . Significance of a Pantry – (Layout, Equipments, Functions, Silver Polishing):

Pantry is the adjoining area or room to the kitchen from where the finished food or a drink is ready to be served. This area serves as an ancillary capacity of the kitchen. The food is given final touch-up for presentation, and then handed over to the serving staff. The pantry is often equipped with a sink attached with normal water and hot water taps.

The pantry mainly keeps the following necessary items –

- Refrigerator
- Electric oven
- Toaster
- Coffee Brewing Machine
- Blender
- Electric food whisk
- Knives and chopping boards
- Hollowware like casserole, bowls, and dishes of various sizes
- Crockery
- Drink ware
- Cutlery

3.4.1. Sideboards in Pantry:

Sideboards are mainly shelves with drawers. These can be used to store hollowware and glassware. The following are the different varieties of sideboards –

- **Buffet** – It has high legs than the sideboard.
- **Credenza** – They are the storage cabinets without legs. They mostly have sliding glass doors.
- **Server** – A server is smaller, shorter, and more formal than a buffet or sideboard.
- **Sideboard** – It has short legs.

3.4.3. Silver Polishing: CLEANING AND POLISHING EPNS

The methods depend on quantity and size of items being cleaned and the cost involved. Some of the silver cleaning methods include:-

Plate Powder Method: - this method is ideal for articles like cruets, toast rack, trolley parts, etc. The articles to be cleaned must be free from grease .Plate Powder which is pink in colour is mixed with spirit and rubbed over the surface of the article to remove tarnish. If the spirit is not available, water may be used. Once the paste has dried, it is rubbed with a clean piece of cloth. A small brush may be used to remove the paste that may have lodged into the engravings. It is then rinsed well in hot water and dried with clean cloth. This method demands more time and labour. Readily available metal polish may be used to clean articles in the same way.

Polivit method:- The polivit plate , which is made of aluminium is place in container together with washing soda. The silver to be cleaned is placed in such a way that at least one piece of silver is in contact with the polivit . Piping hot water is poured to cover the silver. Chemical action of soda and aluminium removes the tarnish. After a few minutes the article is thoroughly rinsed in boiling water and wiped dry with a clean cloth. The method is suitable for larger pieces of silver such as salvers, trays, entrée dishes, jugs, etc.

Silver Dip: - The silver to be cleaned is kept in a wire basket and immersed in the silver dip, which is a pink coloured liquid. It is left in the solution for a very short period remove, rinsed, in warm water and wiped dry with clean cloth. This method is quick but may damage the silver due to chemical reaction between silver and solution.

Burnishing machine:- It consists of a revolving drum half filled with small ball bearing . It may be divided into compartments to hold silver articles of particular kinds. The silver to be cleaned is placed inside the drum, which is then half filled with water and a certain amount of special detergent and closed tightly. The machine is switched on and slowly rotated for 10 minutes. As the drum revolves the mixture of water and detergent acts as a lubricant between the silver and ball bearings and gently removes any tarnish on the silver without leaving any scratches. The silver should be rinsed and dried manually after removing from the drum. The drum is lined with rubber to avoid any damage to the silver during the cleaning process.

3.5. Outlets in a F&B Department- Restaurant, Bar, Banquet, Poolside, Coffee shop, Pastry shop, Night club

Food and beverage outlets are the areas in a hotel where food and beverage are sold to both in-house and outside guests. The following types of food and beverage can be seen which may or may not attach to a hotel.

3.5.1. Specialty restaurant:

These restaurants deal in a particular type of cuisine like Chinese, Italian or French etc. Each and every aspect of the restaurant is typical and related to the area of region of community whose food is being served. The food, service, uniform, décor etc. are ethnic and authentic of the area whose cuisine the restaurant specializes upon. When one enters into such kind of restaurant one can feel the culture and tradition of that area. These restaurants may be attached to a hotel or may independently exist. They have specific hours of function and normally more expensive than ordinary restaurants.

3.5.2. Multi cuisine restaurant:

These restaurants deal with more than one cuisine like Indian, Chinese and Continental etc. They are not as exclusive as the specialty restaurants. There is no emphasis on adherence to the culture and tradition of a particular area of region or community. They may be attached to a hotel or may independently exist. They generally have specific time of operation when attached to a hotel. They may be operating on a straight shift from morning till night when independently existing. They are not as highly priced as a speciality restaurant.

3.5.3. Bar:

These food and beverage outlets deal with the alcoholic beverages only. They may be attached to a hotel or independently existing. They have certain specific hours of operation and the law strictly governs the operation. Their hours of operation, inventory, location and client to whom they should serve etc are governed and regulated by the law-enforcing agency.

3.5.4. Room Service:

This food and beverage outlet is attached to a hotel and caters to the F and B requirements of the guests who are staying in the hotel only. These F and B outlets cannot independently exist. The service in room service is always in trays and trolleys. In a five star hotel the room service operates round the clock. The prices in the room service are generally more than the coffee shop.

3.5.5. Banquets:

This is generally attached to a hotel of restaurant. This outlet generally caters to a huge gathering of people who assemble in the banquet hall for events like reception, marriage party, birthday, conference, seminar etc. The service is generally from a buffet when a lot of guests have to be served within a short span of time. Sometimes formal lunch, dinner etc also takes place in banquet halls. This is the highest revenue producing F and B outlet in any commercial hotel. Sometimes banquet halls can independently exist where an outside contractor does the catering part.

3.5.6. Coffee Shop:

This is generally attached to a hotel. In a five star hotel the coffee shop operates round the clock. It cannot independently exist. The service is very informal and emphasis is on pace of service. Service is generally snacks and very light meals. The meals part is not as elaborate as the restaurant. Prices are not as exorbitant as the restaurants. Although the coffee shop is operational round the clock there are meal timings when the certain items are available which are not available at other times. There are some dishes, which are available all 24 hours.

3.5.7. Pub:

A pub generally independently exists, which serves only beer. The atmosphere in a pub is generally very informal most pubs have a very informal seating arrangement and generally designed to suit the likings and requirements of the youth. They also have specific hours of operation and the law like a bar governs operations. Books of inventory and accounts are maintained as per the government regulation and are supposed to produce them before the concerned authority as and when required.

3.5.8. Discotheque:

This may be attached to a hotel or may independently exist. The ones, which independently exist, are open to anybody who can pay but most allow only couples. The ones, which are attached to the hotels, are not only opened to the members but guests accompanied by members are also allowed. They also have specific hours of operations and are normally attached with a bar.

3.5.9. Pastry Shop:

They may be attached to a hotel or may independently exist. They deal with only pastry or pastry related products. Those, which are attached to hotels, deal with pastry prepared in the same hotel. The ones, which are not attached to hotels, have their own bakery either in the same premises of outside the premises. Service is done across the counter. Very limited seating arrangements may be provided if space permits.

3.5.10. Cafeteria:

These generally independently exist and are found in railway stations and airports etc. The service is generally self-service. Food is displayed in the counter and the guests helps himself in picking up the food as per his liking as he moves along the counter and finally pays the bill at the end of the counter. Sometimes payment of the bill may be through coupon also. Very informal atmosphere exists in these outlets and prices are not very high.

3.5.11. Poolside barbeque:

These are generally attached to the hotels and operate near the poolside. They generally operate for lunch and dinner only. There are adequate lighting arrangements to take care of the dinnertime. The menu is not very elaborate and comprises a lot of grilled and barbequed items. Some light meals are also available. These outlets are generally attached with their own kitchens, which are more often than not makeshift. A bar may be attached to the outlet or alcoholic beverages may be served from the service bar. Once again the décor is very informal like a coffee shop. Service is very much similar to the coffee shop as well.

3.5.12. Grill Room:

These kinds of hotels are generally attached to the star hotels although they can be found independently existing also. They specialize in grills and barbequed items only. The kitchen is separated from the service area by a glass partition so that guest can see the chef preparing the food. This give rise to impulse buying. The guests are normally assured of better hygienic condition as they can see the actual food preparation.

3.5.13. Permit Room:

They are generally found in restaurants and in hotels existing in the dry states like Gujarat. In a restaurant there is a specific area where one can serve alcoholic beverages. The restaurant cannot pour alcoholic beverages an area outside this. Same set of rules and regulations are applicable to the permit room as applicable to the bar. Prior license have to be secured from the appropriate authority before starting a permit room.

3.5.14. Night Club:

They are generally attached to hotels and are open to members only. The operation starts late in the evening and goes on till late in the night. Stripes, cabarets and floorshows etc. are performed as a part of the entertainment. These are not seen in recognized star and commercial hotels. An elaborate menu is offered and the service is quite formal and extensive. It opens only for members. Alcohol is served to the members.

3.5.15. Fast Food Outlets:

They are generally not attached to a hotel and are found independently existing. They serve fast foods, which are easy to prepare to easy to carry and eat. These outlets provide very limited seating arrangements and people are not encouraged to sit and pass time in these places. Service is done in disposable plates and packets. Patrons are supposed to get their food from across the counter. There may be one person to look after the clearance and cleanliness of the place. Very limited service is provided.

3.5.16. Coffee Bar:

This is a very recent development and becoming very popular. These outlets deal with only coffee. They specialize in different types of coffee. Both alcoholic and non-alcoholic coffees are served here. The alcoholic coffees are commonly called as speciality coffee.

3.5.17. Cyber Café:

These are also very recent developments and fast growing in popularity. Each outlet provides computers with Internet facility and the guest can surf the Internet for a specific period of time paying certain amount of money. The outlet also provides light refreshments like tea, coffee and snacks to keep the people engaged when there are two different sessions with the computer.

3.5.18. Vending machine:

Such kind of a service involves service from a machine is requiring a coin or token of a particular denomination and the product comes out through an outlet in the machine itself. These machines are not extensively used in India and the use is still confined to tea, coffee and packed milk etc.

3.5.19. Pizza outlets:

These are outlets that mostly stand-alone. These outlets have been a recent development in India over the past decades. Their food mainly deals with pizzas. They also offer food & beverage like pasta, garlic bread, soft drinks, ice-tea etc. In India chains like Pizzeria, U .S pizza, Pizza hut, Smoking Joe's etc are very popular. This trend has given rise to the franchising business, hence making pizza a youth food trend along with family and office treat zones. Basically covering all age groups of people. These outlets also deal with home delivery and take away. They usually have a moderate or minimum seating arrangement in an informal manner or tables are attached to walls with high chairs. Here one can enjoy hot & fresh food. One also has the optional at most places to plan their own pizza as per the available ingredients in the menu.

3.5.20. Home delivery/ take away:

This has been a recent trend over the past few years. As the name suggests, these outlets deal with delivery of food till your doorstep. These are stand-alone restaurants (kitchen only) that emphasize only on quick preparation of food & its delivery. There is no seating arrangement available here. The staff may contain chefs, order taker, cashier and delivery boys. The order taker takes orders over the phone or of walk in guest, notifies the kitchen and hands over the food packets to guest or delivery boys. He also might take the cashiering responsibilities at the counter, which might be overlooked by the manger. Normally such outlets do not charge for home delivery. Food is provided in plastic containers, aluminum foils, plastic bags etc. These outlets must not be confused with restaurants, which provides services of home delivery.

3.5.21. Drive-Inns:

These are developing outlets, which have not yet made a strong base in India. In places like U.S, U.K etc they have already make their mark and are best accepted. Mc Donald has started this type of service in few of its outlets. This kind of restaurant may be attached to a hotel or stand-alone. They are normally situated at highways or near petrol pumps etc. This kind of outlet has no seating arrangement only a path around the outlet for vehicles to enter and exit. It has one or two counters where the attendant takes your order and payment, at the other counter if any pick up / delivery of the food is order is done. These outlets are time saving and economical.

3.5.22. Chai- bars:

Just like coffee bar these outlets also deals with only one kind of beverage i.e. tea. In India, tea in the Hindi language is known as "chai". These outlets may mostly have an informal atmosphere and seating arrangement. The menu here includes variety of tea based on different regions, method of preparation etc. These outlets may also provide light snacks on the menu to go along with the beverage. These outlets may be stand-alone or may be attached to a restaurant. If attached to a restaurant the same premises is used for service with a different menu card or tent card only for tea.

3.5.23. Bakery:

These outlets may be attached to a hotel, pastry shop or may be stand-alone. They may or may not have a seating arrangement. They may have a kitchen/ place attached to the outlet where bakery items are prepared. The ready to eat food items are then put at the counter for display. . The food items mainly deal with various bread preparations .The guests can then choose his food and make payment over or at the end of the counter.

3.5.24. Grill and eat:

These are restaurants, which give a lot of emphasis on guests and their interests in food. The main attraction being the fact that guest has to pick ingredients, raw meat, vegetables etc of their choice from the counter & cook food himself on grillers / cooking range provided on the table itself. The grillers or cooking range is a part of the décor. The chefs are available for assistance at all times. The guests may not have knowledge of cooking & might harm themselves hence safety and first aid is also given importance. These kinds of restaurants may be attached to a hotel or stand-alone. Here they do have an elaborate seating arrangement. The restaurant may or may not a theme for itself depending upon the country, region or cuisine they are dealing with.

3.5.25. QSR: quick service restaurant:

Theses are fast food outlets, which give importance not only to the pace but also to the quality of service delivered. These are basically stand-alone restaurants that might have a brand name attached to them; hence quality plays an important role here. The seating arrangement and ambience is usually informal. The service staff may or may not collect order from the table as some of these restaurants have counter service available.

3.6. General Layout of F&B Outlets:

Appropriate architecture of F&B outlet makes it prepare, present, and serve in optimum way and increase productivity. These are few basic considerations for various sections of F&B outlets:

Kitchen

It is farthest from the customers.

Store

It has large fridges, cupboards with multiple shelves, and lockers. It is attached to the kitchen.

Pantry

It is being the area where food or beverage is prepared ready to serve, it is located between the dining area and the kitchen.

Restrooms

There are two different schools of thought for location of restrooms – some experts consider that the restrooms must be near the entrance and some think that it should be isolated from entrance or dining area.

3.6.1 General Considerations for F&B Services Layout:

While designing an F&B outlet, one needs to consider every factor that contributes to the smooth running of operations right from food preparation, cooking, dish presentation, serving, and all allied tasks.

While designing commercial F&B outlets, the following points are important:

- Target customer segment (Youth/Men/Women/All).
- Type of food (Light Food/Fast Food/Fine Dining).
- Manner of food production (Cooking/Grilling/Boiling/Baking/Steaming).
- Type of food distribution (On/Off Premise).
- Availability of carpet area.
- Number of staff required.

The kitchen is designed not to be directly visible. The chef cannot directly communicate to the guests. The guest tables and chairs are placed away from kitchen.

CHAPTER FOUR

Unit 4: Preparation for Service

4.1. Mise-en-place:

Mis-en-Place means putting in place and is the term attributed to the preparation of work place for ultimate smooth service. To ensure that the restaurant is ready for service the waiter makes sure that his station has been effectively prepared for the service. A station comprises of a given number of tables which are attended by a given team of waiters. Thus a restaurant may have several stations, each with a team of waiters. In large restaurants each station may be headed by a Captain or Chef –de-rang. Mis-en-Place or preparation in which part of activity may be carried out immediately and part left for the morning or an hour before opening of a restaurant.

4.1.1. The various steps involved are:

- Shut the doors and windows and draw the curtains.
- Keeping the light to the brightest level, set the tables and chairs according to reservations if necessary or required.
- Spread the table cloths and all other linen as and where required like slip cloth (napperon), napkin (serviette), runner etc.
- **The activities of back area includes:**
- Washing, cleaning, wiping, sanitizing, drying, and polishing of cutlery, crockery, glassware, china, stoneware etc.
- Removal of all wilted flowers, foliage from buds or flower vases for the purpose of substituting with fresh ones next morning (This may be done by the housekeeping)
- In case of candle sticks, scrap the wax, wipe, clean and polish, less than half burnt candles are scraped, cut and fit in.

- Sauce bottles are replenished by discarding half filled and made into one, washed under running water. The neck from inner and outer side wiped, the cap cleaned and replaced.
- Cruet set polished and wiped. The free flow checked, perforations cleaned. The cellar or salt/pepper shaker should not be more than 2/3rd filled for convenience of shaking.
- Check, count, cluster and tie the linen, make a bundle, exchange from the linen room. Stack fresh linen in sideboard for recycling.
- Carry the cutlery, crockery, glassware from back area and stack them in the sideboards.
- Check all the cupboards, counters, doors, windows and lock before leaving in case restaurant remains closed for some time. Switch off the air conditioner and lights and deposit the keys with time office security (This is done only when restaurant is open only for lunch and dinner or open for dinner like in case of night clubs or discotheques).

4.2. Mise-en-scene:

The dining room is the hub of several activities before the actual arrival of the guests as well as at the point of his arrival followed by satisfactory service and his departure, further winding off operations. This also involves part preparation for the next meal. It is ideal to know the components not from beginning, but from the end because end is the beginning of preparation of fresh service.

Mis-en-scene refers to preparing the environment of the areas in order to make it pleasant, comfortable, safe and hygienic for the restaurant service. For the restaurant serving staff the restaurant is considered as the service area and it is expected from him to ensure that it should be made presentable enough to accept guests before each service session.

In a regular restaurant where all the three meals are served with a pause of few hours, the dinner is over around midnight. At this stage, the clearing of tables, sideboards, displays and decorations are over. A group of staff with a supervisor carries out the following activities step by step.

All the doors, windows are opened, curtains are withdrawn. All the lights are put at the brighter level, in case there is a regular dimmer. The whole dining room is thoroughly observed and scrutinized.

4.2.1. The scrutiny is made on following lines:

- Check for dirt

- Check for unpolished metal surfaces
- Check for stains on the carpets, curtains and tapestry
- Check for all the electrical gadgets like bulbs, tube lights, power points, hot cases, display counters, pasta trolleys, pastry trolleys, microwave ovens etc.
- Check for glass panes, fountains, artificial landscapes, water bodies, flora etc.
- Check for damaged, broken furniture and fixtures.

4.3.2. Activities Performed During Mis-En-Scene in a Restaurant:

- Carpets are well brushed or hoovered.
- All tables and chairs are serviceable.
- Table lights or wall lights have functioning bulbs.
- Menu cards are presentable and attractive.
- Tent cards or other sales material are presentable.
- Doors and windows are thrown open for some time to air the restaurant. This should be followed by closing the windows and doors and setting the air conditioning or heating to a comfortable temperature.
- Exchange dirty linen for fresh linen.
- Table cloths and mats are laid on the tables.
- Wilted flowers are discarded and fresh flowers requisitioned

4.3. Rules of laying a table:

A cover is the space on the table for the cutlery, crockery, glassware and linen for one person. Each cover requires 24"x18" of space. Cover set-up is based on the type of service being offered by the restaurant. It is important for a server to check the standards required by the establishment.

The basic principles of cover layouts are:

- Each cover should be well balanced on the left and right of the guest's plate.
- All cutlery and other table appointments should be placed at least 2" away from the edge of the table.
- Knives and spoons must be placed to the right of the plate and all the forks on the left, except the butter knife which is on the side plate.
- The cutting edge of all knives should be towards the plate except for the butter knife, which should face away from the plate.

- The water goblet or tea-cup (for breakfast service) must be at the tip of the knife.
- The butter knife should be at the top of the forks along with a utter knife and on an under- plate.
- The napkin should be placed in the centre of the cover or on the side plate.
- Cruet sets must be placed on the top of the cover at the centre of the table.

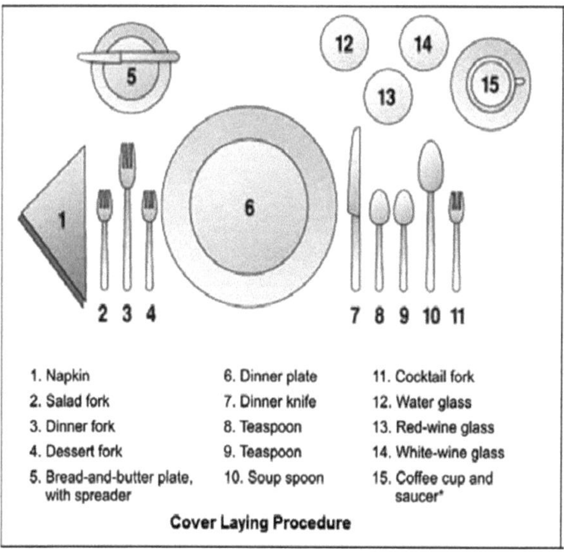

Cover Laying Procedure

<u>4.4. Basics of tray set up:</u>

<u>4.4.1. Setting Up Trays and / or Trolleys:</u>

Once the order has been distributed, a suitable present tray or trolley should be selected and set-up appropriately. The set-up will depend on:

- The number of covers.
- The food and beverage items ordered, and
- The meal or snack requested.

<u>4.4.2. Collection of the Ordered Food & Beverage:</u>

When the trays or trolleys have been correctly set up, collect food and beverage items promptly and in the right order, with the appropriate accompaniments.

Food and Beverage items should be checked, with attention to such details:

- Food and beverage temperatures
- Portion sizes
- Visual presentation as per recipe standards
- Wine details, including vintages

Food temperatures must be maintained from the time the food is collected to the time it is delivered to the guest. Plate covers, food warmers and hot boxes should be used to keep food at the right temperature.

Collect the guest's account and confirm that it matches the order. This account must be taken to the guest's room along with the items ordered.

When all items have been checked, like service equipment, food and beverage as ordered, and the account, they should be taken to the guest's room without delay.

4.4.3. Entering the Guest Room:

Respect for a guest's privacy is the primary consideration when entering a room. The following procedures will usually apply:

- Approach the room quietly.
- Knock firmly and say, "Room Service" clearly.
- Listen for the guest's response and react accordingly. If there is no response, knock and announce, "Room Service" again. Don't go in until the guest opens the door or you have been asked to enter.
- When you have entered, address the guest by name.

"Good Morning, __________. Here is your breakfast."

- Continue to use the guest's surname while making polite conversation throughout the room service procedure.

4.4.4. Presentation of Room Service Food and Beverages:

Exactly where trays are placed and trolleys are set up will vary accordingly to circumstances, depending on the equipment being used, the design of the room, the position of the furniture and the guest's particular wish. Appropriate procedures are as follows:

- Confirm that the tray or trolley is being placed where the guest wants it.
- Set them up where directed. Advice the guest of any potential hazard, for example, the hot box or the coffee pot may be too hot to touch.
- Position the furniture properly.
- Light a candle, if applicable.
- Explain the contents of the tray or trolley.
- Serve the food and beverages.
- Ask the guest if they need anything else.
- Present the account for signature.
- Explain the clearing procedures. Typically, guests are requested to put trays or trolleys outside their room when they have finished.
- Bid goodbye to the guest in a friendly but courteous manner.
- Present the signed charged account to the cashier.

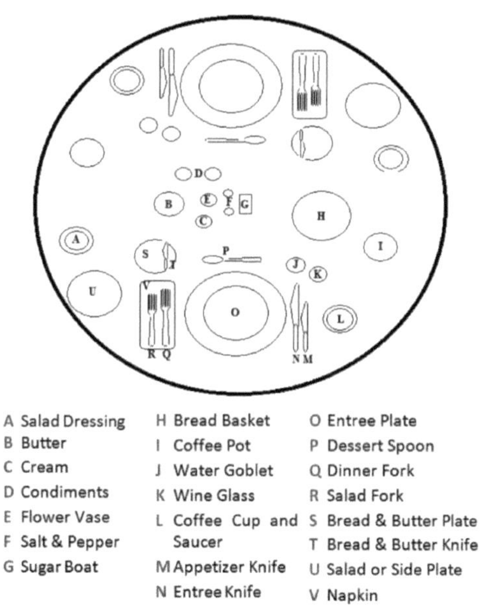

CHAPTER FIVE

Unit 5: Menu and Courses

5.1. Types of Menu:

The menu has become a very important component of restaurant planning because entire gamut of sales and reputation depends upon designing and execution of the menu. Menus may be classified in four different ways i.e. pricing, schedule and meal times.

Brief descriptions of different types of menu are given below:

5.1.1. Menu Classification on the Basis of Price:

Under this category, menus are led by the way they are priced to meet the varying budgets of customers. Menu items may be individually priced or a whole meal priced i.e. A la Carte and Table d' hote menu.

A la Carte Menu: An —A La Carte Menu‖, is a multiple choice menu, with each dish priced separately to give the guest choice to suite his or her tastes and budgets. Each course has a number of choices. If a guest wishes to place an order, an a la carte is offered, from which one can choose the items one wants to eat. The courses generally follow the sequence of the classical menu. Traditionally, the original menus that offered consumers choices were prepared on a small chalkboard, a la carte in French; so foods chosen from a bill of fare are described as à la carte, "according to the board."

In an a la carte menu all items are cooked to order including the sauces that are made with wine, cream or mustard. Depending on the dish chosen by the guest, the cooking time will vary. It is necessary to inform the guests about the time the preparation might take. An extensive a la carte menu is impressive but involves a huge amount of mise-en-place.

Table d' hote Menu: Table d'hôte is a French phrase which literally means "host's table". It is used to indicate a fixed menu where multi-course meals with limited choices are charged at a fixed price. Such a menu may also be called prix fixe ("fixed price"). It usually includes three or five courses meal available at a fixed price. It is also referred to as a fixed menu. Because the menu is set, the cutlery on the table may also already be set for all of the courses, with the first course cutlery on the outside, working in towards the plate as the courses progress.

Fixed menus or table d' hote menus are still used in various forms such as buffet menus, conference packages and on special occasions. A table d' hote menu comprises a complete meal at a predetermined price. It is sometimes printed on a menu card or as in the case of banquets, it is agreed upon by the host of the party. A banquet style of fixed menu has more elaborate choices ranging from the soup to the dessert. For the banquets, the host invariably fix or selects the menu in consultation with the hotel staff in advance.

Most of the banquet food served in India is normally of Indian food. For this, a printed format offering a choice of vegetarian and non-vegetarian dishes is prepared, from which the guests make their choice. Western style fixed menus normally provide the choice of a starter or soup, a main course, and finally a dessert. In each course there could be a choice of dishes to suit the tastes of individual guests.

Table d'hote menus should be well planned and balanced. As the guest is not given a chance to plan his own meal, the meal should be interesting, without any similarity in the colour and taste of the courses as well as being palatable, delicious and well presented.

If the main course is heavy, then the first course should be lighter, and act as an appetite stimulant for the courses to follow. Dishes that are heavy and hard to digest should be avoided. The colour, varieties of ingredients used, and the garnishes should, if possible, be different for each course. Fixed menus are prevalent in transport catering which include air, rail, and sea passengers. The guests have a variety of fixed or table d'hote menus, with virtually no choice offered to the passengers (except the first class air passengers). Cruise liners may have elaborate fixed menus with multiple choices built into each course.

5.1.2. Menu Classification on the basis of Schedule:

This category focuses on the frequency of menu revision. Some establishments offer menus that last months while others are changed daily.

Fixed Menus: A fixed menu is one which is used daily for a period of months or a year, like most restaurants. The restaurants that use such menus either have a large variety of items within each course or when the frequency of repeat guests is less. Establishments like transit hotels, specialty restaurants or weekend resorts may choose fixed menus because the guests are in for a short visit or visit the restaurant for variety from the usual. The best that a restaurant with a fixed menu can do in offering variety is to have dish du jours or specials of the day. Franchised operations may stay with fixed menus that are time-tested and standardized. A KFC or Burger King will have their stock items in the menu for years.

Cyclic Menus: These are designed to offer frequent guests a variety. The cycle of menus can be on a daily, weekly or monthly basis. These menus may be found in downtown lunch restaurants frequented by a dedicated business clientele. Isolated resorts may offer cyclic menus to their guests who do not have anywhere else to go. Cyclic menus will require multi-skilled cooks, flexible purchase and production schedules.

5.1.3. Menu Classification on the basis of Meal Time:

The traditional meal times of breakfast, brunch, lunch, tea and dinner have their special types of meals justifying separate meals for each. There may be restaurants specializing in a particular mealtime. Business centre outlets may specialize in lunch menus because the business district closes in the evening. Many hotels may offer only bed and breakfast. They would naturally specialize in breakfast menus. Fine dining is normally done at night and is located near shopping malls, entertainment centres or in hotels. These restaurants only open at night in which case they would specialize in dinner menus. Night Clubs and Discotheques are a good example of this category.

Breakfast Menus: Breakfast menus are fairly standardized. Most restaurants will offer a choice of juices, cereals, eggs to order, breakfast meats like bacon, sausages or ham, waffles or pancakes with maple syrup, for the sweet toothed. The bed and breakfast establishments generally serve a choice of breads, jam and marmalade, tea and coffee. The breakfast is an important meal to many cultures and guests want a cheap and wholesome meal. Being the first meal, guests are in a hurry and want a quick service. Therefore, breakfast buffets are common in outlets with brisk morning business.

Lunch Menus: Lunch menus can vary from elaborate meals or light meals depending on the purpose and culture of the guest. Business-persons prefer sandwiches, salads and soups due to limited time at lunch breaks or are weight-watchers. Salad bars have become an important part of must luncheon restaurants. Those restaurants that have dedicated clientele may choose to go for cyclic table d' hote luncheon menus, to break the monotony of one single menu. They may even offer specials of the day displayed along with their regular menu.

Dinner Menus: These menus are elaborate as guests have more time and leisure for eating. Dinner menus are an entertainment and people are willing to pay extra for these meals. Alcoholic drinks are an essential part of dinner menus. A well-stocked wine list is offered in addition to the dinner menu. Dinner menus will have house specialties and a real chance to sell their expensive items. Appetizers are more accepted at the evening meal than during the day. Similarly desserts are preferred at dinner time.

Supper Menu: The term 'supper is used in the European continent but it varies in purpose around the continent. It can be a light dinner for either early evenings or late nights. It can be filler between two major meals lunch and dinner or dinner and breakfast. A typical early evening supper meal can be a soup, meat dish with vegetables and a light dessert. A late night supper can consist of a sandwich with hot cocoa or fruit.

Brunch Menus: Are designed for the family or guests who wish to wake late. They are popular on holidays and weekends as also at vacation spots where the pace of life slows down. Brunches (which is a combination of breakfast and lunch), are spread well beyond breakfast hours. The brunch will have combinations of breakfast and lunch items to suit the mood and taste of the individual.

5.2. French Classical Menu:

The classical French menu contains thirteen courses. Today, a menu of this size is hardly ever offered. But even today's shorter menus follow the structure of the classical French menus as far as succession of courses is concerned. They always start with something light to stimulate the appetite, build up to the main course, and then become lighter toward the end of the meal. The thirteen courses of the French Classical Cuisine menu for are given below:

5.2.1. Hors D'oeuvre: Being of a highly seasoned and piquant in nature, this course is used to manipulate the appetite for the dishes that are to follow. In recent years, hors d'oeuvres have gained in popularity, and now appear even on simple menus in modest eating places. Although the actual term —hors d'oeuvres‖ applies to the service of various cold salads and morsels of anchovy, sardines, olives, prawns, etc., it also covers whatever items are served before the soup.

5.2.2. Potage: The French have three separate words for soup. Consommé is a clear, thin broth. Soup refers to a thick, hearty mélange with chunks of food. Potage falls somewhere between the two in texture, content and thickness. A potage is usually puréed and is often thick, well-seasoned meat or vegetable soup, usually containing barley or other cereal or a pulse (e.g. lentils). Today, the words *soupe* and *potage* are often used interchangeably. On good-class à la carte menus, a fish soup is also usually offered for selection, the two most common being —Bisque d'Homard‖ or —Bouillabaisse.

5.2.3. Oeufs: Oeufs are the dishes made from egg. The omelette is the most popular item, but there are other styles of cooking and preparation of eggs such as boiled, en cocotte, poached or scrambled. This course is not included in the dinner menu. Some examples are omelette, Espagnole, Oeuf en Cocotte a la crime, Oeuf poche florentine.

5.2.4. Farineux: This is Italy's contribution to the courses of the menu. It includes different kinds of rice and pasta. Pasta dishes are spaghetti, lasagne and gnocchi. Pasta is made from durum wheat semolina or milled durum wheat to which water is added to form a dough. It can be coloured and flavoured in various ways. There are more than 200 varieties of pasta. The ingredients, size, shape and colour determine the type of pasta. Some examples include Spaghetti Bolognaise, Lasagne Napolitaine and Macaroni au gratin.

5.2.5. Poisson: Poisson are the dishes made from fish. Fish, being soft-fibred, prepares the palate for the heavier meats that follow. Deep-fried or grilled fish dishes do not generally occupy a place on the —classical dinner menu,‖ but are freely offered on the shorter-coursed luncheon menu. This also applies to the coarser members of the fish family, and the dinner menu is usually comprised of the finer fish prepared and cooked in the more classical manners. Ideal fish for dinner menu compilation are: Sole, Salmon, Halibut, Escallops, etc. Rarely seen on a menu for the evening meal are: Cod, Bass, Haddock, Brill, Hake, and Plaice. One deep-fried fish dish, which normally finds itself on the dinner menu, however, is Blanchaille and this only because Whitebait is so light and in no way too filling for the comfort of the guest.

5.2.6. Entrée: This is the first of the meat courses on a menu. It is always a complete dish in itself. It is despatched from the kitchen garnished and sauced in the manner in which it is intended to be served. The entrée is always cooked and garnished in an artistic manner and usually served with a rich sauce. The entrée can be devised of almost anything light. This course consists of all the small cuts of butcher's meats, usually sautéed, but never grilled. Grilled steaks, cutlets and chops invariably replace the joints as the roast (roti) course.

5.2.7. Relevé: This is the main meat course on the menu, and is commonly known as the —piece de resistance.‖ It may consist of joint of any of the following:

Lamb (Agneau), Chicken (Poulet), Beef (Boeuf), Duckling (Caneton), Veal (Veau), Fowl (Poulard), Ham (Jambon), Tongue (Langue), Pork (Pore).

These joints would be cooked by the sauce cook in a first class hotel or restaurant, by any method except roasting. They are usually cooked on casserole, braise or poêle. Generally cooked in a sauce and served with it.

5.2.8. Sorbet: This course is a rest between courses. It counteracts the previous dishes, and rejuvenates the appetite for those that are to follow. Normally served between the releve / remove and the roti, it is water and crushed ice slush flavored as a rule with champagne and served in a glass. A frozen dessert made primarily of fruit juice, sugar, and water, and also containing milk, egg white, or gelatine. Some examples are Sorbet Italian and Sorbet crème de menthe. Russian or Egyptian cigarettes are often passed around during this course.

5.2.9. Roti – Roast: This course normally consists of game or poultry and is often included in the entree. Each dish is accompanied with its own particular sauce and salad. Some examples are Roast chicken, Braised duck and Roast quail.

5.2.10. Legumes: These are vegetable dishes that can be served separately as an individual course or may be included along - with the entrée, relevé or roast courses. Some examples are Cauliflower Mornay, Baked potato and Grilled tomatoes.

5.2.11. Entremets: Entremets on a menu refers to desserts. This could include hot or cold sweets, gateaux, soufflés or ice-cream. Some examples are Apple pie, Chocolate soufflé and Cassata ice-cream.

5.2.12. Savoureux: A dish of pungent taste, such as anchovies on toast or pickled fruit. They are served hot on toast or as savoury soufflé. Welsh rarebits, Scotch woodcock, Canape Diane are some of the examples. Fromage (Cheese) is an alternative to the outdated savoury course, and may be served before or after the sweet course. It is usually served with butter, crackers and occasionally celery. Gouda, Camembert and Cheddar are some examples of cheese.

5.2.13. Desservir: Dessert is a course that typically comes at the end of a meal. The French word desservir mean "to clear the table." This is the fruit course usually presented in a basket and placed on the table, as part of the table decor, and served at the end of the meal. All forms of fresh fruit and nuts may be served in this course. Common desserts include cakes, cookies, fruits, pastries and candies.

5.2.14.Café: Coffee may be served upon the Guest Request and his choice of coffee may be checked beforehand.

5.3. Example Table for dishes from the above courses:

Course	French	English	Example
1.	Hors d'oeuvre	Appetizer	Melon with port, rémoulade, oysters, smoked salmon, shrimp cocktail
2.	Potage	Soup	Consomme brunoise, crème of tomato soup
3.	Oeufs	Egg	Omlette Espagnole, Omelette aux tomates
4.	Farineaux	Rice and pasta	Spaghetti Napolitaine, Ravioli,Cannelloni
5.	Poisson	Fish	Sole de bonne femme
6.	Entrée	First meat dish	Fillet of sole Joinville
7.	Relevé	Main meat dish	Saddle of Iamb
8.	Sorbet	Flavoured ice water	Champagne Sorbet
9.	Roti	Roast with salad	Guinea hen stuffed with goose liver, salad
10.	Legumes	Vegetables	Tomato farcis
11.	Entremets	Sweet	Charlotte russe
12.	Savoureux	Savory	Welsh rarebit, Ivanhoe
13.	Desservir	Dessert	Jellied fruit
14.	Cafe	Coffee	Black coffee usually

CHAPTER SIX

Unit 6: Forms of Service

6.1. English Service / Silver Service:

This usually includes serving food at the table. It is a technique of transferring food from a service dish/platter or flat to the guest's plate from the left. It is performed by a waiter usually using service fork and spoon, although occasionally two forks, two fish knives or some other type of specialist service equipment.

This technique requires much practice. It is almost always used, for a banquet, in many top class hotels, restaurants and cruise liners. The food is always served to the guest from the left side of the guest using a service fork and spoon.

6.2. French Service / Butler Service:

A very exclusive and personalized service in which emphasis is on the presentation of the food as much as is on the quality and taste. The food is individually presented on dishes, platters or flats to each customer by staff and they help themselves from a serving plate held by the waiter (butler) or can be placed directly on the table. It requires highly skilled staff and is found in luxury dining establishments. The food is always presented on the platter first and then the food is served to the guest from the left side of the guest.

6.3. American Service / Plate Service:

This type of service is found in a wide variety of catering establishments and is probably the most common style of food service. Food is pre-plated in the kitchen and served to customers, sometimes under cloche/plate covers which are removed in front of the guests.

The advantages of this type of service include the maintenance of food presentation and portions, and the possibility of a faster turnover of customers. The food is always served from the right side of the customer. Dishes are prepared and decorated in the kitchen and then served directly.

6.4. Russian Service:

It is a manner of dining that involves courses being brought to the table sequentially. The table is laid with food and the customers help themselves. The food is prepared and portioned in the kitchen and placed on to silver salvers which are then brought into the restaurant. Food is served from the platter to the plate.

6.5. Trolley Service:

The various trolleys used in the food and beverage service outlets are:

1. Hors D‘ Oeuvre Trolley
2. Gueridon Or Flambé Trolley
3. Carving Trolley
4. Dessert Trolley
5. Room Service Trolley
6. Wine Trolley
7. Salad Trolley
8. Cheese Trolley
9. Liqueur Trolley
10. Fruit Trolley

6.6. Buffet Service:

Buffet is a method of food service which is a modification of true self service. It is a food service arrangement in which foods are displayed attractively on one or a series of tables, and presentation is an all important factor. Customer collects a plate from one end of the table and move along it helping themselves to the food of their choice.

In **finger buffet** most of food is kept to fairly small mouth size Pieces.

In **fork buffet** cutlery is provided for the customer with which to eats the food.

The guest either helps themselves or is served by chefs standing behind the buffet table. Cold buffet are usually arranged with decorative dishes such as –Pieces can be of Ice carving, butter moulding. U- Shape, L –shape or V- Shape and other shapes of table arrangement can be assembled to accommodate the food to be served and the numbers to be catered for Buffet Service also enables a facility to feed large number of people in given time with less staff requirements

6.7. Cafeteria:

The traditional cafeteria system consists of a straight line of counters containing a variety of hot and cold dishes. The customers start at the end of a line, pick up a tray and move along the length of the counter as they select dishes they want to have. The cashier who is seated at the end of the counter makes bills for the items selected and collects payment.

This form of service is widely followed in institutional and industrial establishment.In cafeteria arrangements beverages are included in the main counter line, usually at the end, just before the cashier. The serving of beverage is recognized to be one of the slowest points in the cafeteria line and the tendency is to separate the beverages out from the main line completely and to serve them from a separate counter.

In some cafeteria arrangements the beverage counters may actually be sited in the dining area. This is an attempt to speed up through put of customers in the main cafeteria area to the dining area, such beverage stations may either be manned by counter staff or vending machines.

6.8. Family Service:

It is a service where a butler is involved in helping the guest to conduct the service smoothly. The bowls and the platters are brought on trolleys or trays kept before the host to portion out and carve the items and holding the plate for him to place the food and serve as directed.

The first portion is offered to the Head Lady of the family followed by other members. The butler takes the trolley around for second helpings. Clearing is done side by side. It is a very informal and private kind of service which normally does not exceed 15 – 20 people. It is customary for the host to show his closeness and favourites through his portions offered.

6.9. QSR:

Quick service restaurant (QSR) is a restaurant which offers certain food items that require minimal preparation time and are delivered through quick services. Typically, quick service restaurants or QSRs cater to fast food items over a limited menu as they can be cooked in lesser time with minimum possible variation.

QSR restaurants are known to have standardized, modular and efficient processes which help them in reducing the lead times to fulfil the orders but still maintain the quality expected by the customers. Preparation methodology and usage of technology are pillars of a Quick service restaurant (QSR).

6.10. Room Service/ In Room Dinning:

Room service provides guests with food and beverage service in the privacy of their own room or suite. Room service is a feature in some way in establishments that offer accommodation.

Different establishments including Hotels, Resorts, serviced apartments or Villas and residential clubs offer different types of room service ranging from a full compendium Menu with 24-hour service to Breakfast only served in the room. Some establishments will have a separate Room service kitchen and production area in others it may be part of the Restaurant operation.

CHAPTER SEVEN

Unit 7: Breakfast Service

7.1. Breakfast:

According to Oxford Advanced Learners Dictionary, 'breakfast' means 'the first meal of the day'. It is very important meal of the day. Breakfast dishes includes bread (plain/toasted), egg (boiled, poached, scrambled, omelette, etc.), porridge, cornflakes, fish, meat and poultry and beverages like tea, coffee, milk, hot chocolate and canned/fresh juices of fruits and vegetables. Breakfast dishes should be very nourishing to provide energy needs of the guests.

Most of the hotels offers meal plans and provide complimentary breakfast in Continental Plan, American plan, Modified American plan and B&B plan. The dishes of the breakfast changes according to plan. Most of the hotels provide breakfast in restaurants, coffee shop, and dining room or even through room service in to the guest rooms.

7.1.2. Why have breakfasts?: We need to have breakfast because:

- Breakfast breaks your overnight fast
- Breakfast refuels your glycogen (energy) stores
- Breakfast kick starts the metabolism
- Breakfast provides us with the energy to keep us going throughout the day

7.1.2. Benefits of regular breakfast: The benefits of breakfast are listed as under:

- Improves your energy levels
- Improves metabolism
- Provides many beneficial nutrients, and boosts your fibre and calcium intake (compared to no breakfast).

- Reduces you chance of over-consuming high kilojoule foods later in the day
- Stabilizes your blood sugar levels
- Improves memory and concentration

7.1.3. Healthy Breakfast: Breakfast should provide about 20-25% of daily nutritional requirements, and it's not just about having any breakfast – it's about having a healthy breakfast. A healthy breakfast should include following:

- **Starchy foods such as bread, cereals, rice, potatoes, and pasta** provide energy, B vitamins, some iron and fibre. Cereals are a really good choice: as well as being quick and easy to prepare, they often are fortified with vitamins, iron and calcium to contribute to your daily nutritional requirements.
- **Fruit and vegetables** are good sources of vitamins and fibre. Breakfast is a perfect time to boost your 5-a-day intake. On your cereal, try chopped fresh fruit, like a banana, or some dried, stewed or canned (in juice rather than syrup) fruit, or add half a grapefruit or fruit salad to your usual breakfast. A small glass (150ml) of pure fruit juice also counts as one serving of your 5-a-day. Alternatively, give vegetables a try at breakfast time, mushrooms, baked beans or tomatoes on toast make a tasty change when you have a bit more time.
- **Milk and dairy foods** give you protein, calcium and B vitamins. Calcium is essential to keep your bones strong and healthy, whatever your age, and a serving of milk on your cereal can give you up to one third of your daily calcium needs. Natural yoghurt is delicious topped with fruit and a sprinkle of muesli.
- **Meat, fish, eggs, beans and other non-dairy sources of protein** give you protein, iron and vitamins. These foods are not essential at breakfast, but they can add variety. Poached, boiled or scrambled eggs, baked beans, grilled kippers or smoked haddock are healthier options than bacon and sausages, which are higher in saturated fat.
- **Beverage.** Water, milk, pure fruit juice, tea and coffee all supply vital fluids. Use low fat milks and ask for 'skinny' coffee when out and about. Being well hydrated also helps you to concentrate better.

7.2. Types of Breakfast provided in Hotels:

Breakfast is generally provided through buffet laid in coffee shop of restaurant. Apart from buffet breakfast is also provided in a la carte service. A wide variety of breakfast is offered in hotels including English breakfast, continental breakfast, American breakfast and Indian breakfast. Each of these types of breakfast has its own variety of dishes.

7.2.1. American Breakfast:

According to Buinessdictionary.com, American breakfast is, _A hotel breakfast that includes most or all of the following: two eggs (fried or poached), sliced bacon or sausages, sliced bread or toast with jam/jelly/ butter, pancakes with syrup, cornflakes or other cereal, coffee/tea, orange/ grapefruit juice‘. Coffee is most preferred beverage in American breakfast.

7.2.2. Cover Required for American Breakfast: Following items are needed for laying American breakfast cover:

- Side plate and side knife
- Large knife and fork
- Dessert spoon and fork
- Tea cup and saucer with tea spoon
- High ball glass
- Napkin

7.2.3. American Breakfast Menu:

- Choice of fresh Fruit Juice Or Cut Fruits Or
- Stewed Fruits
- Choice of Cereals (Rice flakes, wheat flakes etc)
- Served with hot/cold milk
- Eggs (Fried, boiled, poached, omelette)
- Meat (Bacon, Sausages, Salami etc)
- Choice of assorted bread Served with butter and preserves
- Beverages (Tea, Coffee, Hot Chocolate, Horlicks etc)

7.2.4. A brief description of few American Breakfast dishes: The various dishes served in American breakfast includes breakfast cereals, egg, ham, steak, sausages, grilled vegetables, bread with butter/preserves and beverages like tea/coffee.

A brief description of few dishes is as under:

7.2.5. Egg to Order: Egg is one of the most versatile items that are served in breakfast. The egg may be served as hard boiled, poached, scrambled, fried, baked, omelette etc.

American-Style or Folded Omelette: This style of omelette is often called a French omelette, but it is not a French omelette. It was probably devised by cooks who hesitated to tackle the French method. It is made somewhat like a French omelette, except low heat is used and the eggs are not stirred or agitated. Instead, the edges of the cooked portion are lifted with a fork or spatula, allowing the uncooked portion to flow underneath. The finished omelette may be folded in half or like a French omelette. The advantage of this method is that it is easier to learn. The disadvantages are that the omelette is not as light or delicate in texture and the method is much slower.

7.2.6. Waffles and pancakes: Bread items probably play a more important role at breakfast than even eggs. Waffles and pancakes, also called griddle cakes and hot cakes, are made from pourable batters. Pancakes are made on a griddle, while waffles are made on a special tool called a waffle iron. Both items should be cooked to order and served hot. Waffles lose their crispness very quickly, and pancakes toughen as they are held. However, batters may be prepared ahead and are often mixed the night before. Serve with butter and with maple syrup or syrup blends (pure maple syrup is expensive). Other condiments that may accompany these items are fruit syrups, jams and preserves, applesauce, and fruits such as strawberries or blueberries.

7.2.7. Ham: Ham for breakfast service is almost always precooked. Slices in 3- to 4-ounce (90- to 115-g) portions need only be heated and browned slightly on a griddle or under the broiler. Canadian bacon is boneless pork loin that is cured and smoked like ham. It is handled like ham in the kitchen.

7.2.8. Sausage: Breakfast sausage is simply fresh pork that has been ground and seasoned. It is available in three forms: patties, links, and bulk. Because it is fresh pork, sausage must be cooked well done. This does not mean, however, that it should be cooked until it is just hard, dry, shrunken little nuggets, as it often is.

7.3. Continental Breakfast:

According to Buinessdictionary.com, A hotel breakfast that may include sliced bread with butter/jam/honey, cheese, meat, croissants, pastries, rolls, fruit juice and various hot beverages. It is served commonly in the continental Europe, North America, and elsewhere, as opposed to the

English breakfast served commonly in the United Kingdom. It is most simple breakfast. It is served complementary by hotel offering room tariff on Continental Plan and also by B&B operators.

7.3.1. Café complet: The term 'café complet'is widely used in continental Europe and means a continental breakfast with coffee as the beverage. The term **'thé complet'** is also used, with tea provided as the beverage. **Café simple or thé simple,** Café simple or thé simple is just a beverage (coffee or tea) with nothing to eat.

The traditional continental breakfast consisted of hot croissant, brioche or toast, butter and preserves and coffee as the beverage. The current trend in the continental breakfast menu is to offer a wider variety of choice, including cereals, fruits, juices, yoghurts, ham, cheese, assorted bread items and a wider selection of beverages.

7.3.2. Full breakfast: A full breakfast menu may consist of from two to eight courses and usually includes a cooked main course. Traditionally this was a very substantial meal and included such items as chops, liver, game, steak, kippers and porridge as the main part of the meal. This type of breakfast was traditionally known as an English Breakfast, but is now also known as Scottish, Irish, Welsh or more simply British Breakfast. The term _full breakfast' is also becoming more common. Modern full breakfast menus have changed to include a much more varied choice of items. Today customers expect to see such items as fresh fruit juices, fresh fruit, yoghurt, muesli, continental pastries, homemade preserves, margarines, decaffeinated coffee and mineral waters on the full breakfast menu.

7.3.3. Continental Breakfast Menu:

- Choice of Fresh Fruit Juice
- Choice of Assorted Bread (toast, croissants, rolls, brioche, muffins etc)
- Served with Preserves (Jam, marmalade), Honey
- Beverages (Tea / Coffee / Chocolate)

7.3.4. Cover Required for Continental Breakfast: Following items are needed for laying continental breakfast cover:

- Side plate and side knife
- Tea cup and saucer with tea spoon
- High ball glass
- Napkin

7.3.5. A brief description of few continental Breakfast dishes: The various dishes served in continental breakfast include bread with butter/ preserves and beverages like tea/coffee. A brief description of few dishes is as under:

- **French toast** in different versions is popular in many regions, and it has the advantage of being an excellent way to utilize day-old bread. Basic French toast consists of slices of bread dipped in a batter of eggs, milk, a little sugar, and flavourings. French toast is cooked on a griddle like pancakes. Variations may be created by changing the basic ingredients:
- **Bread:** White Pullman bread is standard. Specialty versions can be made with French bread, rich egg bread, or whole-grain breads.
- **Batter:** Milk is the usual liquid, mixed with egg in various proportions. Deluxe versions may include cream or sour cream.
- **Flavourings:** Vanilla, cinnamon, and nutmeg are popular choices. Other possibilities are grated lemon and orange rind, ground anise, rum, and brandy.
- The most common fault in making French toast is not soaking the bread long enough to allow the batter to penetrate. If the bread is just dipped in the batter, the final product is just dry bread with a little egg on the outside. French toast is dusted with powdered sugar and served, like pancakes, with accompanying butter, syrups, preserves, or fruits.

7.4. English Breakfast:

English breakfast is heavy and includes variety of dishes like fruit juices, stewed fruits, breakfast cereals, egg to order, fish, meat, bread with butter/ preserves and beverages like coffee, tea, hot chocolate etc.

7.4.1. Cover Required for English Breakfast: Following items are needed for laying English breakfast cover:

- Side plate and side knife
- Fish knife and fork
- Large knife and fork
- Dessert spoon and fork
- Tea cup and saucer with tea spoon
- High ball glass
- Napkin

7.4.2. English Breakfast Menu:

- Choice of fresh Fruit Juice (orange, pineapple, tomato)
- Cut Fruits (grapefruit, melon, papaya, pears, bananas)
- Stewed Fruits (plums, apples, figs, prunes)
- Choice of Cereals (Muesli, Porridge, Rice flakes, wheat flakes etc) Sen/ed with hot/cold milk
- Fish: (Boiled, Grilled, Poached, Steamed – Sole, Herring, Haddock)
- Eggs: (Fried, boiled, poached, plain or savoury omelette)
- Meat: (Bacon, Sausages, Salami etc – fried or grilled)
- Choice of Assorted Bread (toasts, brioches, croissant, rolls, brown bread Served with butter and preserves (honey, jam, marmalade)
- Beverages: (Tea, Coffee, Hot Chocolate, Milk, Horlicks, etc)

7.5. Indian Breakfast:

India is a country of vast diversity in culture and tradition. Food being part of culture, provides a large variety of dishes in breakfast. It includes dishes like Idli-Sambhar, Vada-Sambhar, Poori-Bhaji, Chole-Bhatoore, Nahari-Kulcha, Stuffed/Plain Paratha with Curd, Poha, Khaman Dhokla with variety pickles and Chutneys.

7.5.1. Indian Breakfast Menu:

- Dosa
- Idlli
- Puttu
- Appam
- Idiyapppam
- Upma
- Wheat Dosa
- Poori
- Pongal
- Egg Roast
- Veg. Khorma
- Kadala Curry
- Veg. Stew
- Aloo Bhaji/Masala
- Red Coconut Chutney
- While Coconut Chutney

7.5.2. Cover Required for Indian Breakfast: Following items are needed for laying Indian breakfast cover:

- Side plate
- All-purpose knife and fork
- Dessert spoon
- Tea cup and saucer with tea spoon
- High ball glass
- Napkin

7.5.3. A brief description of few Indian Breakfast dishes: The food of Punjab and Haryana, rich agricultural states in northern India, is simple, robust, and closely linked to the land. In rural areas, the day may start with a hearty breakfast of sautéed bread called *parathas,* sometimes stuffed with potatoes, cauliflower, or grated radish. Sometimes breakfast is supplemented with *halwa,* a dish of grated vegetables cooked in butter and sugar syrup. In Gujarat in western India, breakfast is served around 7 a.m. and includes tea with wheat or millet bread; *papri* (crisp little squares made from chickpea fl our); or puffed rice.

In southern India, the core cereal is rice. Breakfast is an important meal for Hindus and typically features *idlis* (soft, steamed, disk-shaped cakes) or *dosas* (fl at, round, crispy crepes lightly sautéed in oil). The doughs are made by grinding rice, black lentils, and water into a paste. The standard accompaniments are *sambar* —a spicy lentil soup that sometimes includes vegetables—and coconut chutney. The standard breakfast drink is strong filtered coffee mixed with milk. Another popular breakfast dish is *uppuma,* a semolina porridge with tomatoes and onions. Hyderabad, the capital of Andhra Pradesh, has a large Muslim population. A breakfast in a middle-class Muslim household might include parathas served with fried eggs, an omelet, or minced meat and/or sautéed potatoes.

7.6. Buffet Breakfast:

Of all hotel meals, it is often the service of breakfasts which seems to give the management the most headaches, generally because the majority of guests arrive for breakfasts within a very few minutes of each other, all requiring fast service.

However well planned the service may be, this sudden influx of customers can cause havoc, which may be further aggravated by staff shortages. To overcome these problems and to meet the needs of their guests, many hotels have in recent years introduced a self-service breakfast buffet, which successfully provides a fast break-fast service.

In-house breakfast is generally offered by hotel at a fixed price, dishes are laid on buffet and guests are allowed to choose their favourite breakfast dishes from the buffet. It includes fresh/canned juices, hot chocolate, sweet/sour lassi, milk shakes, croissants, doughnuts, sandwiches, canapés, pan cakes, sausages, egg to order, poori bhaji, chole bhature, nahari kulcha, dhokla, poha, idli sambhar, vada sambhar, dosa(paper dosa, masala dosa), vada pao etc. with hot beverages like tea and coffee. There may be regional variation in dishes on buffet.

CHAPTER EIGHT

Unit 8: Kitchen Stewarding

8.1. Kitchen Stewarding:

This department is involved in the general cleanliness and upkeep of the kitchen. It has a pot wash where large vessels are cleaned and a wash area where service equipment is cleaned, washed and stored .This department also deals with the shortage and issue all service and kitchen equipment and hence the controls are also part of this department. The kitchen stewarding departments is headed a chief executive steward or steward manager. The requisitions of the service equipment are done through a kitchen stewarding indent book with signature from the outlet manager, F&B Manager and chief Executive steward.

8.2. Role:

Kitchen stewarding is essential charged to maintain and preserve the cleanliness and condition of the china, silver, glassware, Equipment and working area of the kitchen. It usually has a pot wash where large vessels are cleaned and a wash area where service equipment is cleaned, washed and stored. In doing so that the steward department maintains inventories and supplies of all equipments, china and silver, scrubs and clean all the working surfaces and floor of entire kitchen. Kitchen stewarding Department are mainly in the back area, it is still one of the most Important Department. Strict vigilance can control wastage and keep costs down by monitoring, breakage, controlling supply of Gas and coal to the kitchen and co-operate with the maintenance Department and monitoring the **Garbage Disposal system** (G.D.S). Also the care of the employee's cafeteria is the charge of the steward Department. This Department plays an important role in the functioning of both the Food production and F&B service Department. It is headed by steward manager, who reports to the F&B manager.

8.2.1. It performs the following functions:

• Washing kitchen pots and pans(scullery/pot wash)
• Maintaining kitchen equipment
• Cleaning all kitchen equipment and ensuring hygiene
• Garbage disposal
• Washing all service equipment including the ones used in banquets
• Polishing silverware
• Sending damaged silver ware for plating
• Pest control
• Carrying transporting heavy articles
• Indenting for new crockery cutlery
• Gas connections and upkeep of tandoor
• Maintaining ppm levels for sanitizing knives and chopping boards
• Replenishment of service ware to various outlets

8.3. Hierarchy of Kitchen Stewarding Department

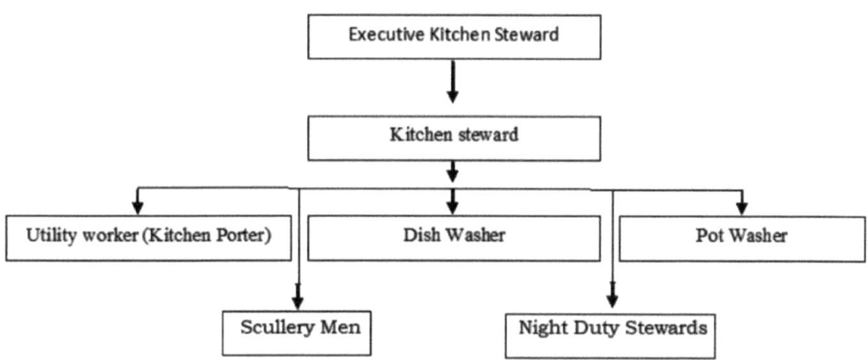

8.3.1. Duties and Responsibilities of the Kitchen Stewarding Staff :

Executive kitchen steward is responsible for the supervision of all silver, dish, and glass washing and the maintenance of high standards of kitchen cleanliness. They report directly to the executive chef. They must be familiar with all kitchens and service equipment, their usage, maintenance and storage, and government laws enforced by the health and sanitation department.

Kitchen Steward: They assist the executive kitchen steward and supervise the utility personnel in the absence of the chief steward. He/she is a working supervisor and normally collects the carts, room service trays, and cafeteria dishes. He/she scraps and stacks dishes and racks up glasses. They also make the coffee, fill up ice trucks, rack ice, and mop up spilled fluids. They distribute clean silverware in their proper storage area.

Dishwashers: They are responsible for cleaning and feeding the stacked dishes into the dish washing machine, to pull out the washed and dried dishes from the machine and stack them into carts, and to run the glasses and silver utensils through the glass machine.

Pot men: They clean all pots used by kitchen. During slack periods, they empty the kitchen garbage.

Ware men: They clear, polish, and burnish all silver flatware and hollow ware. During slack periods they clear all copperware.

Scullery men: They are responsible for the wash up of metal kitchen vessels and implements. The kitchen scullery is known as plonge, and the scullery man as the plongeur.

Night duty stewards: The peak workload occurs at different sections at different times during the work shift; therefore, the related stewards in each section pitch in and help each other under the directions of the supervisor on duty.

8.4. Equipment:

Keeping the equipment spick and span and clean not only contributes towards cleanliness and hygiene, which in turn contributes to ensuring the making of good and healthy food. Maintenance of equipment results in its efficient working as also lower consumption of energy. But all this heavy physical activity is largely mechanized and done with the help of huge machines, and a range of chemical agents and cleansers

8.4.1 List of Equipments Used In Kitchen Stewarding Department:

1. Automatic dish washing machine
2. Ice cube machine
3. Glass cleaning machine
4. High pressure spray cleaner
5. Floor scrubbing machine
6. Mobile Bain Marie
7. Auto lift
8. Racks
9. Loaders (all sizes)
10. Warming cabinet
11. Three sinks dish washing

12. Silver polishing machine
13. Dish landing table
14. Garbage container

Other detergents/cleaning agents/chemicals

- · Liquid shop
- · Liquid bleach
- · Silver dip.
- · Cleaning powder

8.4.2. KITCHEN STEWARDING: The Process.

THE SILVER ROOM & THE PLATE ROOM :

The Silver and the Plate Room is the store room for all the clean earthenware and metal tableware. In small hotel this room is combined with the wash up. They maintain an adequate stock of all the tableware, earthenware and glassware for service together with a slight surplus stock to handle emergency situations. The room is equipped with cupboards and shelves. The inventory of all the articles is regularly taken and tallied with the book stock. The shelves and the cupboards are so designed so as the larger silver items like platters and entrée dishes are stored on the shelves while earthen ware articles are stored in the cupboard. While stacking the heavier items should go at the lower shelves while the lighter items are stored higher up. Smaller items such as ashtrays, menu card holders, table numbers, cruet set, butter dishes are best stored in drawers lined with green baize.

Procedure for washing kitchen utensils and equipments:

Kitchen utensils can be manually or machine washed in the pot wash following the same principles of Wash, Rinse and Sanitize. It is advisable to use a 3 sink system and the utensils and chopping boards are to be dipped in chlorine solution of 100 ppm (parts per million) before being re used.

1. Scrape and pre rinse to keep the washing water clean for a longer time.
2. Wash with detergent in preferably hot water.
3. Rinse in hot water to remove detergent to avoid chemical poisoning.
4. Sanitize in warm water using chlorine or directly in steam or hot air.
5. Drip dry.

The wash up is carried out mainly in two methods:

i) Manual Washing Method: The first method is known as three sink washing method. The first sink contains a hot water and soap solution, and the second sink contains hot water to rinse and the third sink contains tepid warm water with a sanitized solution. The stacked and grouped dirties come in their groups to the first sink and here they are manually scrubbed with the hot water solution after which they are passed to the second sink where they are rinsed and ultimately to the third sink with tepid water where they are sanitized. The equipments can also be sterilized by hot steam and then wiped and send to the plate room and silver room accordingly.

ii) Machine Washing Method: The second method is washing by dish washing machine. The machine itself is very expensive and should be maintained and operated strictly as per the instructions given in the manual. The plates and other earthenware are stacked and put in a wired basket, and the glass wares in a separate similar basket to avoid breakage. The machine is aided by a conveyor belt running through it. The baskets are loaded on the conveyor that takes them to the inner part where they are sprayed with soap solution, and then rinsed, and depending upon the type of machine the articles can even be sterilized and dried as they come out from the other end of the machine.

8.4.3. MACHINES USED FOR CLEANING AND POLISHING:

8.4.3.1. DISHWASHERS: There are 3 types of dishwashers on the basis of the use:

A. Glass washers: used primarily used in bars for there is a frequent use of the glassware and the same glass cannot be used to serve cocktails every time the guest asks for a repeat. The process of dish washing would be the hot water rinse -soap solution-final hot water rinse-wiping if required.

B. Single rack dishwasher: the racks are used to put in cutlery or line the plates and other crockery. It is a box type machine and has a cover of sorts which can be pulled up or down to stop or start the machine respectively.

C. Conveyor belt type dishwasher: this is the dishwasher used now days in all 5 star properties wherein there is a conveyor belt and all the cutlery and crockery is lined in the racks. Dividing curtains highly resistant to chemical agents and heat are present. It is loaded from one end and the process of cleaning is carried out.

<u>Three types on the basis of working:</u>

A. Spray Type: Dishes are neatly stacked in racks which slide into the machines where they are sprayed with hot water and detergents (48 degree C-60 degree C) from above and below. The rack then moves to the sterilization section where the dishes are subjected to a hot water shower (of 82 degree C).Dishes sterilized at this temperature dry quickly when passed out into the air.

B. Brush type: dishes are scrubbed in hot detergent water (48-60 degree C)with revolving brushes. Then they are rinsed and sterilized in another section of the machine.

C. Agitator water machine: In this method, baskets of dishes are immersed in deep tanks and cleaned by mechanical agitation in hot detergent water. The baskets are given a final hot water rinse for sanitization.(82degree C).These machines are usually operated by two people, onc for sorting soiled items and to feed the machine and the other

to collect the
clean ware.

8.4.3.2. BURNISHING MACHINE:

There is a large drum which is half filled with ball bearings and there is a rod in the centre used for putting the handles of the cups and jugs. The cutlery is directly put into the drum. The soap solution is added to avoid friction which could cause scratches. This machine is either attached to a water supply or else water is poured manually. The machine takes around 15 min to complete the polishing process.

8.4.3.3. SILVER PLATING MACHINES:

There is a separate room that is used as the silver plating room where machines are used to electroplate the silver articles.

CHAPTER NINE

Unit 9: Function Catering

9.1. Function Catering:

Function catering can involve anything from the simple service of sandwiches and coffee or tea to gala banquets, and the functions can take place, anywhere, indoors of a private home to a grand ballroom. Today the guest do not only need lodging facilities but also other facilities such as place for meeting, exhibition, wedding, etc. Banquet section is also important to increase the income of the hotel.

9.2. Banquets:

In catering terms a 'function' means a meal served as a special occasion in a room set aside for these purposes and usually for a large number of people. Any party of customers larger than can normally be seated at one table in a restaurant may be given a private room, where available, and a meal served to a larger number than that may be termed a banquet. A banquet is special meal supplied to a group of persons who belong to a particular association and who wish to meet and eat together because of their like interests, usually annually. This makes it a special occasion and the menu and service should therefore be of higher standard than for the normal daily routine. A banquet can be held at lunch or dinner time and the pattern of operation may vary from one kind to another but it is a formal occasion and traditional protocol should be followed.

9.2.1. Types of Banquets:

All functions are categorized into three main categories:

Formal function: In this type of function, certain procedures, such as seating the host, chief guest, guest of honour and the invitees, serving the food and beverages are decided by the host. This should be strictly followed during the function. Formal functions always include speeches at a specified time. Dress code for the invitees may be insisted upon. Controlled behaviour of the guests prevails in the formal catering. State dinners have their own guidelines that vary from state to state and there are different rules governed by the protocol. In most cases, formal dress code, four-to-five-course menu, musical entertainment, speeches and toast made on behalf of the head of state hosting the state dinner as well as the foreign head of the state.

Semi-formal function: These functions are less formal in comparison to formal functions. The most common examples of such functions are the annual general meetings, seminars, national and international conferences, press conferences to launch new products, convocation ceremonies, dealers meetings, etc.

Informal Function: In an informal function, no formalities and procedures are followed on seating, serving the dress codes. The service is indiscriminate of sex and ranks. These functions normally include entertainment. One can witness casual behaviour of the guests in the informal functions. More of normal functions are organized in the presents days. As the name suggests there are informal parties or get-together parties, such as reception parties, cocktail parties, marriage ceremonies, birthday parties and alumni parties.

9.2.2. Seating:

On the total number of people attending a function it must be determined how many will be seated on the top table and how many on the sprigs, round or oblong tables, making up the full table plan. It must be known whether the number of guests on the top table includes the ends, and care should be taken to avoid seating 13 people on this table. All tables, with the exception of the top one, should be numbered again avoiding using the number 13. It is permissible to use 12A in place of 13. The Table numbers themselves should be on stands at such a height that may all the seen from the entrance of the banqueting room; the approx. height of the stands being 30 inches. After the guests are seated and before the service commences, these stands are sometimes removed. As far as possible, when formulating the table plan, one should try to avoid seating the guests with their backs to the top table. There are three copies of the seating plan. Spacing means space between two sprig tables including the width of the chairs and gangway from wall to back of the chair and gangway. To calculate the space required for any particular function, one must know some standard measurements of the furniture used in a banquet department. There some standard guidelines to be followed while doing seating arrangement.

The basic types and sizes of banquet furniture are as follows:

a. Rectangular/ buffet table (Big) : 6‘ x 3’ x 2.5‘

b. Rectangle/ buffet table (Small): 5’ x 3‘ x 2.5’

c. Conference table : 6‘ x 1.5’ x 2.5‘

d. Half moon table : 2’ Radius

e. Round table: 5‘(Diameter) 2.5’ (Height)

f. Serpentine table : 8‘ (Outer Diameter) 3’ (Inner Diameter)

g. Banquet chair dimension: 1‘ – 9‟ x 1’ – 7" x 2.5’ (L x W x H)

Standard guidelines for leaving space while planning a banquet set-up are as follows:

a. Aisle: 3‘

b. Space from the wall to the table: 5’

c. Space between rows: 1.5‘

d. Space between the head table and the row tables: 6’

e. Space between a table and a chair: 1'

9.2.3. Menu:

A banquet menu is a fixed menu at a set price offering usually no choice whatsoever to the customers, unless the client informs the caterer in advance that certain guests require, say, a vegetarian or non-vegetarian meal, and is available to all guests at a predetermined time. Meals are served in courses, which may vary from four to six. The price ranges offered should suit the pocket of the target clients. The banquet menus are complied by a team of managerial staff considering cost, profit margin, style of service, production skill, service skill, equipment availability, dietary needs, availability of raw ingredients and guest preferences. The complied menus are neatly printed and filed in the folder which will be discussed with the potential client at the time of booking. The banquet manager may assist the host in selecting the dishes during the booking of function. The categories of dishes offered in Indian menu are salads, soups, Indian breads, fish, chicken, mutton, paneer, vegetables, rice or biryani, dal, sweets and ice cream. Each of the categories have more than eight dishes thus offering more options to the host to choose from. The number of categories and the dishes under each category a host can avail are predetermined by the hotel. The number of choices offered will vary according to the price.

9.3. Outdoor Catering:

Outdoor of Off-premise catering is a banquet service at external sites. People choose off premises catering to personalize an occasion. All social, professional or state functions can have off premises at their own premises.

A housewife may order off premises catering at her villa for a large gathering of friends, or a corporate house may call for an in-house meeting, training program or conference. The banqueting procedures remain the same. The organization and management needed by these off premises catering companies are very similar to a banqueting department in a large hotel or a conference centre and in addition would have to take into account a number of factors specific to off premises catering:

- The location of the event, whether a semi permanent site is being used where limited services are already in situ in terms of water, sanitation, heating and lighting.
- The transportation of the food beverage items, the distances involved and whether heated or chilled trucks are needed.
- Hygiene problems associated with food being transported and held at the correct temperatures and the added worry of possible power failures on a temporary site; the losses and pilferage that can occur at any stage during transportation and the setting up and the difficulties of ensuring back up facilities and supplies and staffing miles away from the organization's main base.

9.4. EVENTS:

Events create opportunities for people to connect with an area, spend time together, celebrate and experience the diversity of cultures and foster creativity and innovation. They allow a community to come alive and provide an opportunity for a destination to showcase its tourism experience and increase economic activity. Events contribute significantly to community building, lifestyle and leisure enhancement, cultural development, tourism promotion and increased visitation, volunteer participation, fundraising and economic development. Most importantly, events create a sense of fun and vibrancy, resulting in a strong sense of community connectivity, pride and a sense of place.

Events are a dynamic and fast-growing sector that has obvious synergies with tourism. If managed and hosted effectively, they can expand the visitor economy, provide media exposure, promote regional development, and stimulate the upgrading of infrastructure and the emergence of new partnerships for financing sport, tourism, culture, and leisure facilities. The hosting of major events, therefore, represents a unique opportunity to rethink or reposition a destination and to support the development of modern infrastructure. As such many countries now view the successful hosting of such events as a vehicle for economic growth, job creation, branding, well-being, and urban regeneration.

From a tourism perspective, many cities, regions and countries are now devoting considerable resources to developing, attracting and supporting major events as part of a wider strategy to increase visitor numbers and expenditure. However, hosts cities, regions and countries of such events face a range of challenges including funding, effective governance, and the ability to accurately evaluate the economic, social, environmental, and other added value of tourism events

9.4.1. Types of Events:

- CULTURAL CELEBRATIONS: Festivals, Carnivals, Commemorations, Religious events.
- POLITICAL AND STATE: Summits, Royal occasions, Political events, VIP visits.
- ARTS AND ENTERTAINMENT: Concerts, Award ceremonies.
- BUSINESS AND TRADE: Meetings, conventions, Consumer and trade shows, Fairs, markets.
- EDUCATIONAL AND SCIENTIFIC: Conferences, Seminars, and Clinics.
- SPORT COMPETITION: Amateur/professional, Spectator/participant.
- RECREATIONAL: Sport or games for fun
- PRIVATE EVENTS: Weddings, Parties, Socials, Business events and tourism.

CHAPTER TEN

Unit 10: Specialised F&B Catering

10.1. Airline Catering:

Catering for people on the move is a much more demanding job than when doing so in the usual static environment; it is a job that calls for skills and knowledge above and beyond the norm. Doing a job whilst moving at speed or on an undulating floor brings a need not just for good equilibrium but also be able to cope with a rush of passengers, all of them wanting to be severed in a hurry.

Airline catering is concerned with the provision of food to air passengers. A characteristic of airline catering is that pre-cooked or frozen food is loaded into the aircraft galleys and later heated in specially fabricated ovens. The catering for airline food may be undertaken by the airline company or contracted to a specialist firm which may be supplying a similar service to many airlines.

Airline catering is probably one of the most complex operational systems in the world. A large scale airline catering production unit may employ over 800 staff to produce as many as 25,000 meals per day during peak periods. A large international airline company may have hundreds of take offs and landing everyday from just their main hub. While the way food is served on trays to airline passengers bears some resemblance to service styles in restaurants or cafeterias, the way food is prepared and cooked increasingly resembles a food manufacturing plant rather than a catering kitchen. The way food and equipment is stored resembles a freight warehouse, and the way meals and equipment are transported and supplied has a close affinity to military style logistics and distribution system.

Airline catering starts with an understanding of the number of passengers and their needs, such information is available from both market research and actual passenger behaviour. On the basis of this, airlines, sometimes in consultation with caterers and suppliers, develop their product and service specifications. Such specifications determine exactly what food, drink and equipment items are to be carried on each route for each class of passenger.

At the heart of the airline catering system is the airline production unit, which is part warehouse, part food manufacturing plant, part kitchen and part assembly belt. In response to forecasts of passenger's numbers on any given flight, the production unit follows a series of complex steps to produce trayed meals and non-food items ready for transportation to the aircraft. Loaded trolleys and other items need to be stowed on board to ensure the microbial safety of edible items and the security and safety of the crew passengers, and aircraft. At the designated time during the flight, the cabin crew then carries out the service of meals, snacks and other items.

On arrival at its destination, each aircraft is then stripped of all the equipment and trolleys, which are returned to the production units for cleaning and re-use. It is necessary to understand the impact of flying on the physiology of the passenger to manage a complex supply chain, assure the safety of the food and drink, and apply the principles of international logistics.

10.2. Hospital Catering:

Patient meals are an integral part of hospital treatment and the consumption of a balanced diet, crucial to aid recovery. Proper food service and nutritional care in hospitals has beneficial effects on the recovery of patients and their quality of life. Hospitals have several other factors which need to be taken into account when considering the provision of a meal service:

- For the majority of hospital patients there are no alternative catering facilities available to them so that, in effect, they become captive consumers.
- Modified therapeutic and medically prescribed diets are often needed in addition to the normal dietary meals being produced.
- Flexibility is needed in terms of production and service in the event of additional admissions from casualty, early discharges, large scale emergencies etc.
- The catering service is not seen as a priority in the overall planning and financial budgeting of hospitals, although customer satisfaction with

hospital meals is recognized as being beneficial in terms of patient recovery- good presentation, quality and service of hospital food encouraging patient to consume and enjoy their meals.

- Hospital meals are not sold in cash terms to the patients but form an integrated part of the total hospital package of customer car.

A menu for each patient is sent to the wards, so that the patient can select the dishes and specify the portion sizes. Alternatively the nutritionist decides the menu depending on the needs of the patient and sends the requirements to the kitchen. These menus are sent back to the department for summarizing and totalling the number of meals required for the various meal times. Food is plated on the trays by various catering staff using a moving conveyor belt at the rate of 6-8 trays a minute. This speed may be reduced depending on the efficiency, as each tray has to be checked for consistency in portioning. A 300 bed hospital should take about one and a quarter house to serve their meals.

The food is kept hot in a variety of way either by insulating the trolleys, having an electrical plug in all the wards, or regeneration of cold food if the food transported is of the cook-chill type. The food is usually served at staggered timings considering the length of service but always ensuring that the meal interval remains the same. This system lends itself to better advanced selection of food, advance planning in terms of production and service leading to foods being cooked closer to delivery time and reducing the service gap and customer dissatisfaction. Hospital catering is a continually evolving service changing and adapting to new instructions and constraints, new markets, innovations and concepts, in particular that of total facilities management.

10.3. Cruise Line Catering:

Catering plays a vital role in the modern era; catering provides food and beverage services to the people. The people organize parties at their homes, office or nearby banquet hall or hotels. The sea catering is a luxury service which facilitates the person & provides comfort to that extent level. People who are travelling for business purpose or/& vacations from one country to another, they choose this kind of transport facilities.

There are two types of sea transports, which provide the catering facilities: –

CRUISE LINERS: In cruise liners, trips are sold as a package including food, accommodation and many other facilities. However, liquor and tobacco are paid individually.

Most of the cruise liners have their own pastry shops, dining halls, bar, etc. Hence the menus are best and they may differ to suit international tourist.

Table d' hote menus with a wide choice in each course are popular. There is a central kitchen known as "galley", in which there are various sectors such as butchery, pastry, the raw material is packed up from ports in advance, service could be a fine plated buffet.

CARGO VESSELS: Cargo vessels are merchant ships that carry commercial goods.

- No. of staff is usually limited.
- A cyclic menu is prepared to provide meals to the staff.
- Hours of operations are pre-decided.
- The cost of food should be within a budget figure.
- A healthy and wholesome meal is provided.

10.4. Railway Catering:

Catering to passengers during the journey and at halts at stations is called railway catering. This catering may be conveniently divided into two major areas: terminal catering and in-transit catering. Catering at the terminals usually comprises licensed bars, self-service and waiter service restaurants, fast food and take-away units, supplemented by vending machines dispensing hot and cold food and beverages.

10.4.1. IRCTC:

(Indian Railway Catering and Tourism Corporation) was formed on 27th Sept 1999 with an objective to 'enhance customer services and facilitation in railway catering, hospitality, travel and tourism with best industry practices'. Today company has made a significant mark in its customer-services oriented business like setting up of Food Plazas on Railway premises, 'Railneer', 'Rail Tour packages' and 'Internet Ticketing' bringing great deal of professionalism into the operations.

IRCTC deals in two kinds of catering i.e. Railway catering and Non-Railway catering includes departmental catering, static catering, food plaza, jan ahars, hotels, executive lounges, base kitchen and minor units. Non Railway catering includes institutional catering, consultancy services, kiosks, food courts, housekeeping etc. Static catering means catering on platforms, jan ahars, refreshment rooms, stalls, trolleys etc falls under this category.

Retiring room complex is also operated by IRCTC. At present 554 stations are operated with 2000 rooms. IRCTC is having 244 catering units to serve customers. It has four base Kitchen in New Delhi, Noida, Patna and Howrah. IRCTC Noida Kitchen in central Kitchen which supply food to railways as well as corporate sector. IRCTC is managing 59 trains under on board catering license and 33 trains through departmental operation.

10.5. Catering Services in Armed Forces:

Indian Army Service Corps: The ASC is mainly responsible for the provisioning, procurement and distribution of Supplies of food ration, fresh & dry eatable items, FOL(Fuels, oil, lubricants), Hygiene Chemicals and items of Hospital Comforts to Army, Air Force and when required for Navy and other para military forces. The operation of Mechanical Transport except first line transport and fighting vehicles and the provision and operation of first and second line Animal Transport is also the responsibility of the ASC. The other responsibilities include carriage and distribution of ammunition including mines, forward of the Corps Maintenance Area in the field in case of plains, and forward of Divisional Maintenance Area in case of mountain formation, packing of commodities for supply, loading of aircraft and ejection of loads, training and provisioning of clerks for all branches of staff at formation headquarters and the training and provisioning of catering staff in the army. This Corps is a versatile one designed for the role with wide parameters for multifarious activities of immediate concern to the troops. The Corps also handle postal services in forward areas.

All chefs and stewards in the Indian army receive their training at the Army Service Corps (ASC) Centre in Bangalore. Chefs and stewards go through three levels of training. The 6-month long Level 1 course for chefs teaches them the basics of cooking and hygiene. Those who excel in Level 1 go on to become mess chefs and are immediately enrolled into a 3-month Special Training course where they learn to cook different types of starters, soups, mains and desserts that fall under Indian, Continental and Chinese cuisines. After the completion of the Special Training course, they are ready to return to their respective regiments, and join army messes situated across the country.

Sometime between 2-10 years of their tenure as a mess chef, they return to the ASC centre for training at Level 2 and 3. Each of these courses lasts 28 days, and teaches the chefs more about Continental, Chinese and regional

Indian cuisines. Nearly every mess chef in the army can turn out dosa, sambar, biryani, noodles, fish curry, kadhi and rajma with the same amount of confidence.

The stewards, in a similar training drill, are taught skills related to steward duties and responsibilities — how to make basic cocktails and mocktails; the many ways of folding a napkin; knowledge of cutlery and glasses, along with each specific purpose; how to serve beverages (always from the right) and food (from the left); whom to serve first (always the lady); how to set a table for an Indian, Continental or Chinese meal; nuances on the placement of cutlery if an officer wants to be served, is waiting for his senior to finish, or is done eating and hence has 'closed the plate', and so on.

Some of the most important lessons shared between the chefs, stewards and their instructors are about the formal parties that are organised every so often in an army mess. The quintessential example of elegance, tradition, order and precision, formal parties in the army are all the charm one needs to experience. The menus for these parties are curated with thought, the dishes named with ingenuity and the tables laid out with skill. The pristine white china is framed with a delicate gold border and, in some cases, stamped with the regiment monogram. The glasses are crystal. The menu is often continental; a tradition that was started during the British rule for the simple reason that it's the least messy cuisine to eat with cutlery. Everyone closes their plate when the senior most officers is finished eating. And finally, dessert is served.

The menu for a formal party holds a special place in most army messes, as they represent craft and knowledge on the part of the mess committee that designs them. Sometimes old menus are referred to, to commemorate victories, recreate a bygone special dinner, or simply to please a guest. The menus are a matter of pride — even keepsakes. If you take a walk from one end of the dining hall in the National Defence Academy (NDA) to the other, you will see menus from pre-independence times and special occasions that hosted important dignitaries, kept safe on a bed of taut velvet and covered with glass.

10.6. Welfare Catering:

The major purpose of these services is philanthropy and social welfare. Persons / organisations who undertake these services, aim to ensure that people are well and properly fed, and if any profit is made through their business, it is of secondary importance.

Examples of such catering services are feeding people at workplaces, the armed forces, in schools, in supplementary feeding programmes implemented by the government or for sick people who are in hospitals. Industrial catering is one form of welfare catering. Many industries provide food to their employees as part of their welfare activities. It is believed that work output is related to the welfare of the employees. Well-fed workers produce more and better work. Workers receive free food or food at a price much lower than its actual cost (subsidised), with the rest of the cost being borne by the company. In industrial, institutional and welfare outlets the objective is mainly to provide a necessary service. Caterers / managers of these services may be given limited budgets within which they are required to successfully manage the operations. In such situations, the caterer may not be in competition with other caterers for business since the functions 'belong' to the employing organisation. Also, in such establishments, the service is not available to the public, but only to the members of the institution/organisation for which the service is operated.

The catering facility may range from vending machines supplying a limited variety of beverages and snacks, to a waiter silver service restaurant with an extensive menu. Catering amenities are an important aspect of industrial situations and as a department in an organization can evoke the emotional feelings of the employees. Companies are appraised on the type of facilities they provide for their staff, and it is a service that once provided should not be allowed to fall below its initial standards. This is particularly important where companies have developed and employed more staff over a number of years without due consideration to the catering service which has long since become over-stretched.

The catering facilities in industrial & institutional situations such as factories, office block etc are an ancillary service to the main function of the organization. The two methods by which catering may be organized in such industrial or institutional situations are direct management or contracted out. Direct management is where the parent company chooses to establish and operate the catering facilities itself. The second method involves the parent company employing a firm of contract caterers to operate and manage the catering department for them. In the first situation the parent company is completely responsible for the type and standard of catering service it provides; the catering department thus becoming another department in the organization that is under its direct control and management.

Contract caterers are usually engaged for a specific period of time, after which the contract may be renewed or dissolved as both parties wish. Contract caterer are involved in all types of industrial catering situations, ranging from the small independent concerns to the large multi-national organizations and may become involved for different reasons.

Establishing and operating catering services are the main functions of contract caterers and as such they can have a more professional approach than many of those organizations who try to operate their own catering facilities; this professional attitude and approach are reflected in the standards of facilities provided and in more effective cost control in addition to a well organized catering department, other financial benefits can accrue because of the purchasing power of large contract caterers, such as cost saving products prepared to the company's own specifications.

Companies consider the provision of a catering service as a valuable and important contribution to the welfare of their employees and are proud of the standards they achieve. The total market available for industrial catering facilities may be quite restricted and this may be further limited as the individual catering facilities usually cater to quite specific groups of employees. Customers in industrial & institutional situations require a meal of a good standard and quality, at an acceptable price, and one that can be comfortably consumed in the amount of time they have available for their meal. In industrial & institutional cafeteria the menus are generally more limited in terms of choice than are the menus offered in comparable commercial operations.

Paty B: BEVERAGE SERVICE

"*Beverage Service*"

CHAPTER ELEVEN

Unit 1: Non-Alcoholic Beverages

Non-Alcoholic Beverages are potable drinks which may be nourishing, stimulating, refreshing may have thirst quenching properties. They also help in maintaining of body ph balance. Non alcoholic beverages provide supplement diet to invalids, infants and convalescents. Some non alcoholic beverage eg. Mocktails (considered as equivalent to cocktails) are consumed by teetotaller at social gatherings.

Some non alcoholic beverages provide instant energy after exertion from sports/games or other activities. They prevent dehydration and help in maintaining blood volume in case of bleeding, heat stroke, vomiting, excess sweating or diarrhoea. In this unit we will concentrate on all the basic non alcoholic drinks, which may be taken as a single drink or modified and mixed to make it tastier, refreshing and a new appearance.

We will read about tea, coffee, juices, squashes, cordials, mixed drinks etc. where you will also know about the basics of these drinks and how these can be taken in different ways and enjoyed. Certain ingredients in milk like theobromine induce sleep. It decreased body temperature when taken chilled resulting in refreshed feeling.

1.1. Classification of Non-alcoholic Beverage:

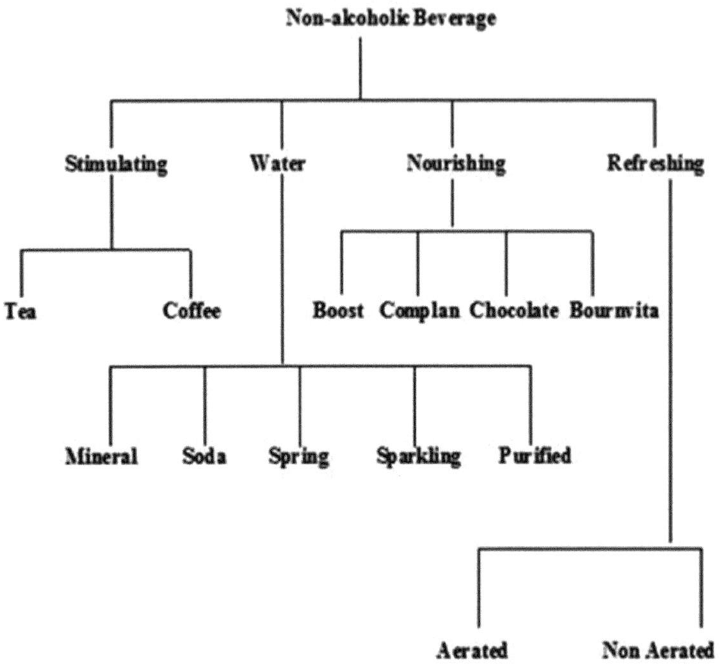

1.1.1. Stimulating Drink/Beverage:

These are consumed to stimulate our mental and physical activities. Eg. Tea and coffee

Refreshing drink/beverage:

These are drinks that are taken to make up for the fluid loss (due to perspiration) of our body. Eg. Nimbu Pani, water, syrups, soft drinks, tonic water, etc.

Nourishing drink/ beverage:

Beverage consumed to provide nutrients to the body. Ex. Milk-based products like a milkshake, chocolate drinks, juices, etc.

1.1.2. Non-alcoholic (examples):

- Hot-Tea, coffee, cocoa, etc.
- Cold-Dispense beverages
- Aerated water
- Mineral water and spicy water

- Squashes
- Juices
- Syrups

Just as the name suggests, Non-Alcoholic Beverages contain no or less than 0.5% alcohol. They are potable drinks which have one, two or all of the 3 qualities of being refreshing, stimulating and nourishing. Non-Alcoholic Beverages may be either HOT or COLD.

Cold non-alcoholic beverages can be further Germany), Vichy Celestine (France) and Badoit (France) are examples of beverages which naturally contain carbon dioxide gas.Coca Cola, Fanta, 7up, Limca, Tonic Water, Ginger Ale, etc. are beverages which are artificially charged with carbon dioxide gas.

Hot non-alcoholic beverages, the prime examples of which are Tea, Coffee and Hot Chocolate, are consumed primarily as stimulating beverages around the world. Though most of the hot non-alcoholic beverages have substantial levels of nutrients, their consumption for nutritional or refreshment purposes is very limited. Categorized as either Aerated or Still (Non-Aerated).

Still Drinks are plain liquids which may be flavoured or unflavoured. Mineral water, fruit & vegetable juices, squashes, cordials, crushes, slushes, shakes, smoothes, syrups, nectars, ethnic drinks like lassi, nimbu-paani, aam-panna, coconut water, jaljeera, etc., all come under the of Still or Non-Aerated Beverages.

Aerated Beverages, also called Sparkling Beverages, are the drinks which contain Carbon Dioxide, either occurring naturally or added artificially. Spring waters or Mineral waters like Appolianaris.

<u>1.1.3. Tea:</u>

Tea is a non-alcoholic beverage obtained by processing the leaves of Camellia Sinensis or Camellia Assamica, which are tropical plants of the Camellia family. The processed tea leaves are infused with steaming hot water to release the rich aroma and flavour of tea and then combined with cream, sugar, lime juice or a huge array of other herbs, flavours and mixers. Tea is the second most popular non-alcoholic beverage in the world after coffee. It is the most commonly consumed drink in India, China, Japan, Korea, Sri Lanka, West Asia, Great Britain and France.

<u>Types of tea:</u>

Black Tea: This is the most commonly available and the most widely consumed variety of processed tea in the world. Black tea is produced when the production method described above is followed without variations. As the name suggests, it is black in colour and is characterized by strong aroma and flavour. A variation of the Black Tea is the CTC (Cut, Tear and Curl) Leaf Tea. This variation is produced when, during the Rolling stage, the rolling cylinder in the crushing machine has grooves and spikes on its rolling surface. When the leaves pass under the cylinder, they not only get rolled but also get cut, torn and curled. The CTC Leaf Tea leaves have a pellet-like appearance and are browner in colour compared to Black Tea. Though having lesser flavour than Black Tea, CTC Leaf Tea produces stronger liquor.

Oolong Tea: - The Oolong Tea is very popular in its country of origin, China. It is produced by reducing the time of the Withering and Fermentation processes by half. The liquor of the Oolong Tea is golden-amber in colour and, even though it isn"t very strong, it gives off a highly refreshing aroma and contains a fine, delicate flavour.

Green Tea: - Green Tea is produced by steaming the leaves immediately after plucking. The stages of Rolling, Withering and Fermentation are completely eliminated. After steaming, the leaves are dried, rolled and packaged for sale. Green Tea leaves, when infused with hot water, turn it a light golden in colour and give off a delicate, enticing aroma. Green Tea is gaining popularity all over the world due to its high content of vitamins and minerals as well as its anti-oxidant properties. In India, Green Tea is grown in the Kangra valley and in Dehradun and is used to make the popular Kashmiri Kahwa.

Making Tea:

- Use a good quality tea.
- Use fresh water, which is freshly boiled. The water should be lime free. Tap water makes tea cloudy.
- Heat the tea pot, i.e., rinse out the teapot with boiling water before putting in the tea. One teaspoon of tea per person + one for the pot (depending upon the quality of the tea).
- Pour the water onto the tea just as it reaches boiling point, taking the pot to the kettle, as the water must be as near boiling point as possible to enable the leaves to infuse properly. Water should be 950C (just below boiling point), before it is poured over the tea leaves.

- Infusion becomes bitter if boiled longer.
- Brew the tea, never stew it. Allow the tea to brew only for 4-5 minutes, and stir well before pouring.
- Just before serving, stir the tea in the teapot with a spoon. Use a strainer.

1.1.4. Coffee :

Coffee is a hot non-alcoholic beverage which contains a strong stimulant called CAFFEINE. It is made by infusing the crushed processed beans of the "Coffea" plant with hot water. Many different mixers, herbs, sweeteners, juices, etc. are added to the coffee liquor according to the consumers" tastes to make the bitter coffee more palatable. Coffee is the most popular beverage, particularly as an after-dinner drink, in the world.

Making Coffee:

1. Use freshly roasted and ground coffee.
2. Buy the correct grind for the right type of machine
3. Clean the equipment
4. Use a set measure.
5. Add boiling water to the coffee.
6. Infusion time is according to the type of coffee being used and the method of making
7. Control the temperature. Do not boil it.
8. Strain; serve.
9. Add/milk/cream separately.
10. Serving temperature – Coffee – 820C, Milk – 680C

1.2. Nourishing Beverages:

1. **Bourn vita:** Mixture of malt, sugar, glucose, cocoa powder, dried milk, dried egg, salt and flavouring. Blended together; cooked under a vacuum until brittle. Carefully broken up.
2. **Horlicks:** Malted milk made from wheat flour, malted barley and milk.
3. **Oval tine:** Made from barley, malt milk, cocoa powder, soya flour, eggs and vitamins.
4. **Milo:** Made from condensed milk and malt extract with cocoa power, milk products and added vitamins.

Other Patent Beverages:

1. Boost
2. Complan
3. Mistura – real almond, chocolate, rich protein mixture.

1.3. Refreshing Beverages:

Iced Tea: Make strong tea. Chill well. The iced tea may be strained and stored chilled until required. This may be then served in a glass, on a doily, with a teaspoon on a side plate.

Garnish: A slice of lemon and sprig of mint.

Alternate method: Place crushed ice in a tall glass. Bring cool black tea in a teapot. From the right, pour it over the ice.

Cold Coffee: Strong coffee (black) should be made in the normal way. Strained and chilled well until required. It is served with an equal quantity of chilled milk for a smooth beverage or with cream in a tall glass with ice cubes added and with straws. The glass should stand on a doily on a side-plate with a teaspoon and wherever necessary, some cream should be served separately. It could be topped with ice cream.

1.4. Milk Drinks:

1. **Plain cold milk** – It is refreshing and nourishing. Generally served in a tall glass with an underliner and doily in between and a sundae spoon. Sugar syrup is given separately. A straw is also provided.
2. **Milk shakes** – A mixture of fresh milk, ice cream and flavouring syrup, rapidly whisked. May be topped with ice cream.
3. **Ice cream sodas** – A combination of fruit syrup and fresh cream in a long glass filled with soda water and topped with ice cream.
4. **Egg nog** – These are beaten eggs with fruit syrup and sugar added, mixed with hot/cold, and garnished with nutmeg power.
5. **Iced chocolate** – Make a hot chocolate with melted chocolate, castor sugar and milk. Cook it, whisking it all the time. Allow it to cool completely. Put it in a blender with crushed ice.
6. **Flavoured milk** – In tetra packs.

1.5. Mocktails:

A non alcoholic beverage containing all properties of a cocktail except alcohol. Some famous mocktails are given below:

- **Virgin Mary** – Tomato juice with salt, pepper, worcester sauce. May be garnished with a wedge of lemon. Served in a salt rimmed old-fashioned glass.
- **Non-alcoholic Pina Colada** – Pineapple juice and coconut cream, shaken well and strained. Served in a Collins glass. Garnished with pineapple. Served with a straw.
- **Shirley Temple/Roy Rogers** – A mixture of ginger and grenadine. Served on the rocks with a full fruit garnish and straws.

- **Tropicana** – Pineapple juice + orange juice.
- **Pussyfoot** – Orange juice, lemon juice, lime cordial, grenadine, egg yolk and soda, shaken well. Served on ice in a Collins glass and topped with soda.

1.6. Squashes and Cordials:

These are all concentrated fruit extracts, meant to be broken down with fresh or aerated water into a long drink and may be served hot or cold.

A fruit squash is made from fruit juice, sugar and preservative. Fruit cordial is a fruit squash from which all suspended matter is completely eliminated and is perfectly clear. It is filtered and clarified using fining agents. It is preserved by adding Potassium Meta-bi-sulphide and Sodium Benzoate or pasteurized by freezing.

1.7. Fruit Syrups:

These are concentrated fruit juices preserved with sugar or manufactured from compound colourings and flavours, eg. orange, lime, cherry, etc. Grenadine syrup is made from pomegranate.

1.8. Waters:

Soft Drinks: Drinks are acidified, sweetened, coloured artificially, carbonated and often chemically preserved. The formulation and flavouring of many well-known brands are a guarded secret. The water used should be well-purified, and free from micro-organisms, dissolved metals and organic compounds.

Synthetic flavours are generally used because:

- Natural flavours added to the drinks do not give standard products.
- Natural flavour extracts undergo changes in the presence of light, acid and storage.
- Natural flavours do not transport pigments of sufficient depth.
- Natural flavours are unstable in acidic conditions. Acids used are Citric, Malic, Tartaric and Phosphoric. Dissolved carbon dioxide also produces acidity.

Sodium Benzoate is a common preservative used in soft drinks.

Tonic – It is an aerated drink, sweetened and flavoured with natural fruit and plat extracts including quinine. It is drunk straight with ice and a slice of lemon or added in a cocktail. It is generally used with gin.

Ginger ale – Consists of aerated water with colouring and ginger essence.

Lemonade – Consists of lemon juice, sugar and aerated water.

Bottled Water: It is of two types:

1. **Mineral** – This has a mineral content, which is strictly controlled.
2. **Spring Water** – This has fewer regulations apart from those concerning hygiene.

Waters can be classified as:

1. Still
2. Naturally sparkling
3. Carbonated during bottling.

The capacities of the bottles vary from 1.5 litre to 220 ml. Glass and plastic bottles are available.

Natural Spring Waters: This is obtained from natural spring water in the ground. The water itself is impregnated with the natural minerals found in the soil. It is sometimes charged with an aerating gas. The uniqueness of this mineral water is that they have medicinal value. Where natural spring waters are found, it is usually termed as „Spa". Here the water may be drunk or bathed in, according to the cures they are supposed to effect. Many of the best-known mineral waters are bottled at the springs.

Mineral Waters: According to their chemical properties, they are classified as :

- **Alkaline Waters** – Help treatment of gout and rheumatism.
- **Aperients Waters** – Have saline constituents like sulphate of magnesia or sulphates of soda.
- **Chalybeate Waters** – Mineral waters are of two kinds : carbonated or sulphated. They act as a stimulant and as a tonic.
- **Lithiated Water** – Rich in lithia salts.
- **Sulphurous waters** – These are impregnated with hydrogen.
- **Table Waters** – These are less mineralised than other natural spring waters and are mainly alkaline. They may be taken between meals or at meal time, either alone or mixed with light wine or spirits.

1.3. Brand Names of Mineral Waters :

- French : Badoit, Contrex, Evia, Perrier, Vichy Saint
- England : Ashbourne, Abey Well, Ashe Park, Malvern, Aqua Pura

- Ireland : Bally Gowan, Glenpatrick
- Italy : San Pellegrino, Ferrarelle, Crodo Lisiel
- Germany : Apollinaris, Uberkinger, Petrusquelle
- Belgium : Spa
- Switzerland : Aqui
- Sweden : Ramlosa
- India : Himalaya, Pondicherry

CHAPTER TWELVE

Unit 2: Wines

Wine is an alcoholic beverage made with the fermented juice of grapes. Technically, any fruit is capable of being used for wine (i.e., apples, cranberries, plums, etc.), but if it just says "wine" on the label, then it's made with grapes.

2.1. Classification of Wines:

The wines are classified on following basis:

- BY COLOUR – Red, White, Rose
- BY NATURE – Still/Table, Sparkling, Fortified, Aromatized
- BY TASTE – Sweet, Dry
- BY YEAR – Vintage, Non-Vintage
- BY BODY – Light ,Medium, Heavy bodied wine

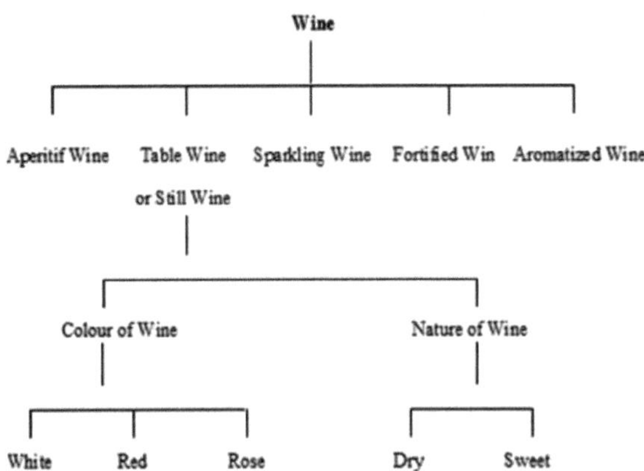

2.2. Production of Wine:

The process that turns the grape juice into Wine is called Fermentation. This is process associated with the conversion of natural grape juice sugar into alcohol and carbon-dioxide caused by the action of yeast, the minute organisms which are found on the skin of the grapes. The yeast feeds upon the grape sugar.

2.2.1. Production of wine involves following steps:

1. Harvesting
2. Grading
3. Weighing
4. De Stalking
5. Crushing Or Pressing
6. Chaptalisation
7. Sulphuring
8. Fermentation
9. Cellaring
10. Second Pressing
11. Racking
12. Finning
13. Filtration
14. Blending
15. Maturing Wines
16. Bottling
17. Pasteurisation
18. Ageing
19. Storage

1. **HARVESTING:** Grapes are plucked when the density of the bloom or natural yeast on the skin taken from a number of bunches is constant so that the grape is fully ripened and has nothing to gain more from the plant. Dry weather is chosen for harvesting. Some wines are left on the vines (shrub) a little longer to develop a greater concentration of sugar. From these finest dessert wines are obtained.
2. **GRADING:** Grapes are graded according to the quality which segregates ripe mature grapes from spoiled grapes.
3. **WEIGHING:** Grapes are weighed, to determine the quantity required for fermentation.

4. **DE STALKING:** The ripe grapes are plucked off from the stalks. Modern methodology incorporates a de stalking machine. The stalks have a bitter taste due to the presence of tannin, which should not come in contact with the juice.
5. **CRUSHING OR PRESSING:** Grapes are traditionally crushed with the feet by wearing special type of shoes called Zapatos di pisar or more conveniently by mechanical presses to extract the juice called must. At this stage the wine maker uses a hydrometer to measure the specific gravity of must, which indicates the sugar content and therefore the projected alcoholic strength. During the crushing stage, if red wine has to be made, then the skin is allowed to come in contact with juice till it gets colour from the skin. In case of White wine, skin in is removed immediately (if it is made from red grapes). Rose wine is made by allowing the skin to come in contact for a short while to get the pink colour.
6. **CHAPTALISATION:** If in case the *Must* shows the insufficient amount of sugar, then the sugar is added to enrich the must. This process is called chaptalisation.
7. **SULPHURING:** Sulphur dioxide is added early in the fermentation process to prevent air from oxidizing the juice and converting the alcohol into vinegar. Sulphur dioxide takes up all the oxygen to let the wine yeast which is anaerobic (able to work in absence of oxygen) to convert grape sugar into alcohol. Sulphur dioxide forms a coating on the surface of juice to prevent the air from entering the juice and thereby letting the wine yeast to do its work.
8. **FERMENTATION:** Fermentation is the process of adding wine yeast (technically termed as Saccharomyces Ellipsoideus) to fresh grape juice to convert the natural sugar in the grape to ethyl alcohol. The fermentation is done in stainless steel vats nowadays against the traditional wooden vats. In this process carbon dioxide is simultaneously released making fermentation violent at first and then slows. The yeast added is 3-5 % of the volume of juice. The fermentation process two days to two weeks. Fermentation occurs only as long as there is sugar to ferment or when the alcohol content rises to 14% because at this point alcohol kills the remaining yeast. If sugar remains with alcohol content then the wine tends to be sweet. A wine is considered sweet when it has 2% sugar content. During the process the temperature is maintained between 64-70 degree F for red wines and 44 degree to 59 degree F for

white wines. The wine maker may control the acidity caused by grape acids by adding water acidifying agents such as gypsum.

9. **CELLARING:** Once fermentation is complete the _running wine‘ or vin de goutte is run off into the casks for maturing. The casks are filled to the full to exclude air. The filled casks are put in cellars for the wine to mature. This is called Cellaring. The suspended particles are allowed to settle to the bottom of the cask as sediments or less.
10. **SECOND PRESSING:** The residue of pips and skin (called marc) left in the fermentation tank or vat is sent for further pressing and the resultant juice, called vin de presse to which is rich in tannin. The wine maker may decide whether to add vin de presse to vin de goutte. The left over i.e. pips and skins are sent for a third pressing and the juice fermented and distilled to produce eau –de –vie- de- marc. Nothing is wasted and the sugar in the grape is completely utilized.
11. **RACKING:** The wine must be separated from the dead yeasts which decompose and give an odd flavour to the wine. The wine is carefully pumped into another cask without disturbing the lees leaving some wine at the bottom. This is sent for distilling into eau- de- vie- de- marc. Racking removes some acidity. The colour is brilliant and flavours blend together and smooth out.
12. **FINNING:** This is the process of converting cloudy wine into clear fine wine. This may be done with a gelatinous substance such as-

- Ising glass (bladder of sturgeon fish)
- White of egg beaten with salt
- Colloidal silica
- Gelatin or Bentonits
- They collect (attract) all the impurities and protein haze in the wine.

13. **FILTERATION:** After fining the wine may passed through fine filters to get crystal clear wine. The young wine is pumped to the refrigeration unit to stabilize the wine.
14. **BLENDING:** Experienced specialist improve the quality of wine by blending wines of different vineyards and vintage (different years) to produce wine that is consistent in quality.
15. **MATURING WINES:** It is natural process by allowing the wine to rest in oak barrels for 1 or 2 years to gain maturity and pick up a soft mellow character from the oak wood. Maturisation can be induced artificially

by agitation, heating, refrigeration and electrical impulses. During maturation wine tends to evaporate. So the loss of wine during maturation is called Angels share. There is a stopper (usually cork) that fits into the opening at the top of the barrel. The stopper must be opened from time to time to allow the gas to escape.

16. **BOTTLING:** Wine is poured into sterilized bottles during cool and dry weather. The bottles are closed with corks and sealed with Spanish wax or foil. The selection of cork is very important as poor quality of cork can spoil the wine. After 40 years the cork tree develops a thick, spongy, semi hard bark, several inches thick. Portugal primarily and then Spain and Italy produces the best cork.

- The corks are obtained from bark of tree called _Bark oak‘.
- There are different colours of bottles for different wines.
- Green & Transparent For white wine
- Brown red wine
- Transparent rose wine

17. **PASTEURISATION:** Pasteurization is the process to free the wine from further fermentation. The wine bottles are immersed upright in double boilers with water, heated to temperatures between 180 degree F & 190 degree F. The immersion is for 1 to 2 minutes.
18. **AGEING:** Wine is matured in bottles. The period of maturing may differ from house to house, till it achieves its characteristics, aroma and flavour.
19. **STORAGE:** Wines are stored in cool conditions at temperatures of 50 degree- 65 degree F. The storage area must be as light can ruin the wine. The wines must be moved as little as possible before they are shipped out.

2.2.2. Methods of making sparkling wine: There are 4 methods of making sparkling wine:

- Carbonation or Impregnation Method
- Cuve Close or Charmat-Process or Tank Method
- Transversagé Method or Transfer Method
- La Méthode Champenoise or The Champagne Method

- **Carbonation or impregnation method**: In this method wine is chilled in closed vats, so that frost forms outside. A special apparatus injects CO2↑into the still, chilled wine and the wine is then bottled under pressure. The resulting wine resembles fizzy drinks in the glass with large bubbles which do not last long. This is the cheapest and least durable way of making wine sparkle and is used for the cheapest of all sparkling wines.

- **Cuve close or charmat-process or tank method**: This method of making sparkling wine was started in France by M. CHARMAT and involves secondary fermentation which takes only 10 days to complete in contrast to the years of waiting required by Métho-de-Champenoise. In this method the still wine is pumped into tanks together with a measured quantity of yeasts and sugar. Secondary fermentation is allowed under controlled temperature and wine is circulated in closed tanks by propellers. After 10 days of violent and quick fermentation wine is drawn off through filters, still under pressure and bottled. Its advantages are that it is very much cheaper, faster and less labour intensive than the other processes and is better suited to base wines which lack much capacity for aging. This method is not permitted to be used for Appellation Côntrolée wines; it is permitted for German and Italian wines. The bubbles are little larger in these wines than in those made by Métho-de-Champenoise and usually do not last as long in the glass. SEKT from Germany and ASTI from Italy are made from this method.

- **Transversagé method or transfer method**: In this method secondary fermentation takes places in bottles and the wine is matured or ripened lying down in cellars just as in Métho-de-Champenoise, but at this the method changes, instead of undergoing the expensive —Remuage and —Degorgement processes, the bottles are taken very cold straight to the point of Degorgment. As soon as the corks are removed the sediment rise up in the wine and clouds it. All clouded wine is passed through filter then dosage is added in filtered wine, which is bottled under pressure, corked and muzzled. This method is not preferred as it takes away bouquet and body of the wine.

- **La métho de champenoise (MAY-TUD SHAHM-PEN-WAHZ) or the champagne method or méthode traditionelle:**

HARVESTING: The grapes used for manufacture of Champagne are Pinot Noir, Pinot Meunier and Chardonnay. The normal harvest usually takes place in late September or early October.

PRESSING THE GRAPES: Pressing has to very quick in large shallow presses, especially for red grapes so as to avoid or prevent the wine from being coloured by the skins.

- 1st Pressing – —Vin De Cuvée‖ – Superior wines
- 2nd Pressing – PremiéresTaille
- 3rd Pressing – DeuxiémeTaille
- 4th pressing – Rebéche

Only two pressing of the grapes are permitted. Prestige Cuvée Champagne is usually made exclusively from the first pressing. The second pressing is generally blended with the CUVÉE to make vintage and non-vintage Champagne and rest are used for making ordinary wines.

PRIMARY FERMENTATION: This takes places in casks which may be either traditional oak casks or stainless steel or glass lined cement vats. Fermentation starts about 8 hours after pressing. The first fermentation takes two to three weeks and produces still wines.

RACKING: The wine is then drawn off into new casks leaving behind the sediments (Lees) casts off during the fermentation, this is called Racking.

BLENDING: The most important step in Champagne production is the blending of the still wines. Each of these still wines is made from a single grape variety from a single village of origin. Non-vintage Champagne blends contain on an average 40-50 wines from as many as 10 different years, whereas Vintage Champagne is made almost totally from a blend of just one year. A small quantity of wine is permitted from other years in Vintage Champagne to ensure correct balance is achieved.

LIQUEUR DE TIRAGE (LEE-KERR DEH-TEER-AHZH) / **DOSAGE** (DOH-SAHZH): After the blending process the winemaker adds Liqueur De Tirage (a blend of sugar and yeast) which will begin the wine‘s second fermentation.

SECONDARY FERMENTATION: The wine is bottled in spring in special strong bottles. The bottlers are temporarily sealed by an Agrafe – a metal clip, which can be adjusted as necessary and laid down. The secondary fermentation takes place inside the bottles slowly which are placed in the cellars where the temperature is maintained at 50˚F. It is during secondary fermentation gas formed builds up a pressure of 5-6 atmosphere (95 pounds per square inch). This is done as pressure inside the bottle will push the cork out.

AGING: These bottles are kept in —MIS SUR LATTE‖ position (bottles are placed horizontally) and kept in deep caverns (caves). These caverns have constant temperature and are now called wine cellars by wine producers. Fermentation takes place after six months of bottling. The bottles are kept in —MIS SUR LATTE‖ position for 4-5 years. For non-Vintage wines minimum time is one year, for Vintage ones minimum time is 3 years.

RÉMUAGE: As a result of secondary fermentation sediments are also formed and this must be removed. The process of removing sediments from the bottle by shaking is RÉMUAGE. The object of RÉMUAGE is to remove sediments in the bottle on to the cork. This process was developed by widow Clicquet in 1800. Traditionally bottles are placed in special adjustable wooden racks called —PUPITRES‖. Every 3 days they are given a shake by skilled workers called —REMUERS and angles of Pupitres are altered. As Remuers shakes each bottle every 3 days, he/she tilts it gradually, degree by degree from horizontal up to vertical. The bottle reaches Sur la pointe or mis en masse position. It takes 2-3 months to change the angle from 45° to 90°. Now a day's mechanical frames called —GYROPALETTES are used to shakes and twist the bottles and gradually turn them upside down but effect is same, the sediment or Lees ends up in the neck of the bottle. The bottles are kept in sur la point position for one year and sometimes are allowed to rest for 10 years.

DÉGORGMENT (DAY-GORZH-MOWN): The necks of bottles are refrigerated, traditionally by being placed in a freezing brine solution, so that a small block of Ice forms in them trapping the sediments. To remove the sediments one has to hold the bottle against stomach and cut the wire, open the cork slowly. The cork with frozen sediments is allowed to push out of the bottle.

DOSAGE (ADDITION OF LIQUEUR d' EXPÉDITION): Champagne which was lost during Dégorgment is replaced by more similar wine and a sugar solution is added known as Liqueur d' Expédition if required in final wine. At this point the winemaker can determine whether he/she wants sweeter or drier Champagne.

RECORKING: The bottle is finally re-corked with a new cork and sealed with a wine cage (wired up and dressed in foil). Wine is then stamped and labelled.

2.3. New world vs. Old world wines:

Regions

Old World regions are winegrowing areas found in Europe, North Africa, and the Middle East. These include (but are not limited to) France, Italy, Spain, Hungary, Portugal, Germany, Lebanon, Croatia, Israel, and beyond.

New World regions are areas that have adopted winemaking practices from Old World regions to create their own industries. (In other words, basically everywhere else that isn't Europe, North Africa, or the Middle East.) New World regions include all of North America, South America, Australia, South Africa, and more.

Flavour Profiles

Old World wines tend to be lighter-bodied, lower in alcohol, have brighter acidity, and show more earth-driven flavors. New World wines are usually fuller-bodied, higher in alcohol, have lower acidity, and are much riper on the palate.

Winemaking Styles

Winemaking styles also play a major role in the Old World vs. New World contrast, specifically with regards to oak usage. New oak is more commonly used in New World regions, whereas Old World regions tend to stick with neutral wood.

Labelling

Another Old World vs. New World style to note is the way in which wines are labelled. Most Old World regions reference their wines by region, whereas New World wines are generally identified by grape variety.

2.3.1. Old World Examples:

Countries like France and Italy. Here are a few examples of how these countries have influenced the rest of the world.

France: Whatever your opinion on French wine may be, to study wine is to study France. It is here you will find the origin place of grapes like Cabernet Sauvignon, Pinot Noir, and Chardonnay. These grapes are so influential that they're often referred to as "international varieties."

France's best blends (Bordeaux, Champagne, etc) have defined what makes a balanced wine for hundreds of years. And French traditions have shaped the tastes of winemakers all over the world.

Italy: Italy's winemaking influence has spread far and wide, particularly in that new world Mecca of California. California's earliest European settlers were Italian, and you can still see their fingerprints on many regions there.

Portugal: Their fortified Madeira was incredibly popular with the early Congress of the USA. This influenced the man some have called America's first winemaker: Thomas Jefferson.

Spain: Spain has a massive number of native grape varieties. Plus, they've dedicated more of their land to the growing of grapes than any other country in the world. This has led to their own individual takes on about every style of wine: from red blends to sparklers.

Germany: Germany is far more than just Riesling, but this country's most popular grape has gained traction all over the world. Riesling grows everywhere from South Africa to the Finger Lakes of New York.

Others: Hungary, Croatia, England, Etc

2.3.2. New World Examples:

Countries in North and South America, as well as South Africa, Australia, New Zealand, and now: China! Let's take a look at how these countries have set themselves apart from the old school crowd.

North America: California immediately comes to mind. California's wine industry proved that it could stand shoulder-to-shoulder with Europe during the famous Judgement of Paris.

And since then, it's opened doors for the rest of the New World to get credit where due. Everything from the plush, fruit-forward wines of the Pacific Northwest to the gold colour of Canada's Ice Wine has received its due in the years since.

South America: If there's one thing wine fans know South America for, it's taking French grapes and making them their own.

Argentina's answer to Malbec and Chile's version of Carménère are some of the best known. Both wines are unique and original when compared to their European counterparts.

Australia: Settled by Europeans in an environment that couldn't be less like Europe if it tried, Australia's wine industry was a testament to willpower and determination.

Australian Shiraz is very popular in every bar.

New Zealand: Perhaps the best example of the transformation of a grape based on territory is that of the battle between French and New Zealand Sauvignon Blanc.

Climate and winemaking practices have proven that the Kiwis can take a steely French white and transform it into a cornucopia of tropical fruit.

South Africa: As far as "new world" goes, South African wine is definitely the oldest, having been first planted in the 1600s. It's hardly new here.

But the combination of European influence and gradual transformation forces it into the new world category by definition. Not to mention the fact that most non-South African wine drinkers knew nothing about South African wine until the 1980's at best.

China: A relative newcomer to the worldwide wine stage, China's history with fermentation and culture goes back further than any other country on this list. Still, they've adopted the "French Model" mostly with their recent transformations.

2.4. Grape varieties:

2.4.1. Red Wine Grapes:

Shiraz:

This grape variety originated from France, as well as Cabernet Sauvignon. This grape, compare to Cabernet sauvignon, is often come with full-bodied, darker in colour and tannin, with the silky finish. The grape varieties usually have a strong taste of fruits such as blueberries, sweet Black olives and are spicy.

In addition, the grape varieties it has been found that they are very high in antioxidants too.

Food pairing: You can pair it with anything made of Blue Cheese; such as burgers, with barbecue sauce and pepper and foods with spices or herbs because these foods will help pull the flavour out.

Merlot:

This variety comes with outstanding softness with bright red colour and soft tannin, usually medium to full-bodied. Nevertheless, the taste and quality is based on region and climate. If it comes from an area with a warm climate, usually it will provide a high astringent. But, if it comes from an area where the weather is warm it is always a little astringent and dominant with fruit flavour.

Food pairing: The food suitable to be paired with red wine Merlo (Merlot) includes fish, fresh vegetables, including food with fewer spices as the spicy flavour of wine to drown away. Dishes prepared from white meat like chicken or red meat cooked with less spices are recommended.

Pinot Noir:

Pinot Noir are often priced higher than red wine grape varieties. Since it is relatively weak infections and easy-to-mutate which needs attention. It provides a red light collared wine; the body is quite light, touch rather dry and refreshing fruit flavour. Thus, giving the final touches to a long and gentle finish.

Food pairing: Often Light Bodied but highly complex. This grape variety is was good with red meat, and fish.

2.4.2. White Wine Grapes:

Sauvignon Blanc:

Translated as "white wood" or "White Wild" has its origins in Bordeaux. Usually colored green intense flavour, similar to apple green, lemon, kiwi, and peach, which varies according to the ripeness of the grapes in the making of wine. The thing that makes this grape variety for striking is the smell (Aroma) herbs, paprika, basil, parsley and lemon grass and so on.

Food pairing: Recommended foods should be paired with this wine varieties include Goat Cheese, Cream Cheese and focused on food spices like Mexican food and Vietnamese food which is compatible with the smell of herbs in wine.

Chardonnay:

Chardonnay have been referred "Queen of the grapes," commonly used to make white wine often indispensable in making Champagne or sparkling wine. Chardonnay comes with the aroma of vanilla, coconut, butter and white wine from. It's creamy and smooth, which varies according to the fermentation process.

Food pairing: Chardonnay is great with creamy cheese, white meat, chicken, pork, seafood, herbs, mushrooms and cream sauce.

Riesling:

Riesling is often characterized by the aroma that resembles the fruit with sour (Acid) and Dry similar to lemonade. However, you can also find Riesling, Semi-Dry or Dessert Wine as well as wines from this grape. Often smells of green apple, peach, lemon, freshly cut grass, and oil, but sweet sling. It has aromas of honey, flowers and ripe fruit with.

Food pairing: Riesling often are less sweet, notable sour but there is a balance (Balance) so. It is suitable to be paired with Asian cuisine. With flavours like spicy Indian food, food Thailand by a classic that fits Marie include duck leg sling it. If you are looking for a glass to pair with fragrance white wine like Chardonnay, we presented you with "Lucaris Desire Rich White" which would be the ideal choice. The innovative Aerlumer will also help spread the aroma of wine as well.

2.4.3. Sparkling Wine Grapes:

Glera:

A white grape variety originally from Italy, often used to make sparkling wine (Italian Sparkling Wine) as a process Vigo (Prosecco), mostly grown in the Veneto, Italy.

Food pairing: Paired with foods such as mushrooms or taste it like cream sauce, beans, almonds, potato chips or pop popcorn butter flavour. It also includes various seafood and Spicy Asian cuisine too.

Moscato:

The oldest grape varieties can be grown all over the world. Focus by smell, sweet unique. There is a chemical compound called "Linalool" found in mint, orange and cinnamon becomes a description of the special aroma of grape varieties. if you want fresh, sweet and relatively low alcohol content (5-7%) Sparkling, Moscato is a great choice.

Food pairing: The Sparkling wine from Moscato tend to have low alcohol content and high sweetness ideal with spicy Asian dishes like Chinese, Thailand and Vietnam are often smells of ginger, cinnamon, pepper or be paired with white meat such as chicken or fish as well.

Pinot Blanc:

Pinot Blanc is a white grape variety which developed from Pinot Noir. In the past in Burgundy, this grape variety is use for making white wine and as an ingredient to make Champagne. In present, Pinot Blanc has become a key ingredient in the making of Sparkling in a variety of areas. The prominent Pinot Blanc is the aroma of fruits; apples, limes, including flowers.

Food pairing: Such as fish, white meat, poultry, eggs and soft cheese, Ricotta or Goat Cheese and so on.

(Sparkling wine have different types and names depending on the area of production. The name of each grape variety. This information will help you to select sparkling wine that you are looking for easily. And the type of sparkling wine, including the famous Champagne from France or Cava from Spain, Asti from Italy and Prosecco from Italy.)

2.5. Wine Brand names:

2.5.1 Indian Red Wines:

Sula Rasa Shiraz

Sula Rasa Shiraz is best served at 16-degree Celsius and is produced from the estate vineyards of Sula. A complex wine, Sula Rasa is stored for 12 months in premium French oak barrels and then further matured in the bottle before release. To fully enjoy this special wine, it is recommended that the bottle is opened and poured out 30 minutes prior to being served slightly chilly. This wine is best enjoyed with barbeque dishes and cheese like gouda and parmesan.

Myra Misfit

Myra Vineyards was founded by ex-banker, fine food, and beverage enthusiast, Ajay Shetty. Operating with its founder's belief that 'Wine Is All Heart', Myra Misfit is a limited edition bottle which is a blend of Classic Sauvignon and fruity Shiraz aged in French oak barrels for 18 months. The aroma comes with a strong berry whiff and has a spicy & fruity taste. This tastes best with pizza, pasta, and meat and is also India's first unfiltered wine.

Fratelli SETTE

Relatively highly priced, Fratelli SETTE is a flavoursome and smooth wine with rich flavours of smoky coffee and chocolate. This is one of the most popular brands in India and tastes amazing with spicy Indian dishes. SETTE means 'Seven' in Italian which indicates that it is a dream that the seven brothers of Fratelli had. The top 1% of the grapes from the Fratelli's estate-owned vineyards in Akluj near Pune go into fulfilling this dream. SETTE is a barrel-aged red wine, matured in French oak for 14 months.

Grover La Reserve

Manufactured in Nandi Hills of Bangalore, Grover La Reserve is aged for 16 months in new French oak. This is a well-balanced medium-bodied wine with complex layers and is best enjoyed with hard cheese and roasted red meat. It delivers a smoky aroma, with notes of bacon to the dark plum and roasted cherry flavours. The soft finish features some peppery notes and combines grace and majesty on the palate.

YORK Arros

YORK Arros wine from Maharashtra's York winery, produced by a young winemaking team, is a limited production blend of the winery's best Shiraz (55%) and Cabernet Sauvignon (45%). The wine is aged 13 months in American and French oak, and another 12 months in the bottle before release. The sweet vanilla notes of the American oak dominate, along with bright fruits and Indian spices.

KRSMA Sangiovese

KRSMA Sangiovese comes from the vineyards of Hampi. The wine has a promising first whiff of juicy red fruit which then follows through with a hint of spiciness on the palate. A nice balance of fruit and acidity, leading to a good finish. This wine has a lot of cherries and clove notes.

Charosa

Charosa wine is filled with rich coconut, vanilla, chocolate, and raspberry aromas and has a dark ruby red colour. This medium-bodied wine is aged for a year and has a concentration of warm red fruit flavours. Charosa wine tastes best when paired with grilled red meat and sautéed vegetables.

2.5.2. Indian White Wines:

J'NOON White

The J'NOON range of wines emerged when passion met inspiration. This is the first collaboration between Jean-Charles Boisset and Kapil Sekhri in the Indian wine industry where the wines are made on Indian soil and then are served all over the world. J'NOON is an artistic take on the Urdu word 'Junoon', meaning 'passion' and is a limited edition collection.

Belstar Cult Prosecco

Prosecco is an Italian white wine and the new addition to the Prosecco portfolio is the Belstar Cult Prosecco which comes from the grand old house of Bisol. The sweetness varies from very dry to medium-sweet and has rich fruitiness which is balanced with a crisp acidity. Apart from the taste, the luxurious bottle will make sure that you are coming back for it.

Crios Torrontes

Susana Balbo has been called the 'Evita of Wine' and the 'Queen of Torrontes'. Her Crios Torrontes which is made in Argentina is a floral and fruity drink with apple blossom, peach, orange citrus, and lime. This wine works with smoked meats and seafood.

Riesling

Hugel wines are made from grapes purchased from winegrowers in a dozen of the most favoured localities around Riquewihr. Riesling white wine is dry and elite and is best paired with seafood and grilled or poached fish.

Sula Chenin Blanc

Made in Sula vineyards, Sula Chenin Blanc is as sweet white wine and adapts to a variety of tastes. This wine works well with Indian dishes, salads, and shellfish. A notable acidity and hint of sweetness give this wine a balanced structure and refreshing character.

2.5.3. Indian Sparkling Wines:

Zampa Soiree Brut

One of the best sparkling wines available in the county, Zampa Soiree Brut has floral aromas. Pale pink in colour, this wine is light and creamy with fine beads and persistent mousse and red cherry and strawberry fruits that define the fruit character.

Carpene Malvolti Prosecco

Antonio Carpene founded his winery in 1860, having been fascinated with Champagne. Carpene Malvolti Prosecco is a full flavoured wine made in North East Italy. Fine and continuous bubbles, the wine is fruity and appealing with a floral and fresh fruit bouquet and a lemony finish. The wine works best with fish dishes.

Les Cordeliers

Like all other great Bordeaux wines, Les Cordeliers is full -bodied and well structured and is quite vivacious. This is a fruity, attractive wine, without excess acidity. It derives its remarkable freshness from the Semillon.

2.5.4. Popular International Wine Brands:

Barefoot

Selling upwards of 22.5 million cases of product per year, it is safe to say that Barefoot has definitely established themselves as one of the world's most famous wine brands. Owned by E&J Gallo, Barefoot is, by some estimates, considered the largest selling wine globally.

With a wide range to choose from, they offer a large selection of reds, whites, and bubbles. The brand has managed to achieve a laidback and fun identify, perfect for the casual drinker who wants something tasty, approachable, but doesn't take the nuances of wine too seriously.

Lindeman's

One of Australia's most famous wine producers, Lindeman's is owned by Treasury Wine Estates and has been around since the mid 1800s, when Henry Lindeman planted his very first vine in New South Wales. It has been on a steady climb ever since and is now among the wine brands with the widest name recognition in the world.

Enjoying a good reputation as far as mass producers go, Lindeman's is known as a reliable, good quality wine at a decent price. Perfect for those looking to explore some of the more common grape varieties, Lindeman's consistently makes it on to the top sellers list for their sauvignon blanc and chardonnay.

Concha Y Toro

One of the Chilean wine industry's biggest claim to fame, Concha Y Toro is in fact the largest producer of wines from Latin America. Headquartered in Santiago, it is estimated that this prolific winery produces over 16 million cases of wine a year.

Their wine is sold in 140 countries around the world and has had a reputation for quality since they were founded in 1883. Boasting some truly fine wines, Concha Y Toro isn't afraid to get experimental and is widely praised for their modern approach to wine making.

Gallo

Another famous wine brand in the American wine industry, Gallo has been around for less than a hundred years but is currently the largest exporter of wines in California. Currently distributing to over 90 countries, Gallo is known for recruiting highly skilled winemakers that ensure each bottle delivers a consistent colour, quality, and taste.

Yellowtail

Established in 2000, Yellowtail has been quick to make a name for themselves in the Australian market and beyond. With a production capacity of around 300 million litres, their strategic exporting has made them one of the most widely drank wines in the United States. Always looking to evolve, the brand offers a huge selection of wine and alcoholic beverages, from their Jammy Red Roo to their Sangria Blanco.

Great Wall

With a main office located at the foot of the Great Wall of China, this famous Chinese wine brand is estimated to have about 74.8 hectares of vineyard in the country. Growing 10 different grape varieties, they use imported winemaking equipment brought in from places like Germany, Italy, and France. With everything from sparkling to fortified wines, their popular range of products places them firmly as one of the world's top wine brands.

2.6. Service of Wine:

The person associated with wine service is called as Sommelier. While serving wines, he is expected to take care of:

- Right Glassware
- Right Temperature
- Proper handling of bottle.
- Right Quantity

2.6.1. The Procedure of Serving White Wine:

Ordering of wine – The wine waiter should present the wine list to the host, so that he can order for the wine. The wine waiter should write a BOT in triplicate. The top copy goes to the dispense bar in order to obtain the bottle, duplicate copy goes to the cashier for bill and third copy is retained in the book itself for the future reference.

Placing the wine glass – Wine glass is placed just near the water goblet depending upon the policy of the establishment, whether to place the glass at the top or below, the water goblet. Place the wine glass which should be chilled.

Present the bottle of wine to the guest – With your hand cupped under the bottle's —punt‖, or base, and the neck resting in your forearm with label facing out, present the bottle to the —host,‖ or customer who ordered the bottle. Announce the vintage, name, and varietal of the wine to the host and table at this time.

Open the bottle of wine – Open bottle with a corkscrew and offer the cork to the guest. It is an old tradition which allows the customer to examine the cork or sniff the cork, to ensure the wine has not been damaged in any way. Some customers will decline, so simply set the cork on the edge of the table.

Pour wine for tasting - The host is poured a small amount to —taste‖ and, when the host has approved the wine, the guests at the table are served the wine first and then the Host's glass is filled last.

Serve the wine - In a clockwise pattern, move around the table pouring for ladies first, as always. Then move around the table again pouring for the men. To properly pour the wine, hold the bottle by the punt and gently tip the neck down to the glass. Do not overfill glasses: 2/3rd for white wine is an acceptable industry average.

Place white wine in an ice bucket near the table. When the bottle is empty, the Host is asked if they wish another bottle of the same wine or if they wish to see the wine list. Don't forget to top up and refill guest's glasses as required.

2.6.2. The Procedure of Serving Red Wine:

Ordering of wine – The wine waiter should present the wine list to the host, so that he can order for the wine. The wine waiter should write a BOT in triplicate. The top copy goes to the dispense bar in order to obtain the bottle, duplicate copy goes to the cashier for bill and third copy is retained in the book itself for the future reference.

Placing the wine glass – Wine glass is placed just near the water goblet depending upon the policy of the establishment, whether to place the glass at the top or below, the water goblet. Place the wine glass in which red wine is to be served. The glass in which red wine is served should be at room temperature and not chilled. Generally red wine glass wine is kept below the white wine glass.

Taking wine to the table – The wine bottle is brought to the table in a wine cradle or basket or in a bare hand.

Presenting the wine bottle – The wine waiter should present the wine bottle to the host from right at a suitable angle, showing the label. The wine waiter should also mention the name of the wine and vintage wine.

Opening wine bottle – Due to the crust in old bottle certain varieties of wine have to be decanted before they are served. It is a very delicate process and need a very steady hand. The proper method suggest, standing of bottle at least 24 hours before decanting.

Tasting the wine – The wine waiter should pour a little sip into the host's glass for tasting and approval. The host should acknowledge that the wine is in good condition and suitable to be consumed.

Sequence of service – When the host has approved the wine, change his glass with a fresh one and proceed to serve the other guests from the right hand side, ladies first and then the gentlemen, lastly the host.

Leave red wine on the table with the label facing outwards towards the dining room. When the bottle is empty, the Host is asked if they wish another bottle of the same wine or if they wish to see the wine list. Don't forget to top up and refill guests glasses as required.

2.6.3. The Procedure of Serving Champagne / Sparkling Wine:

Ordering of wine – The wine waiter should present the wine list to the host, so that he can order for the wine. The wine waiter should write a BOT in triplicate. The top copy goes to the dispense bar in order to obtain the bottle, duplicate copy goes to the cashier for bill and third copy is retained in the book itself for the future reference.

Placing the wine glass – Wine glass is placed just near the water goblet depending upon the policy of the establishment, whether to place the glass at the top or below, the water goblet. Place the wine glass (Champagne Tulip, Champagne Flute and Champagne Saucer) in which sparkling wine is to be served.

Taking wine to the table – Champagne is to be served chilled. So remember to wrap it with a napkin and then cover it with another one (called as Baby Wrap). The wine bottle is brought to the table in a champagne bucket in a stand with ice. Place it on the right of the host.

Presenting the wine bottle – The wine waiter should present the wine bottle to the host from right at a suitable angle, showing the label. The wine waiter should also mention the name of the wine and vintage wine.

Opening wine bottle – After presentation, keep the bottle in the wine cooler. The neck of the bottle should be kept pointed towards the roof so that if cork is accidentally released, then no one gets hurt. To open the bottle correctly, first cut and remove the foil cover and tourniquet. Then place your thumb on the cork and at the same time remove the cork, harness and hood by twisting the bottle to loosen the cork. This is the best possible way to avoid the bottle pressure growing. Keep the angle of the bottle at 45 degrees and must be pointed towards ceiling.

Sequence of service – After opening, proceed to serve the guests clockwise. Serve ladies first, then to others and at last to the host. Pour 1/3rd of the glass and refill the glasses periodically.

After pouring sufficient amount of champagne, re-cork with a temporary bottle stopper and place in the ice bucket or chillers with a napkin wrapped on it.

2.7. Aperitif / Aromatized Wine:

Aromatized wine is a fortified wine in which herbs, roots, flowers, barks and other flavouring agents have been steeped in order to change the natural flavours of the wine. Aromatized wines includes both dry (French origin) and sweet (Italian) vermouths and the quinined or apéritif wines of the various countries such as DUBOUNET, LILLET, ST. RAPHAEL etc. Vermouth is the name given to those flavoured wines which in theory contained wormwood, which was first used in Germany in sixteenth century. Wormwood in German is wermuth which was pronounced —vermutt hence origin of modern name. Some examples of Vermouth are:

- NOILLY PRAT – French – dry and light in flavour
- CINZANO BIANCO – Italy – sweeter version of white vermouth
- VOTRIX & DUVAL - England

2.8. Fortified Wines:

These are the wines which are fortified with spirit like brandy during vinification when fermentation process is going on. If fortification is done in the beginning of fermentation the end product is sweet fortified wine.

If fortification is towards the end of fermentation, the resultant wine is dry fortified wine. The addition of spirit increases the alcoholic content; therefore fortified wines have an alcoholic strength of 15% - 24% and also good keeping quality. Fortified wines may be sweet or dry, white, rosé or red. SHERRY, PORT, MADEIRA, MALAGA and MARSALA etc. are the best examples. —HEAVY WINE is the official term for fortified wine; it is also used to describe wines which have too much alcohol and fruitiness.

CHAPTER THIRTEEN

Unit 3: Spirits

The production of distilled spirits is based upon fermentation, the natural process of decomposition of organic materials containing carbohydrates. It occurs in nature whenever the two necessary ingredients, carbohydrate and yeast, are available. Yeast is a vegetative microorganism that lives and multiplies in media containing carbohydrates—particularly simple sugars. It has been found throughout the world, including frozen areas and deserts.

Distilled spirits are all alcoholic beverages in which the concentration of ethyl alcohol has been increased above that of the original fermented mixture by a method called distillation. The principle of alcoholic distillation is based upon the different boiling points of alcohol (78.5 °C, or 173.3 °F) and water (100 °C, or 212 °F). If a liquid containing ethyl alcohol is heated to a temperature above 78.5 °C but below 100 °C and the vapour coming off the liquid is condensed, the condensate will have a higher alcohol concentration, or strength.

3.1. Classification:

Spirit: This is potable alcoholic beverages obtained by distillation of a liquid containing alcohol. Some of the spirits are:

a) **Whiskey**: It is derived from the Gaelic term, 'using beatha', meaning, water of life, and is a distillation of fermented mash of grain (maize, barley, corn, rice, etc.) or a combo. It is matured or aged in wooden casks.

b) **Brandy**: 'Brandewijn' in Dutch means 'burnt wine' and it is obtained from the mash of grapes. Brandies can be obtained from other fruits like peach, apple, etc.

c) **Gin:** It is derived from a French word, 'Geneivre', which means juniper berries and it is the prime flavouring agent in gin. The base is a neutral spirit made from grain with other flavourings like coriander, orange and lemon peels added to it.

d) **Rum:** It is obtained from 'Saccharum', a main constituent of sugarcane and was originally made in West Indian plantations.

e) **Vodka:** The term 'Voda' means water. This is a fermented mash of grain/vegetables (potatoes). Re-distillation removes all odour, taste and colours. It is diluted to required strength.

g) **Tequila:** It is obtained from a large pineapple-type plant of the lily family – mistaken usually for a type of cactus – found in abundance in South West Mexico.

3.2. Distilled Spirits: (Six Spirits with Brands and Serving suggestions).

Distilled spirits play a massive role in cocktails, providing a 'base' for us to add various other liquors and flavours to, and are even used in the making of more complex and nuanced spirits.

There are just six 'base' liquors among the many distilled spirits on the market: these include vodka, whiskey, brandy, gin, rum, and tequila, and these six base spirits are enjoyed in a myriad of ways, whether straight up, on the rocks, or mixed into a complex, flavourful cocktail.

Understanding the differences between each of these 6 types of distilled spirits will allow you to use them more effectively in your cocktails and mixed drinks.

3.2.1 WHISKEY:

- Typically 40 to 50 percent ABV (80 to 100 proof) or higher
- Whiskey is typically aged in charred oak barrels
- Can be blended or single malt
- Varieties found all over the world

Whiskey comes in many styles and has a diverse flavour profile making it a versatile cocktail base.

It is produced all over the world, but the various styles are often defined by the country or region in which they're produced, such as Irish Whiskey, Japanese Whiskey, or Tennessee Whiskey.

Whiskey is made from fermented grain mash, and different varieties of the distilled spirit are made from various grains (which may be malted), such as barley, corn, rye, and wheat.

Typically, whisky is aged in wooden casks, usually old sherry casks or barrels made from charred white oak.

Some styles of whiskey, such as bourbon, use new barrels, while others use a mixture of new and previously-used whiskey or wine barrels.

Moonshine (also known as white dog) is the only variety that isn't aged, and while some whiskeys are blended, others are single malts.

Whisky is strictly-regulated all over the world, and comes in many classes and types.

The unifying characteristics usually depend on the fermentation of the grains, distillation process, and ageing in wooden barrels.

Whiskey mixes well with other liquors to create complex drinks, but it also pairs well with dark fruits, and is often used in warm drinks, too.

Despite its many varieties, whiskey has notes of roasted and malted grain with oak undertones, though each style will have distinct characteristics.

Serving suggestion: *Neat, or with water or ice, in an old-fashioned or tulip-shaped glass, or mixed with cola. Use high quality whiskey in three-ingredient cocktails such as Manhattan or Old-Fashioned.*

3.2.2 Brandy:

- Distilled from fruit
- Typically 40 percent alcohol by volume (ABV, 80 proof)
- Typically aged in oak
- Distilled worldwide with several styles distinct to certain regions

Brandy features in several classic cocktail recipes but it is often enjoyed on its own.

While it is produced all over the world, there are specific styles of brandy that are unique to certain regions, such as Cognac, Armagnac, Spanish Brandy, American Brandy, Pisco, Grappa, and Eau-de-vie, to name just a few.

While brandy is traditionally used in drinks with a few simple ingredients, today you'll find it in many modern cocktails which are pushing the boundaries of this classic spirit and experimenting with its complex flavour.

Brandy is distilled from fruit, traditionally from grapes, but it can be distilled from other fruits such as cherries, peaches, apples and apricots.

It has a dark, fruity wine taste with a pleasant oakiness, which is owed to the fact that it's typically aged in oak and often blended.

Other varieties are coloured with caramel to give the impression of aging, and some are produced using a combination of both aging and colouring

There are no distinct worldwide regulations for brandy, though some styles must be produced in certain regions using particular ingredients or methods.

Traditionally, Brandy is served at room temperature, neat, from a snifter, wine glass or tulip glass.

It is often warmed slightly by holding the glass cupped in the palm or by gentle heating, though excessive heating can cause the alcohol vapour to become too strong and overpowering.

Serving Suggestions: *Neat at room temperature or slightly warmed, or in cocktails such as the Brandy Sour, the Brandy Alexander, the Sidecar, the Brandy Daisy, and the Brandy Old Fashioned.*

3.2.3. GIN:

- Dry profile with herbal flavours
- Made from juniper berries
- Typically un aged
- Typically 40 to 47 percent ABV (80 to 94 proof)

Gin has seen a significant rise in popularity in recent years, and it comes in many different flavours and varieties, though the most popular styles are London Dry Gin, Plymouth Gin, Old Tom Gin, New American Gin and Generver.

It's produced worldwide, though it is associated mainly with the UK and Europe (especially the Netherlands).

Gin has a distinctive dry profile which makes it perfect for dry (non-sweet) cocktails such as classics and martinis. It's a good base spirit for cocktails which contain fever ingredients, and pairs well with mixers and fruits.

In order for a spirit to be classed as gin, it needs to be derived from Juniper berries, though gin is distilled from neutral grains such as barley, corn, rye, and wheat and is flavoured with a variety of botanicals, which vary depending on the brand.

Gin has a distinctively herbal and dry taste, with a "piney" aroma, and the old styles of gins such as Old Tom and Plymouth have a subtle sweet hint to them.

Gin's first ingredient is juniper, but it's also flavoured with a variety of botanical or herbal flavours, spice, floral or fruit flavours or a combination.

It's often drunk with tonic water, and is also used as a base spirit to produce flavoured gin-based liqueurs such as sloe gin, which also uses additional flavourings as well as fruit and sugar for a distinctively sweeter taste.

Serving Suggestion:*paired with tonic water, or in cocktails such as Tom Collins, Martini, Gibson, or Negroni.*

3.2.4. RUM:

- Distilled from some form of sugar
- Aging depends on climatic conditions
- Typically 40 percent ABV (80 proof). Over proof rums can reach 75 percent ABV (150 proof)
- Mainly produced in the Caribbean and South America

A popular feature in tropical drinks and warm cocktails, rum's sweeter flavour makes it one of the most versatile spirits. It was one of the first liquors to be mixed into drinks and comes in many varieties.

Rum is mainly produced in the Caribbean and South America, and some varieties are unique to countries, such as Cachaça which must be produced in Brazil.

This spirit is distilled from some form of sugar, with Molasses being a common option, or in some cases, pure sugar cane.

Flavour profile varies depending on style, region and aging process, though typically rum has a sweet, toasted flavour.

Light rum usually isn't aged, but other rums are aged in oak barrels though aging times vary depending on climate, as rum produced in warm climates require less barrel time than rum from colder climates.

Rums are also produced in various grades. While light rums are commonly used in cocktails, "golden" and "dark" varieties were traditionally consumed neat, "on the rocks", or in cooking, but today they're commonly consumed with mixers, too.

Flavoured rums are infused with fruit flavours such as banana, mango, orange, star fruit, pineapple, coconut, or lime, and spiced rums are also popular – these obtain their flavours through the addition of spices and, occasionally, caramel, and tend to be darker in colour.

Serving suggestions: *neat, slightly warmed, over ice with a slice of lime, with cola, or in cocktails such as Mojito, Daiquiri, Strawberry Daiquiri or Piña Colada.*

3.2.5. Vodka:

- Neutral taste
- Rarely aged
- Typically 40 to 50 ABV (80 to 100 proof)
- Clear colouring (but can have flavours/colorants added)

Vodka is a clear distilled alcoholic beverage originating from Europe, with varieties from Poland, Russia, and Sweden.

It is composed primarily of water and ethanol, which makes it one of the most versatile distilled spirits available, mainly because it has a neutral alcohol/ethanol taste that can be adapted to pretty much any flavour profile – whether savoury or sweet.

Vodka can be distilled from almost anything, but the most common methods are distillation from neutral grains such as rye, corn, and wheat, or potatoes, though it's possible for vodka to be distilled from beets, grapes, and other bases.

While it is traditionally clear in colouring, flavoured vodkas are a popular category today.

Some modern brands have also developed more interesting varieties of vodka, using fruits, honey, or maple sap as the base.

Traditionally, Vodka is drunk "neat", meaning it's not mixed with water, ice, or other mixers. In the vodka belt of Belarus, Estonia, Finland, Iceland, Lithuania, Latvia, Norway, Poland, Russia, Sweden, and Ukraine, it is usually served freezer-chilled.

However, vodka is also popular in cocktails and mixed drinks, such as the Vodka Martini, Cosmopolitan, Vodka Tonic, Screwdriver, Greyhound, Black or White Russian, Moscow mule, Bloody Mary, and Caesar.

Serving suggestions: *neat, or freeze-chilled, paired with soda water, cola, or lemonade, or in a cocktail such as Cosmopolitan, Bloody Mary, or White Russian.*

3.2.6. Tequila:

- Typically 40 to 50 percent ABV (80 to 100 proof)
- Tequila must be produced in Mexico
- Can be aged or un-aged
- Distilled from the agave plant

Tequila is best known for being served in shots at the bar and served with salt and lemon, but this distilled spirit has a great flavour profile that works well in a range of cocktails – most famously margaritas and frozen cocktails where the tequila is mixed with any fruit imaginable.

Tequila is also used in spicy cocktails.

Distilled from the fermented juices of the agave plant, Tequila has a distinctive earthy flavor with semi-sweet and spicy tones. It can be aged or unaged:

Blanco (or silver) tequila is unaged, while the Reposado and Añejo varieties are aged, often in used whiskey (bourbon) oak barrels.

Tequila is special liquor as it's the most tightly regulated and can only be made in Mexico.

Spirits distilled from the agave plant that are produced outside of Mexico cannot be sold as "tequila." For example, agave spirits such as mezcal, pulque, sotol, raicila, and baconara, are not considered "tequilas."

The regulations surrounding Tequila are defined under an Appellation of Origin, which was established in 1978, and the industry is overseen by the Tequila Regulatory Council (CRT).

Serving suggestions: *Neat, in a shot glass, or in cocktails such as the Margarita, Tequila Sunrise, The Paloma, Tequila Collins, or Tequini.*

3.3. The Procedure of Serving Spirits:

Spirits are generally served as per the request of the customer in the following patterns:

- Neat: It means that nothing should be added to the drink.
- On the Rocks: It means that the drink should be served on the ice.
- With Mixes: It means some mixers should be added to the drinks such as lemonade, tonic water, dry ginger ale etc.

The standard serve of spirits is 30 ml or 60 ml in India. Light spirits (Gin, Vodka, Tequila etc) are usually garnished with a slice of lemon; whereas dark spirits (Brandy, Whiskey, Dark Rum etc) are not usually garnished.

Neat and on the rocks are served in the Old Fashioned glass or Rock glass (Gin, Whisky, Rum and Vodka) while Brandy or Cognac are served neat in Brandy Balloon or Brandy Snifter. Spirits with the mixes is served in Highball or Collins.

The drinks may either be served over the bar counter or at the table in the bar, restaurant or lounge and should be carried on a tray and placed on a drip mat on the right hand side of the guest. If the drink is to be served with mixes, it should be taken in a carafe and poured over the spirit in front of the customer.

3.4. A brief History of Spirit Distilling:

Because the two ingredients necessary to alcoholic fermentation are widely spread and always appear together, civilizations in almost every part of the world developed some form of alcoholic beverage very early in their history.

The Chinese were distilling a beverage from rice beer by 800 BC.

The Arabs developed a distillation method that was used to produce a distilled beverage from wine.

Greek philosophers reported a crude distillation method.

The Romans apparently produced distilled beverages, although no references concerning them are found in writings before AD 100.

Production of distilled spirits was reported in Britain before the Roman conquest.

Spain, France, and the rest of Western Europe probably produced distilled spirits at an earlier date, but production was apparently limited until the 8th century, after contact with the Arabs.

The first distilled spirits were made from sugar-based materials, primarily grapes and honey to make grape brandy and distilled mead, respectively. The earliest use of starchy grains to produce distilled spirits is not known, but their use certainly dates from the Middle Ages.

Some government control dates from the 17th century. As production methods improved and volume increased, the distilled spirits industry became an important source of revenue. Rigid controls were often imposed on both production and sale of the liquor.

The earliest stills were composed simply of a heated closed container, a condenser, and a receptacle to receive the condensate. These evolved into the pot still, which is still in use, particularly for making malt whiskeys and some gins.

The next refinement was heating the alcohol-containing liquid in a column made up of a series of vaporization chambers stacked on top of one another.

By the early 19th century large-scale continuous stills, very similar to those used in the industry today, were operating in France and England.

In 1831 the Irishman Aeneas Coffey designed such a still, which consisted of two columns in series. Since distillation requires that the liquid portion of a fermentation mixture be vaporized, considerable heat must be applied to the process.

The fuel used in distilling spirits has always been that which has been most readily available at the particular time and place. Peat, coal, and wood were the fuels used historically, while the fuels of choice today are coal, natural gas, and oil. The high steam requirement for continuous-still operation inhibited the development of rectifying columns for production of spirits until after the Industrial Revolution.

Many of the minor components of distilled spirits, which are present only in parts per million, are detectable by the senses of taste and smell, but efforts to identify and quantify these compounds chemically have often been hampered by the lower limits of detection by analytical methods.

Classes of compounds such as aldehydes, organic acids, esters, and alcohols were easily identified by conventional methods, but many of them could not be determined until after the development of chromatography.

The Russian botanist Mikhail Tsvet was an early pioneer of this measurement technique, reporting his first work in 1903. Refinements in both technique and equipment, made during the first half of the 20th century, allowed numerous flavour components in distilled spirits to be identified by gas chromatography.

CHAPTER FOURTEEN

Unit 4: Liqueurs

Liqueurs: Liqueurs are flavoured and sweetened spirits having high alcoholic content. Liqueurs are served in small quantities as digestives at the end of the meal.

4.1. History: Liqueurs were first produced in the monasteries of Europe for medicinal purposes. Many of the herbs with medicinal properties were grown near the monasteries. The medicinal properties of this herb were extracted by steeping them in alcohol. In Europe, the flavored liquids were applied on wounds and were often drunk in small quantities for curing cold and fever. Some were sweetened to make them tastier. These were regarded as the protection against infection and plague, but many pharmacists conflicted with the religious laws because of the claims they made for their potions.

In the fourteenth century, the elixir of the monks was known as a preventive against malaria. The dark red liqueur made from Dijon black currents was considered to cure physical diseases, and the bitter wormwood liqueur of Marseilles was used as medicine for stress until 1915 when the government banned the production. Today there are many distillers who make liqueurs of different flavours and colours. The modern first commercial liqueur industry first developed in France. Marie Brizard is often thought to be its founder. She developed an anisette (an-uh-set) in Bordeaux in middle of 18th century. Although some liqueurs have medicinal benefits and most of them are certainly a help to digestion.

4.2. Liqueurs can be classified as follows:

4.2.1. Generic Liqueurs: Generic Liqueurs can be made by anyone and anywhere. Their names simply indicate what kind of liqueur they are, cream or oil extract from the plants are used. Advocaat, Anisette, Curacao and crème de menthe are example of generic liqueurs.

4.2.2. Proprietary Liqueurs: Proprietary Liqueurs are made by a single distiller who owns the right to make the liqueur of that name. The recipes are trade secret. Grand Marnier, Cointreau, Bénédictine , Kahlúa, Drambuie, Bailley's Irish Cream etc. are example of proprietary Liqueurs.

4.3. Ingredients of Liqueurs:

Liqueurs are flavoured, coloured and sweetened spirits. To produce liqueurs the following ingredients are required: Spirit, Flavouring Agents, Sweetening Agents and Colouring Agents.

- **Spirit**: To produce a fine liqueur, the alcohol used must be as pure as possible. Constituents of alcohol, such as aldehydes that contribute to the aroma are undesirable in a liqueur base. The method and the degree of rectification will determine the purity of the spirit. Whiskey, Rum, Brandy, Cognac, Fruit spirit etc. are all used, although most liqueurs are made from neutral or grain spirit.

- **The Flavouring Agent**: Liqueurs are flavoured with herbs, flowers, fruits, seeds, barks and roots. Following are the examples of flavouring agents used in the production of liqueurs:

- **Herbs:** Basil, Peppermint, Melissa, Rosemary, Sage, Thistle, Thyme, Wormwood etc.

- **Flowers:** Chamomile, Lavender, Lily, Orange Blossom, Rose Saffron etc.

- **Fruits:** Berries, Peach, Oranges, Pineapple, Banana, Citrus Peel, Raisins etc.

- **Barks:** Angostura, Myrrh, Sandalwood, Cinchona etc.

- **Roots:** Angelica, Celery, Ginger, Turmeric, Gentian, Orris root etc.

- **Seeds:** Aniseed, Apricot Stones, Almonds, Caraway, Clove, Cocoa, Coffee, Coriander, Juniper Berries, Musk, Pepper, Star Anise, Vanilla etc.

- **Sweetening Agents**: The sweetening agents used in the production of liqueurs are sugar syrup, maple syrup, corn syrup, and honey. The sugar content of the liqueur distinguishes it from the other types of spirits.

It ranges from 2.5-35% by weight. All liqueurs sold in the U.S.A must contain a minimum of 25% sugar by weight. A liqueur with 10% or less is termed as dry liqueur.

- **Colouring Agent**: Natural vegetable colouring agents or approved food dyes are used to colour the liqueurs. The production of liqueurs starts from the extraction of flavouring agents from the natural substances, then the flavouring agents are impregnated with the base spirit and distilled if necessary, sweetened, fined, and bottled as liqueurs. In the U.S.A, liqueurs are termed as cordials. In reality, all liqueurs are alcoholic drinks, whereas cordials can be alcoholic and non-alcoholic.

4.4. Production of Liqueurs:

- **Extraction of Flavouring**: The flavouring agent must be extracted from the natural substances which are used as an ingredient in the blending process. There are four methods by which the flavouring oil can be extracted, depending on the type of the ingredient. They are as follows:

- **Pressure**: By applying mechanical presses the oil is extracted from the ingredients, e.g. from citrus peel.

- **Maceration**: It is used when soft and delicate fruits are used as flavouring agents in the preparation of liqueur. In this method, the flavouring agents are soaked in cold spirit for long time to gain maximum flavour. The spirit, usually the brandy, is placed in the oak casks with the fruits for up to a year and stirred occasionally for effective maceration. Flavour and colour are extracted during this process. When the maceration is over, the liqueur is transferred, and filtered.

- **Infusion**: This is maceration in warm spirit at a constant temperature for several days. This method extracts more flavour quickly than any other method.

- **Percolation**: In this method, the spirit is continuously passed through the flavouring agent by heating. The spirit is boiled and the vapours are passed up the flavouring agent to get the flavour, condensed and return to the boiling spirit. The extracted natural substance may be blended with the base spirit, allowed to rest, sweetened, fined, and bottled or distilled and processed.

- **Distillation**: The extracted essences or oils are steeped in the base spirit until it is well impregnated with flavour, and then it is distilled under vacuum to protect the delicate essences. During distillation, a colourless dry distillate of high alcohol strength is obtained. This liquid is further purified by re-distillation to remove any impurities which would change the flavour.

- **Compounding**: Compounding is the process of blending the ingredients in strict sequence to produce a desired flavours. Most liqueurs are made according to the secret recipes, many of which are centuries old.

- **Maturing**: Liqueurs must be allowed to rest. The finest liqueurs are matured in oak casks, which assist in mellowing the liquid.
- **Sweetening and Colouring**: Sweetening agent is added according to the style and sweetness required. Liqueurs are coloured to harmonize with the flavour.

- **Fining**: Any suspended matter in the liquid must be removed by fining. The fining process is similar to fining of wine.

- **Bottling**: Spirit is added to liqueur to bring it to the correct alcoholic strength, if necessary. All liqueurs are given a final filtration to ensure star bright clarity before bottling.

4.5. The Procedure of Serving Liqueurs:

Liqueurs are served in several different ways: Neat, With cream, As a Frappé, In a Pousse Café.

- **Liqueur served neat** - Straight liqueurs are served in small glasses of between 20 to 30 ml capacity with 30 ml being the 'normal' amount served. These glasses are filled to the brim, but as liqueurs have a high sugar content their viscosity is high and they don't easily spill over the side of the glass. Examples are Bénédictine, Cherry Brandy, Amaretto, etc.

- **Liqueur served with cream** - These liqueurs, usually coffee or chocolate based, are served in a liqueur glass and topped with fresh cream (unwhipped). The cream is poured onto the liqueur and floats. Examples include Tia Maria and cream, Kahlúa and cream, Crème de Menthe and cream, etc.

- **Frappé** - A frappé is a drink (usually a liqueur) served on crushed ice. It may be served in a cocktail glass and is accompanied by two straws and an appropriate garnish. Examples are Crème de Menthe Frappé, Baileys Frappé, Cointreau Frappé, etc.

- **Pousse café / shooters** - A Pousse Café/Shooter comprises of different liqueurs that are layered on top of each other in the order of the recipe. This ensures that the heaviest items are poured in turn to provide a base for the next ingredient.

4.6. International Liqueur Brands:

1. Amarula
2. Frangelico
3. Chios mastiha
4. Amaretto
5. Disaronno
6. Baileys
7. Rakomelo
8. Limoncello
9. Ginjinha
10. Umeshu

CHAPTER FIFTEEN

Unit 5: Cocktails

5.1. Introduction:

A cocktail is drink where it is a mixture of two or more different types of drink where one must be a spirit. A cocktail is not limited to just one spirit and in many instances a cocktail may have two or more spirits with a non alcoholic mixer (a cocktail can have a mixture of all spirits).

The first "recognised" cocktails, though they were not called cocktails where spirits with the addition of sugar and bitters.

Today even drinks like a rum and coke are technically cocktails for they contain a spirit and a mixer (non alcoholic beverage). These types of cocktails are without doubt the most popular drink apart from beer. The reason for their popularity is mainly due to the drinkability of the product. Most have a mixer which is "sweet" or high in sugar and in some instances, as with Coke, high in caffeine.

The following are traditionally the most popular forms of "cocktails" (Spirit and mixer):

· Bourbon and Coke
· Rum and Coke
· Scotch (Whiskey) and dry (Dry Ginger Ale) or Coke or Soda or water
· Gin and Tonic
· Vodka and orange juice

The above mixers are either made by a person behind the bar or bought in a bottle or can premixed. These premixed versions are called "Ready to Drink" or RTD's.

Cocktails come in all shapes and sizes, flavours and versions. What we might call a cocktail in another country they might have a completely different name. This is usually to do with cultural differences and or the spirit they use to make the cocktail.

5.2. Cocktail Classification:

Cocktails can be classified into two main categories:

- **Short drinks** typically contain between 6 to 12 cl. of liquids and tend to be consumed as a digestive drinks. These Short Drinks are strong and contain a lot of alcohol.
- **Long drinks** typically contain between 12 and 25 cl. of fluids and can be enjoyed as aperitif or as a thirst quenching daytime beverage, as they are less strong than the short drinks.

5.3. Rules of making cocktails:

Make cocktails correctly and efficiently according to organizational and traditional recipes; consider eye appeal, texture, flavour, and required temperature in preparing cocktails and evaluate presentation of cocktails and make adjustments before serving. Many cocktail recipes are straightforward and are exactly the same regardless of where they are made, whilst others can be adapted or mixed to a particular enterprise's recipe. You will need to know the organization's recipe and the expectations that apply to the presentation of cocktails. You will need to understand the various techniques for competently preparing and serving cocktails.

Efficiently made cocktails are those that are made quickly with minimum waiting time for the customer. Knowing your products, the required recipes (or at least having written recipes close at hand), ensuring that the bar mis-en-place has been completed and working quickly will help ensure that the customer receives a quality product in a timely manner.

As cocktails are presumed to be colourful and decorative you will need to know what garnishes to use and how to use them. A garnish is an edible decoration that compliments a drink. Garnishes include lemon or orange slices and peels, strawberries, cherries, cucumber strips, chocolate sprinkles and powder etc.

Glasses can be rimmed with salt or sugar.

Decorations can also be used to enhance the eye appeal of cocktails. Swizzle sticks, fancy straws, cocktails umbrellas and other plastic decorations can be used to enhance the appearance of the drink.

5.3.1. Shaking: When a drink contains eggs, fruit juices or cream, it is necessary to shake the ingredients. Shaking is the method by which you use a cocktail shaker to mix ingredients together and chill them simultaneously. The object is to almost freeze the drink whilst breaking down and combining the ingredients. Normally this is done with ice cubes three-quarters of the way full. When you've poured in the ingredients, hold the shaker in both hands, with one hand on top and one supporting the base, and give a short, sharp, snappy shake. It's important not to rock your cocktail to sleep. When water has begun to condense on the surface of the shaker, the cocktail should be sufficiently chilled and ready to be strained.

5.3.2. Straining: Most cocktail shakers are sold with a build-in strainer or hawthorn strainer. When a drink calls for straining, ensure you've used ice cubes, as crushed ice tends to clog the strainer of a standard shaker. If indeed a drink is required shaken with crushed ice (ie. Shirley Temple), it is to be served unstrained.

5.3.3. Stirring: You can stir cocktails effectively with a metal or glass rod in a mixing glass. If ice is to be used, use ice cubes to prevent dilution, and strain the contents into a glass when the surface of the mixing glass begins to collect condensation.

5.3.4. Muddling: To extract the most flavour from certain fresh ingredients such as fruit or mint garnishes, you should crush the ingredient with the muddler on the back end of your bar spoon, or with a pestle.

5.3.5. Blending: An electric blender is needed for recipes containing fruit or other ingredients which do not break down by shaking. Blending is an appropriate way of combining these ingredients with others, creating a smooth ready to serve mixture. Some recipes will call for ice to be placed in the blender, in which case you would use a suitable amount of crushed ice.

5.3.6. Building: When building a cocktail, the ingredients are poured into the glass in which the cocktail will be served. Usually, the ingredients are floated on top of each other, but occasionally, a swizzle stick is put in the glass, allowing the ingredients to be mixed.

5.3.7. Layering: To layer or float an ingredient (ie. cream, liqueurs) on top of another, use the rounded or back part of a spoon and rest it against the inside of a glass. Slowly pour down the spoon and into the glass. The ingredient should run down the inside of the glass and remain separated from the ingredient below it. Learning the approximate weight of certain liqueurs and such will allow you to complete this technique more successfully, as lighter ingredients can then be layered on top of heavier ones.

5.3.8. Flaming: Flaming is the method by which a cocktail or liquor is set alight, normally to enhance the flavour of a drink. It should only be attempted with caution, and for the above reason only, not to simply look cool. Some liquors will ignite quite easily if their proof is high. Heating a small amount of the liquor in a spoon will cause the alcohol to collect at the top, which can then be easily lit. You can then pour this over the prepared ingredients. Don't add alcohol to ignited drinks, don't leave them unattended, light them where they pose no danger to anybody else, and ensure no objects can possibly come into contact with any flames from the drink. Always extinguish a flaming drink before consuming it.

5.3.9. Cocktail Making Tools:

1. The shaker: There are some shakers that are made of 3 separate parts, with the middle part holding a fixed filter. Those shakers are not always as waterproof as they should be. Using a professional model like the Boston shaker is advisable. These shakers are made of 2 parts: the cup en a top with a filter aka the strainer. Metal shakers are preferred over the glass types.
2. A mixing glass with a long spoon, logically named a bar spoon.
3. An ice bucket
4. An ice tong
5. A fruit press
6. A cork screw that includes a small knife which can be used to remove lids.
7. A bottle opener
8. A fruit knife and plate
9. A siphon with co2 cartridge to make "fresh" soda water
10. A measuring jigger
11. A straw holder
12. A nutmeg grater
13. Small plates (for rimming the glasses with salt or sugar)
14. A sugar sprinkler
15. A very thin & long knife to carve fruit for garnish and side decoration.
16. A bottle cap for opened wine of champagne bottles.
17. A can opener
18. An (electronic) mixer / blender.

5.4. Popular and Classical Cocktail Recipes:

1. **Aviation Cocktail:** 2 ounces London dry gin ½ ounce Maraschino liqueur ½ ounce lemon juice Shake all ingredients with ice and strain into a chilled cocktail glass. Garnish with a Maraschino Cherry.

2. **Bellini:** 1½ ounces white peach puree 4 ounces Champagne (Optional: ½-ounce peach liqueur) gently stir ingredients in a mixing glass and strain into a champagne flute. Optional: float a half-ounce of peach liqueur.
3. **Blood and Sand:** ¾ ounce Scotch whisky ¾ ounce Cherry Heering ¾ ounce Italian sweet vermouth ¾ ounce fresh-squeezed orange juice Shake all ingredients with ice and strain into a chilled cocktail glass. Garnish with an orange peel.
4. **Bloody Mary:** 1½ ounces vodka 2 dashes Worcestershire sauce 4 dashes Tabasco sauce salt and pepper ¼ ounce fresh lemon juice 4 ounces tomato juice Combine all ingredients in mixing glass and roll back and forth to mix. Strain into a chilled goblet. Garnish with a wedge of lemon, olives and a stick of celery. Celery salt and horseradish are optional.
5. **Caipirinha:** (Caipirissima with Rum or Caipiroska with Vodka) 2 ounces cachaça ¾ ounce simple syrup ½ lime, quartered Chill a rocks glass with cracked ice. Muddle lime and simple syrup in a mixing glass. Add cachaça and the ice into the mixing glass and shake well. Pour the entire contents back into the rocks glass and serve. Garnish with an orange peel.
6. **Collins:** (Tom, John or Vodka) 1½ ounces London dry gin, bourbon, or vodka 1 ounce simple syrup ¾ ounce lemon juice club soda Shake spirits, sugar and lemon juice with ice, strain into an chilled Collins glass and fill with soda. Garnish with a cherry and an orange slice.
7. **Cosmopolitan:** 1½ ounces citrus Vodka ¾ ounce Cointreau ¼ ounce fresh lime juice 1 ounce cranberry juice Shake all ingredients with ice. Strain into a chilled cocktail glass. Garnish with an orange peel.
8. **Daiquiri:** 1½ ounce white rum ¾ ounce simple syrup ¾ ounce fresh lime juice Shake all ingredients with ice and strain into a small cocktail glass. Note: Purists will hold out for the original recipe: juice of half a lime, ½ teaspoon superfine sugar, 2-ounces rum (assembled in that order, stirring the sugar into the lime juice before adding the rum).
9. **Gimlet:** 2½ ounces London dry gin ½ ounce preserved lime juice Shake ingredients with ice and strain into a chilled cocktail glass or over ice in an old fashioned. Garnish with lime wedge.
10. **Gin Fizz:** 1½ ounces London dry gin ¾ ounce fresh lemon juice 1 ounce simple syrup Club soda Shake and strain into a highball glass. Fill with club soda. No garnish.
11. **Irish Coffee:** 1½ ounces Irish whiskey 1 ounce brown sugar syrup 4 ounces coffee lightly whipped unsweetened cream Combine first three

ingredients in an Irish coffee glass. Ladle one inch of cream on top.

12. **Mai Tai:** 2 ounces aged rum ¾ ounce lime juice 1 teaspoon orgeat syrup Shake thoroughly with ice and strain into an old fashioned glass filled with ice. Garnish with lime wheel and mint sprig.
13. **Manhattan:** 2 ounces rye or bourbon whiskey 1 ounce Italian sweet vermouth 2 dashes Angostura Bitters Pour all ingredients over ice in a mixing glass and stir. Strain into a chilled cocktail glass. Garnish with a cherry or a twist. You may substitute dry vermouth for a dry Manhattan with a lemon peel garnish, or half sweet and half dry for a "perfect" Manhattan.
14. **Margarita:** [1930-1940] 2 ounces 100% agave tequila 1 ounce Cointreau ¾ ounce fresh lime juice ½ ounce of agave syrup (optional) coarse salt Lime wedge Combine first three ingredients in a mixing glass with ice. Shake well and strain into a chilled, salted cocktail glass.
15. **Dry Martini:** (*the traditional recipe*) 1½ ounces London dry gin 1½ ounces dry vermouth 1-2 dashes orange bitters Stir all ingredients with ice to chill and an orange or lemon twist on top. Substitute sweet vermouth for a Martinez.
16. **Dry Martini:** 3 ounces London dry gin (or vodka) ⅛ ounce dry vermouth Prepare a tall mixing glass with ice. Pour vermouth over ice and swirl to season, then strain vermouth off the ice. Pour gin or vodka over seasoned ice and stir to chill. Strain into a chilled martini glass. Garnish with an olive.
17. **Mint Julep:** ½ ounce of simple syrup 2 sprigs of mint 2 ounces bourbon gently bruise one sprig of mint in the bottom of a highball glass with simple syrup. Add half of the bourbon and half fill with crushed ice. Swirl with a bar spoon until the outside of the glass frosts. Add more crushed ice and the remaining bourbon and stir again. Garnish with a sprig of mint.
18. **Mojito:** 1½ ounces white rum ¾ ounce fresh lime juice ¾ ounce simple syrup 1 mint sprig and 4 mint leaves 1 ounce soda In a tall mixing glass muddle mint leaves with simple syrup. Add lime juice and rum and fill with ice. Shake vigorously and strain over fresh ice into a highball glass. Top with soda and garnish with a sprig of mint.
19. **Negroni:** 1 ounce London dry gin 1 ounce Campari 1 ounce sweet vermouth Soda (optional) Combine all ingredients in a chilled old fashioned glass and stir. Garnish with an orange peel. Top with an ounce or two of soda or serve straight up, in which case it should be stirred

with ice and strained into a chilled cocktail glass.

20. **Old Fashioned:** 2 ounces bourbon 3 dashes Angostura Bitters 1 teaspoon sugar 2 orange slices 2 maraschino cherries splash of soda Carefully muddle the sugar, Angostura, one orange, one cherry, and a splash of soda in the bottom of an old fashioned glass. Remove the orange rind and add bourbon, ice, and soda. Garnish with a fresh orange slice and a cherry. Note: The old-fashioned Old Fashioned recipe omits the fruit. Simply muddle the sugar and bitters in a splash of soda until the sugar is dissolved, forming a syrup. Add the whiskey and the ice, and stir. Garnish with a lemon twist.
21. **Pisco Sour**: 2 ounces Pisco 1 ounce fresh lime juice 1 ounce simple syrup 1 small egg white Several drops of Angostura Bitters Shake all ingredients with ice and strain into a small cocktail glass. Garnish with several drops of Angostura Bitters on top of the foam.
22. **Rob Roy:** 2½ ounces Scotch whisky ¾ ounces sweet vermouth Dash Angostura Bitters Pour all ingredients over ice in a mixing glass and stir as you would a Martini. Strain into a chilled cocktail glass and garnish with a lemon peel.
23. **Sazerac:** 2 ounces rye whiskey 2 dashes Peychaud's Bitters Splash of absinthe ½ ounce simple syrup Herbsaint Anise Liqueur Chill one rocks glass while preparing the drink in another. Splash the Herbsaint into the second glass, swirl it, then pour it out. Add rye, syrup, and bitters and stir with ice to chill. Strain into the chilled rocks glass and garnish with a lemon peel.
24. **Sidecar:** 1½ ounces cognac ¾ ounce Cointreau ¾ ounce fresh lemon juice Shake all ingredients with ice and strain into a chilled old fashioned glass or cocktail glass. Garnish with an orange peel. Note: If served "up" strain into a small cocktail glass with a sugared rim.
25. **Stinger:** 2 ounces cognac 1 ounce white crème de Menthe Shake both ingredients with ice and strain into an old fashioned glass filled with crushed ice or serve up in a chilled cocktail glass. Note that this is an exception to the rule that drinks with only liquors and liqueur should be stirred.
26. **Whiskey Sour**: 2 ounces bourbon or rye whiskey 1 ounce simple syrup ¾ ounce fresh lemon juice Shake all ingredients with ice and strain into an old-fashioned glass or a special sour glass. Garnish with an orange slice and a cherry speared on a cocktail pick (known as a flag).

CHAPTER SIXTEEN

Unit 6: Beer

6.1. Introduction:

Beer is an alcoholic beverage made by brewing and fermented malted barley and other cereals, with hop added to give flavour and stabilize it.

Making beer is believed to be over 10,000 years old, ancient Egyptian made beer about 6000 years ago and different civilizations made beer from many cereals. Germanic tribes were brewing in the first century AD and in Roman Britain beer (ale) was the national drink. Rich and poor both made beer and preferred beer to contaminated water. Early brewers used simple methods and fermented beer for only short time – one to two days maximum. By around 1100 AD, techniques of brewing had become very much sophisticated.

Introduction of Hops in 15th century in brewing gave distinctive bitter taste to the beer and also increased shelve life of beer. The first beer brewed with hops in England was bitter ale. During industrial revolution in the mid 1800s, beer makers invented a method to dry malt in huge rotating heated drums that made the grain lighter in colour and made a pale, golden beer. In the late 19th century with the introduction of compressed gas refrigeration made fermentation possible at any time in any season and climatic conditions. With time as technology developed few breweries start mass production of beer with latest brewing equipments to produce million barrels of beer per year commercially.

Recently brewers started the older techniques of beer making such as making beer in small quantity batches eliminating filtration and pasteurization to retain flavour and character imparted by the yeast during fermentation. Brewpubs and Microbreweries produce high quality beer in smaller quantity and are start functioning in India as well.

6.2. Beer Classification/Types:

There are three traditional styles of beer:

Top Fermented:

Ales– Generic term for English styles top fermented beer. Copper coloured or darker. Served at room temp.

Porter – Originally local London beer made with roasted un-malted Barley. Strength 5-7.5% v/v.

Trappiste – Ale type beer produced exclusively in Belgium and The Netherlands. Strength 6-8 % v/v

Kolsch– Product of Cologne - Bonn area, usually served with German sausage.

Stout - National beer of Ireland, the famous Guinness brewery of Dublin. Alcoholic strength is 4-7% v/v.

Wheat Beer:

Weizenbier - Originating from Bavaria, served with a slice of lemon. Alcohol content is 5% v/v.

Weisse (Berliner) – Originating from Berlin. Served with the essence of raspberry

juice. Alcohol content is 2.5-3% v/v

Bottom fermented beer:

Muchener - Internationally accepted name for dark brown beer. In home city it is

called Dunkel. Alcohol content is 4-4.75% v/v.

Vienna - Amber coloured beer, In home city it is referred to as Spezial Alcohol

content is 5.5% v/v.

Pilsner- Outside Czechoslovakia usually spelled as Pilsener. Golden colour clear

bear. Alcoholic content 5% v/v

Bock– A strong bottom fermented beer Often labeled with a goat symbol.Alcohol strength not less than 6% v/v.

Dopple Bock- Extra strong bottom fermented beer. First brewed by the Italian workers in Bavaria. Brand names end in the suffix --ator. Alcoholic content is 7.5-13% v/v

There are four main families of beer styles determined by the variety of yeast used in their brewing.

Ale (top-fermenting yeasts)

Ale yeasts ferment at warmer temperatures between 15°C and 20°C (60°F to 68°F), and occasionally as high as 24°C (75°F). Pure ale yeasts form a foam on the surface of the fermenting beer, because of this they are often referred to as "top-fermenting" yeast – though there are some ale yeast strains that settle at the bottom. Ales are generally ready to drink within three weeks after the beginning of fermentation, however, some styles benefit from additional aging for several months or years. Ales range in color from very pale to black opaque.

Lager (bottom-fermenting yeasts)

While the nature of yeast was not fully understood until Emil Hansen of the Carlsberg brewery in Denmark isolated a single yeast cell in the 1800s, brewers in Bavaria had for centuries been selecting these cold-fermenting Lager yeasts by storing or "Lagern" their beers in cold alpine caves. The process of natural selection meant that the wild yeasts that were most cold tolerant would be the ones that would remain actively fermenting in the beer that was stored in the caves. Some of these Bavarian yeasts were stolen and brought back to the Carlsberg brewery around the time that Hansen did his famous work. Lager yeast tends to collect at the bottom of the fermenter and is often referred to as "bottom-fermenting" yeast.

Lager is fermented at much lower temperatures, around 10°C (50°F), compared to typical ale fermentation temperatures of 18°C (65°F). It is then stored for 30 days or longer close to the freezing point. During the storing or "lagering" process, the beer mellows and flavours become smoother. Sulphur components developed during fermentation dissipate. The popularity of lager was a major factor that led to the rapid introduction of refrigeration in the early 1900s. Today, lagers represent the vast majority of beers produced, the most famous being a light lager called Pilsner which originated in Pilsen, Czech Republic (Plzen in Czech language). It is a common misconception that all lagers are light in colour: lagers can range from very light to deep black, just like ales.

Beers of Spontaneous Fermentation (wild yeasts)

These beers are nowadays primarily only brewed around Brussels, Belgium. They are fermented by means of wild yeast strains that live in a part of the Zenne River which flows through Brussels. These beers are also called Lambic beers.

Draft beer

Draft beer is a recognized form of fresh and flavourful beer on tap from a kegerator system. In most cases , this form of beer is served at bars or restaurants as a flavourful and inexpensive beer The word draft is comes from the English for the word “draught” which means ‘to pull’ from a cask with a hand pump. Draught beer often refers to beer ‘on tap’ that comes from containers 5 gallon or less. Click here to see other sizes, less than 5 gallons, that keg beer comes in.

The major difference between bottled / caned beer and keg beer is the pasteurization process in the brewery. Keg beer is almost never pasteurized and that means the keg must be refrigerated. And ultimately this is the way beer should taste; not from a pasteurized can. It is well documented that pasteurized beer, is packaged at very high temperatures that kill the flavour of the beer. *Keg* has become a term of used in the 1950s as pasteurised draught beers were replacing more traditional European style cask beers. The quality of the kegging process at the brewery was not as good as it is today, and sometimes the keg beers are referred to as tasting like 'Plastic Beer'. Some beer drinkers believed that chemicals were used to create a foam head. Despite this consumer concern, keg beer was replacing traditional cask ale in all parts of the Europe, primarily because it requires less care to handle.

6.3.Leading Brands of Beer:

1. Bud light
2. Budweiser
3. Heineken
4. Stella Artois
5. Corona
6. Skol
7. Guinness
8. Aguila
9. Miller Lite
10. Brahma
11. Tsing Tao
12. Tiger
13. Amstel
14. Foster
15. Strohs
16. Kingfisher
17. Kalyani Black label

6.4.Beer Service Techniques:

Beer Glasses:

Beer must be served in the right glasses irrespective of its type, at the correct temperature, and be poured using the correct technique. Beer glasses must be clean and preferably cold. The slightest residue the previous drink can destroy the head that should be part of every beer. The washed beer glasses should not be dried with a tea–towel as the lint may cause the beer to appear flat but should be taken from the glass washer to drip-dry in the refrigerator. The beer glass should be washed after each use and must not be refilled. Normally, the serving temperature of beer is 13° – 15° C. Bottled / Canned beer is normally served in Beer Mugs or Beer Goblets whereas Draught Beer is served in Tankards. Lager glasses are generally used for Lager Beer.

Beer Presentation:

The presentation of a glass of beer is very important to beer drinkers. The beer should form a head of approximately 1 cm. The head should last as long as possible and as such should be composed of fine, small bubbles. As it is drunk the head should leave a fine _lace‘ on the side of the glass.

Pouring Bottled / Canned Beer:

In case of customer willing to be served bottled or canned beer in a glass, then the procedure should include:

- Hold the glass by the stem or by the base. Do not touch the rim of the glass.
- Tilt the glass and pour the beer slowly onto the side of the glass.
- Straighten the glass, continue pouring until approximately a 1cm head forms, but do not overfill.
- If leaving the can or bottle with the customer, place the can/bottle with the label facing the customer, next to the glass.

Pouring Draught Beer:

Pouring procedure of draught beer is as under:

- Hold the glass by the stem or by the base. Do not touch the rim of the glass.
- Hold the glass at a slight angle, with the tap near the inside of the glass.
- Turn the tap to _full on‘ in one quick action.
- After approximately 30 ml of beer has hit the bottom of the glass, the glass should be straightened and the remainder filled, creating approximately a 1cm head on the beer.
- Turn the tap quickly to _full off‘ when the glass is full.

Note:

- If the tap is half open, or turned on or off slowly, beer will squirt out, making it frothy.
- If the beer is pouring flat, it may be necessary to lower the glass away from the tap to create the desired head. Alternatively if the beer is pouring heady, keep the side of the glass as close to the tap as possible to minimise the head.
- If the beer pours excessively heady, do not continue pouring and overflow the glass. Instead, stop pouring, leave the glass to allow the head to settle, then fill the remainder.
- Always pour beer drinks last when serving a mixed round of drinks.

Pouring Stout:

Stout is a very 'heady' beer, and for this reason draught stout is dispensed using a mix of nitrogen and carbon dioxide (as opposed to carbon dioxide as used for 'normal' beers). Nitrogen forms smaller bubbles and helps to prevent the stout from being too heady. Draught stout is poured in a similar way to draught beer except that only approximately ¾th of the glass is filled, then the stout is allowed to settle. The fine bubbles rise to the top of the stout forming a creamy head. Once the stout has settled, the remainder of the glass is filled.

6.5.Beer Storage:

Beer has the shortest storage life of any alcoholic beverages.

- Canned and bottled beer may be generally be stored at temperature between 40*F and 70*F(4.5*C and 21*C)
- Beer kept in storage for too long will lose their flavour and their aroma.
- Unpasteurized beer should be refrigerated at all times and all beer should be kept away from direct sunlight.
- Beer bottles should be stored be stored upright to avoid leakage.
- Beer cans packaged in cases may be stacked.
- All bottles and cans be stored in a way that minimizes the chance for dirt and dust to come into contact with the beer containers.
- Keg beers should be stored in a manner that allows for easy keg movement and taking inventory.

CHAPTER SEVENTEEN

Unit 7: Liquor

> "**Liquor** - *Liquor is simply the name used to describe any distilled beverage. Simply put, staples like gin, vodka, rum and tequila are all forms of liquor. Liquor also is distilled and has an alcohol content of at least 20 percent, although 40 percent is more common. 'Alcohol' is a more general category and can mean different industrial, medicinal, or recreational functions whereas 'Liquor' refers solely to beverages with alcoholic content.*"

7.1. Alcohol and the human body:

Alcohol (ethanol) is a drug, and health professionals should know something of its physiological and pathological effects and its handling by the body. It is a small, water soluble molecule that is relatively slowly absorbed from the stomach, more rapidly absorbed from the small intestine, and freely distributed throughout the body. Alcoholic drinks are a major source of energy—for example, six pints of beer contain about 500 kcal and half a litre of whisky contains 1650 kcal. The daily energy requirement for a moderately active man is 3000 kcal and for a woman 2200 kcal.

7.1.1. Absorption:

Rate of absorption of alcohol depends on several factors. It is quickest, for example, when alcohol is drunk on an empty stomach and the concentration of alcohol is 20-30%. Thus, sherry, with an alcohol concentration of about 20% increases the levels of alcohol in blood more rapidly than beer (3-8%), while spirits (40%) delay gastric emptying and inhibit absorption. Drinks aerated with carbon dioxide—for example, whisky and soda, and champagne—get into the system quicker. Food, and particularly carbohydrate, retards absorption: blood concentrations may not reach a quarter of those achieved on an empty stomach. The pleasurable effects of alcohol are best achieved with a meal or when alcohol is drunk diluted, in the case of spirits.

Alcohol is distributed throughout the water in the body, so that most tissues—such as the heart, brain, and muscles—are exposed to the same concentration of alcohol as the blood. The exception is the liver, where exposure is greater because blood is received direct from the stomach and small bowel via the portal vein. Alcohol diffuses rather slowly, except into organs with a rich blood supply such as the brain and lungs.

Very little alcohol enters fat because of fat's poor solubility. Blood and tissue concentrations are therefore higher in women, who have more subcutaneous fat and a smaller blood volume, than in men, even when the amount of alcohol consumed is adjusted for body weight. Women also may have lower levels of alcohol dehydrogenases in the stomach than men, so that less alcohol is metabolised before absorption. Alcohol enters the fetus readily through the placenta and is eliminated by maternal metabolism.

Blood alcohol concentration varies according to sex, size and body build, phase of the menstrual cycle (it is highest premenstrually and at ovulation), previous exposure to alcohol, type of drink, whether alcohol is taken with food or drugs, such as cimetidine (which inhibits gastric alcohol dehydrogenase) and antihistamines, phenothiazines, and metoclopramide (which enhance gastric emptying, thus increasing absorption).

7.1.2. Behavioural effects:

Alcohol is a sedative and mild anaesthetic. It is believed to activate the pleasure or reward centres in the brain by triggering release of neurotransmitters such as dopamine and serotonin. Alcohol produces a sense of wellbeing, relaxation, dis-inhibition, and euphoria. These feelings are accompanied by physiological changes such as flushing, sweating, tachycardia, and increases in blood pressure, probably because of stimulation of the hypothalamus and increased release of sympathomimetic amines and pituitary-adrenal hormones. The kidneys secrete more urine, not only because of the fluid drunk but also because of the osmotic effect of alcohol and inhibition of secretion of ant diuretic hormone.

7.2. Strength of drinks:

7.2.1. Alcohol by volume:

(abbreviated as ABV, abv, or alc/vol) is a standard measure of how much alcohol (ethanol) is contained in a given volume of an alcoholic beverage (expressed as a volume percent). It is defined as the number of millilitres (mL) of pure ethanol present in 100 ml (3.5 imp fl oz; 3.4 US fl oz) of solution at 20 °C (68 °F). The number of millilitres of pure ethanol is the mass of the ethanol divided by its density at 20 °C (68 °F), which is 0.78924 g/ml (0.45621 oz/cu in). *The ABV standard is used worldwide.*

7.2.2. Alcohol Percentage in common Drinks:

- Vodka | ABV: 40-95%
- Gin | ABV: 36-50%
- Rum | ABV: 36-50%
- Whiskey | ABV: 36-50%
- Tequila | ABV: 50-51%
- Liqueurs | ABV: 15%
- Fortified Wine | ABV: 16-24%
- Unfortified Wine | ABV: 14-16%
- Beer | ABV: 4-8%
- Malt Beverage | ABV: 15%

7.3. Pouring Measure:

The type of alcohol consumed in alcoholic beverages is ethanol, typically produced by yeast during the fermentation process. While there are other types of alcohol – such as isopropyl or butyl alcohol – these are not safe for human consumption.

The amount of alcohol found in beer, wine, and spirits can vary a little based on how high the proof is, which is measured in the U.S. with alcohol by volume (ABV) percentages. Proof for alcohol is generally twice the percentage of alcohol listed. Serving sizes have been standardized for legal reasons to contain roughly 0.6 ounces of alcohol per serving.

7.3.1. Serving measurements include:

- 5 ounces of wine per glass, 24 proof or 12 percent ABV
- 12 ounces of beer per serving, 10 proof or 5 percent ABV
- 1.5 ounces of liquor or spirits per shot, 80 proof or 40 percent ABV

Mixed drinks, cocktails, wine coolers, punch, and other types of combined alcoholic beverages are measured in legal terms using the above servings, although servers themselves may not be as careful about pouring.

For brewing purposes, the average alcohol content of beer is generally between 3 percent and 7 percent ABV; wine alcohol content ranges between 9 percent and 14 percent ABV, unless it is fortified; and spirits begin at around 20 percent ABV, but some states allow up to 95 percent ABV.

7.3.2. Peg Measures/Jiggers:

A jigger is a measure of millilitres / fluid ounces, used to measure liquors for mixed drinks and cocktail. A double ended jigger has a small cup in one end and the large on the other end and sizes for these cups are different. In Indian it is commonly served as 30ml or 60ml of Distilled Spirits.

CHAPTER EIGHTEEN

Unit 8: Bar

A **Bar** (also called a pub or tavern) is a business that serves drinks, especially alcoholic beverages such as beer, liquor, and mixed drinks, tor consumption on the premises. Bars provide stools or chairs for the patrons along tables or raised counters. Some bars have entertainment on a stage, such as a live band, comedians, go-go dancers, a floor show Bars that are part of hotels are sometimes called long bars or hotel lounges.

People are increasingly enjoying socializing over a good drink. Suggestive selling is motivating people to try new combinations or drinks and people are willing to pay for the quality high priced product. The unit deals with aspects related to setup of Beverage operation and service involved therein. Today bartending may not be realized without use of specialised equipments which n9t only bring lot of convenience but also satisfy the hygiene and sanitation regulations of local authorities. The unit will deal with various equipments requires in the Bar operation.

In Hotel, a bar is one of the main revenue generating outlets of the food and beverage department. The key function of bar is to serve alcoholic beverages in proper glassware according to guest's choices. Guest like their drinks with various mixer such as soda, coke lemonade, tonic water, ginger ale and water etc; some like with ice or without ice and some prefer their drinks 'neat' or nothing added. Generally complimentary snacks are served along with the guest preferred drinks in most of the bar, established by the management. The bar must have adequate supply of all kind of alcoholic beverages, non alcoholic beverages, ice, straws, coasters, different glassware and kitchen stock etc. within the reach of bar personnel's. Bar is set for service and storage of all these items mentioned for smooth functioning. Bars also required lighting, drainage, electric supply and water supply with running hot and cold water facility for making ice in ice machine, washing of glassware and to operate other machinery such as fountain soda etc. All bars should be equipped with proper drainage system to ensure that the water drains rapidly.

8.1. Bar Layout:

The first step to think through layout of bar is to ensure that it takes into account customers atmosphere, service and efficiency. Providing a functional space for the employees in which they can perform accurately and quickly is a continuous challenge to the designer the routine work at bar includes taking orders for beverages, mixing and garnishing drinks, wash and sanitize glassware, handle revenues, restock bar supplies with minimum efforts and maximum productivity. At the same time, it has to be kept attractive, clean and hygienic, makes the customer feel comfortable, blends well with the interiors and theme and stimulates beverage sales. Consequently some strategic decisions must be taken to fit in the design within the stipulated budgets.

Bar designs, today, are a subject of changing lifestyle and trends in fashion customers want elegance and are ready to pay for the same. The designing includes all relevant areas refurbished in terms of wood or marble and rich fabric to achieve a feeling of intimacy and comfort. Restaurant type bars try to incorporate simplicity and elegance through elegant wood work, marble tops for the counters and tables, overstuffed chairs which makes the seating comfortable as well as classy. Concept bars, a modern trend, tends to take the customer, into a exotic locale, which otherwise is not generally experience by the customer. Increasingly customers are willing to be a part of the action whether they are playing pool, enjoying video games or stage performances and so bats are increasingly participative. One of the most frequented beverage operations are the night club where the trend is towards use of lighter colours, increased space for people to sit and talk if they wish not to dance, increased eye contact between people.

8.1.1 PARTS OF BAR:

Typical bar is made up of three parts: The front bar. The back bar and the under bar. Often it may have a fourth part – The over bar. Each part has its specific functions. The figure shows all these parts in profile with its standard dimensions. The length of the bar will vary according to need.

The Front

Guests order their drinks and these drinks are served at the front bar, thus it is meeting point for guests and bartenders. The front bar should be functional and have adequate space for the pouring and serving beverages. The width of the bar is 16-18" (inches) with an alcohol proof and waterproof top surface, usually made of laminated plastic or high quality granite and should be easy to clean. Usually a padded armrest runs along the front edge from one end to another. If armrest is provided, around 8" (inches) space must be added up to the width of the bar, hence the total width of front bar is 24-26" (inches).

The last few inches of the back edge of the front bar are usually recessed, and the bartenders pour the drinks here, to demonstrate liquor brands and pouring skills. This recessed area is known by different names such as glass rail, drip rail, spill trough or just 'rail'. The front bar is supported on a vertical structure is known as 'the bar die'. It is like a wall separating the guests from the working area. It forms a 'T' with the bar, making a kind of table on the guest side, with other side shielding the under bar from public view. The guest side may be padded, decorated with attractive carving or left plain. There is usually a footrest running the length of the counter on the guest side, about 9-12" (inches) off the ground; footrest is made of brass rail.

The height of the front bar, normally 42-48" (inches), is a good working height for the bartenders. It also makes the front bar just right for leaning against, with one foot on the footrest. All under bar equipment are designed to fit under the 42-48" (inches) high front bar.

If it is a sit-down bar, it will have stools tall enough (usually seat rung 30" high) to turn the front bar into a table. Each stool is provided a 2' (feet) length of bar. The stool should be comfortable with rugs for footrests, or the footrest of the front bar is within easy reach.

A bar where drinks are served from the main bar for table service or other outlets, the front bar must have a separate pick-up station set away from bar guest's area with the help of railing, where servers turn in, receive beverages order and return empty glasses.

<u>The Back</u>

It is located at the back of the bar counter leaving sufficient space for the bar personnel to do their job comfortably. The back bar is usually 24" (inches) in depth and has two functions i.e. the decorative function of display of liquors and storage function of liquors. Traditionally, bottles of liquors and sparkling assorted glassware are displayed in back bar to enhance the appearance of bar. Usually back bar is lined with mirror, which has two purpose; firstly due to reflection it doubles the splendour of the bottles and secondly it gives the person sitting at bar to view others in the room or bartenders to observe the guests without being noticed.

The mirror also adds depth to the room due to which bar looks bigger in size. Back bar also acts as visual merchandising tool for the bar. New trend in back bar to include posters, pictures, tainted glass, antiques, plants or textured wall etc. to look more attractive and to break the monotony.

Most of the bars are fitted with overhead slotted racks to store stemware which makes the bar more attractive. The base of the back bar is usually 42" (inches) in height and functions as a storage space and the part of it may be a refrigerated cabinet or it may house special equipments such as glass frosting machine, bottle cooler or ice machine etc. Whatever be its uses, since it is visible to guests, it should not only visually pleasant but harmony with décor also. The extra stocks such as napkins, cocktail umbrellas, slavers, jugs, sugar, condiments or drinking straws are stored.

The Under Bar

It refers to the area under the front bar of the bartender's side and is the heart of the entire beverage operations as the bartenders will be facing guests while producing their drinks. The under bar should be designed keeping in mind the equipment required, types of drinks to be produced and mixes required for the drinks. Thus workflow must be considered while designing and utmost care and attention should pay.

According the volume of business and length or style of bar counter, the under bar can be divided in to several pouring station for smooth functioning. Each station should have individual supply of fast moving pouring liquors, ice, mixes, glassware, mixer, blender, sink and garnishes within arm's reach of bartenders. The liquors in each pouring station are grouped into 'Calling Brands' and 'Pouring Brands'. Most of the busy bars should have Bar Guns (automated dispensing machines) for mixes in each pouring station.

If draught beer is sold the beer dispensing units must also provided as per volume of business. The under bar also contains equipment for washing glasses and other bar equipment – sink system with drainage or mechanical dishwasher. Clean bar glasses should be kept group wise according to type and stored in glass racks/shelves or overhead racks near each pouring satiation. Adequate storage area should be provided for reserve stocks of wines, beers, spirits, liqueurs and kitchen supplies. The under bar must also have provision for hand washing sink and waste disposal.

The Over/Above

As the name suggests, it is a fitting or fixture found above the front bar. It solves two purposes, one the function of design or decor and other the function of storage of stemware glasses are hung from slots. Care must be taken while over bar is provided at a convenient and adequate height so as to not impede efficiency. Like every other part of the bar, the over bar also blend well with overall décor of the bar.

All the parts of the bar must be functioning well keeping the requirements of the guests as well as bar personnel in mind. The minimum space from back of the back bar to the front of front bar is 8' (feet) to ensure smooth operations of bar.

8.2. Permitted Hours:

In a bar, a last call (last orders) is an announcement made shortly before the bar closes for the night, informing patrons of their last chance to buy alcoholic beverages. There are various means to make the signal, like ringing a bell, flashing the lights, or announcing verbally.

Last call times are often legally mandated and vary widely globally as well as locally. Legislation's purposes include reducing late night noise in the neighbourhood, traffic crashes, violence, and alcohol related health problems.

India closing time of bars varies in different states. In Delhi it is 1 AM, Mumbai 1:30 AM, Chennai, Hyderabad and Kolkata at midnight. In Chandigarh it is 1 a.m. weekdays and 2 a.m. weekends. In Bangalore it is 11:30 p.m. on weekdays and 1 AM on Friday and Saturday nights. However, it is advisable to check with the Local Municipal authorities for such issues as the Timings may vary from city to city.

8.3. Opening and Closing Duties:

Opening Checklist

Bartenders are typically responsible for opening the bar since they are usually the first ones to arrive. This is a big part of a bartender's duties. First, they can make a quick property check for any visible damage. Then they can proceed to go through the bar opening and closing checklist and complete the following tasks:

- Unlock beer and wine coolers
- Unlock and inspect beer taps to ensure they are functional
- Check bar inventory and restock any items if necessary
- Place floor mats behind the bar
- Cut and prepare garnishes and other perishables
- Prepare mixers and juices
- Assemble, fill, and start frozen drink machine

- Stock glasses, mugs, highballs, pilsners, wine glasses, snifters, etc.
- Double-check all bar drink-making tools and equipment (strainer, shaker, jigger, ice scoop, ice cream scoop, wine opener, bottle opener, stirrer, bar mats, pour spouts, etc.)
- Re-stock ice
- Make sure all trash cans are emptied and liners are replaced
- Restock disposable items (napkins, straws, utensils, coasters, skewers, etc.)
- Restock items for food menu (if the bar serves food)
- Rinse and clean bar sink
- Have backup beverage canisters and CO_2 tanks ready to replace emptied ones
- Wipe down the bar's counter, tables, chairs, and stools
- Turn on the light, music, bar TV, neon lights, and bar signs
- Get and count opening bar bank from the bar manager
- Get a new comp and waste log from the bar manager

Closing Checklist

The first thing to do when closing is ensuring all guests have left the bar and all doors are locked. Having guests linger around can severely slow down the closing process and prevent your bartenders from completing the tasks or leaving on time. While the manager takes care of the bar manager duties, like ordering the full bar liquor list, you can take care of yours. Here is the bar closing checklist for bartenders:

- Lock beer and wine coolers
- Clean and lock beer taps
- Take floor mats to back dock
- Empty trash cans and replace liners
- Melt any remaining ice from the night before in the ice bins
- Cover and store all perishable items in their appropriate places. Discard if necessary
- Cover and store all mixers, juices, sweet and sour, etc., in their appropriate places
- Empty frozen drink machine. Refrigerate leftover and clean machine
- Clean and restock glasses, highballs, pilsners, wine glasses, snifters, etc.
- Clean all blenders and mixers

- Restock disposable items (napkins, straws, utensils, coasters, skewers, etc.)
- Restock beer cooler
- Restock liquor empties
- Wipe down service well liquor bottles
- Wipe bar top, counter, chairs, and stools
- Sweep and mop the floor
- Clean soda gun nozzles
- Empty, rinse, sanitize, and clean the bar sink
- Turn off the light, music, bar TV, neon lights, and bar signs
- Give bar bank to the bar manager
- Close and lock the cash register
- Turn in comp and waste log to the bar manager

8.4. Age and Alcohol:

In most countries, it is forbidden to sell beverage alcohol to a person under a certain age. For example, this threshold is 16 years in Italy, 18 in Hungary and 21 in the United States.

Sometimes, the minimum age differs depending on whether you are drinking the alcohol on the premises or buying from a shop. In Sweden, it's 18 in restaurants and 20 in shops; in Denmark, it's 18 in bars and restaurants, and 16 in shops.

In some countries, the permitted age changes depending on the strength of the drink. In Finland, the legal age is 18 for buying drinks from shops with a maximum of 22% alcohol by volume and 20 for drinks stronger than that. In other countries, the permitted age varies depending on whether or not the person is accompanied by an adult of legal drinking age, such as a parent or a spouse.

The legal age is set because alcohol can be very dangerous to the young. This is because they generally lack the experience of dealing with alcohol and their internal organs haven't finished developing, so a small amount may have a much larger effect than it does on adults.

The legal drinking age in **India** and the laws which regulate the sale and consumption of alcohol vary significantly from state to state. In India, consumption of alcohol is prohibited in the states of Bihar, Gujarat, Nagaland, Mizoram as well as the union territory of Lakshadweep. There is partial ban on alcohol in some districts of Manipur. All other Indian states permit alcohol consumption but fix a legal drinking age, which ranges at different ages per region. The legal drinking age starts usually at 21 years in mort of the states. However, in some states the legal drinking age can be different for different types of alcoholic beverage.

8.5. BAR Frauds and Types:

8.5.1. Frauds by customer:

Customer walking without paying

The primary kind of customer fraud is customers walking out without paying their checks. However, customers may also cheat an establishment by a number of other methods. They may claim that the food was unsatisfactory and thus indicate (usually the manager or host will make the suggestion) that they will not pay for it.

Bringing foreign article

Another possibility, which has occurred frequently, is for customers to indicate that their food contained some foreign matter, such as glass or china, or even an insect (perhaps even brought in by the complaining customers).

Customer making unnecessary complaints

Complaints are generally made to the waiter or waitress, who should in turn call the manager or host to solve the problem. Since there is always the possibility that the events did in truth occur, the normal policy is to grant free drinks or dinners to the guests to avoid embarrassment, to prevent possible lawsuits, and, of course, to encourage the customers to return. In most cases of fraud, the guests will not return to perform the same type of fraud nor will they return merely to buy a dinner.

Only one or two systems of cash collection can eliminate the walkout fraud. Cash prepaid (for fast food) or collected either by a cashier stationed at the beginning of food service (single-price dinners or buffets) or a cashier at the end of the line in cafeteria eliminates customer fraud of this nature. A COD system comparable to those used for beverages is occasionally used in food service.

In every other system there remains a possibility that the customer will walk out despite precautions by management and by employees. It is impossible for a waiter or waitress to watch a table continually. Even with team systems in which two servers work together—-one remaining in the dining room and the other placing orders and relaying food from the kitchen—the team cannot watch every customer continually. A team system, however, certainly is an. improvement over the individual server system. Likewise, a cashier cannot be expected to stop every customer to determine if the check was paid, particularly during busy meal hours.

Using false credit card

Customers may also use credit cards that are worthless or attempt to pay with checks that are not honoured by banks. Unless customers are known, it is best to avoid cashing checks if possible. If a check must be cashed, adequate identification should be provided, and no check should be honoured for more than the value of the dinner.

Counterfeit currency

Occasionally customers will attempt, either intentionally or unintentionally, to give to cahier counterfeit currency. In most cases, this currency will be easy to detect if proper cash handling procedure are followed. All bills should be quickly examined on both sides and placed on the ledge of the register. It is hoped that this cursory examination will detect most of the counterfeit money; although in some cases help of the expert can be taken.

8.5.2. Thefts by waiter and waitress:

Intentional omission of items are omitted from the bill in order to establish a rapport with customers, to increase tips, or perhaps to give free merchandise to friends or fellow employees. This type of fraud occurs when inadequate dupe system or validating systems are utilized.

A full control system in organizations having full services is impractical, since accounting for items with a less retail sales value is too costly. Bookkeeping costs would be excessive in relation to income.

In some cases, the items that are to be sold are already under the control of the service staff, as in the case of milk in individual containers or a 6-gallon refrigerated carton in the service area. No records are maintained when a waitress or waiter pour a glass of milk. Should this charge be omitted from the check, it would be impossible to track down the guilty party, since a number of personnel may have access to the milk supply.

Reusing of checks

This type of theft may occur in any kind of establishment. For high volume operations, it is possible that a large number of sales may be of the small dollar amount. Thus customers presented with a particular check would have no way of verifying whether it was their own or not, since the amount were correct and the items were the same. With the abbreviation normally used on checks it may be impossible for the guest to read a check without an interpreter. So long as the amount is correct, they are satisfied. Unless the amount is higher, most customers do not care if they receive their own check.

Pocketing checks or using unauthorized checks

It is often possible to reproduce the checks that are used by an establishment. Certainly if stock checks (not specially imprinted ones) are being used, they may be readily be purchased by anyone form dealers. It is also possible when checks are not numbered or recorded (and in those cases where the numbers are recorded but not audited) for a waiter or waitress simply to pocket the check and the cash received, if other control systems are not utilized. Checks can be counted automatically by the utilization of a check numbering system similar to UPC(universal product code) or those system s being used by banks. Each check is imprinted with a number that can be read by a machine. If a number is omitted or the check not closed out, the machine will report this omission. These systems are readily available that have been made in electronic technology.

Over charging

This practice may occur when staff members are allowed to make corrections on the checks without supervision. The customers may be charged for merchandise not received. Or higher prices may be entered on the check. After the customer has paid the staff member, the correct prices and amounts are entered, the check is rotated, and the difference is pocketed by the server.

Incorrect addition

Intentionally adding a some amount to each check and pocketing the money when check is properly totalled can readily be performed, particularly if amounts are handwritten on the checks. Should the error be discovered by the customer it is normally excused, since an error is over adding can be quickly explained away as poor arithmetic.

Substitution

In some establishments with fairly tight system of control, it may be impossible for a waitress or waiter to supply friends with free merchandise. However, substitution can be made by ordering higher priced items from the kitchen and charging for lower priced ones. The server orders a higher priced item but records a lower priced item on the check. The friend is presented with a check for the smaller amount.

Falsification of tips or other charges

In some hospitality organisations where many food and beverage sales are complimentary, other incidents occur where a dinner is being paid for by someone other than the guest. Extra amount of beverages or food may be placed on the checks to increase the value of the sale. This extra food can be sold to other guests and the cash received pocketed by the waiter or waitress. This padding of the bill may also be done whenever the tip may be a fixed proportion of the total bill. If the sales are increased by 1000rs the tip may go up to 100rs or more. When given a free dinner the guest does not closely inspect the items on the bill. Instead, he or she merely gives a brief inspection, signs for the full amount, and leaves a tip based on the total value listed on the check.

8.5.3. Bar tenders fraud or errors:

A bar tender who handles cash (using a register) has the same opportunity of theft as a waiter or a waitress- and the same chance of error.

8.5.4. Cashier theft or error:

The possibility of theft for cashier is more restricted than with either bartender, waiters, or waitress, since they normally do not handle the products sold. If the cashier is responsible solely for cash collection, errors or theft may occur under any of the following categories;

- Cashier keeps the money and pockets or destroys a check.
- Cashier changes the total of check after collection.
- Cashier bunches sales, split-rings, or under rings.
- Cashier gives incorrect change.
- Cashier performs incorrect addition.
- Cashier falsifies payout or adds items to complimentary checks and removes them from other checks.

8.6. Responsible Service and trends:
(GOOD PRACTICES)

Providing a safe environment means the adoption of some techniques which will go a long way to deterring trouble.

8.6.1. Spotting Trouble:

If staff are pleasant and friendly when serving patrons, trouble will seem 'out of place'. Getting the right atmosphere is important. An attitude of 'anything goes' can encourage violence and loutish behaviour. Glass Removal Regular removal of glasses and empty bottles is important. It ensures that patrons are aware of staff and security. It reduces possible breakages and broken glass problems, and also removes any potential weapons should trouble break out. Get to know your regulars by getting to know your regular patrons by name, their usual drink, and even perhaps the football team they barrack for, staff will encourage good behaviour through a friendly atmosphere and professional relationship. Quiet corners Particular attention should be given to areas that cannot be easily seen by bar staff or security. Regular collection of glasses or table swabbing will let patrons know firmly that there is passive supervision. It will also act as a deterrent for troublemakers.

8.6.2. Recognising the signs:

Unduly intoxicated means a state of being in which a person's mental and physical faculties are impaired because of consumption of liquor so as to diminish the person's ability to think and act in a way in which an ordinary prudent person in full possession of his or her faculties, and using reasonable care, would act under like circumstances. Penalties apply if the sale, supply or consumption to the person display signs of intoxication is permitted.

The following signs which, in combination, may indicate that a person has had too much to drink.

- Mood changes
- Slurring or mistakes in speech
- Raised speaking voice
- Clumsiness, fumbling with change
- Swaying or staggering
- Confusion, lack of ability to hear or respond
- Bumping into or knocking over furniture
- Dozing while sitting at a bar or table
- Crude behaviour
- Spilling drinks or the inability to find one's mouth with glass
- Inappropriate sexual advances
- Aggression or belligerence
- Inability to light a cigarette

8.6.3. Tips to prevent intoxication:

The licensee is not immune from action being taken if a police officer or licensing investigator believes the circumstances and, particularly, the undue intoxication level of patrons generally warrant further action. The following suggestions can help prevent intoxication Have glasses or jugs of water available for patrons who want to 'space' their drinks, or for those that are driving. Encourage the consumption of low alcohol and non-alcoholic drinks. Provide free food or cheap snacks. Reconsider bulk sales. In the case of beer, be discriminate in the use of jugs. With wine, consider offering all wines by the glass as well as the bottle, or stock a wider range of half bottles. Ensure that customers understand that even at "all inclusive" nights (e.g. $50 banquets with food and drink supplied) you reserve the right to refuse liquor to any patron who appears to be unduly intoxicated Adjust your prices to encourage moderation rather than intoxication. This may include low and non-alcoholic drinks that are priced lower than full strength drinks.

8.6.4. Refusal of Service:

As part of your job, there may be times when you have to refuse service. Service may be refused at any time for non-discriminatory reasons. For example, you may refuse service when patrons do not meet dress standards. However, there are times when you are required by law to refuse service of liquor, e.g. where a patron is unduly intoxicated, or you suspect the patron is less than 18 years.

The main reasons for refusal of service are:

- The law requires it - e.g. Minors or unduly intoxicated or disorderly persons;
- Safety of the patron - the consumption of liquor is placing their safety in jeopardy;
- Safety of others - the consumption of liquor by a particular patron is placing the safety of other patrons in jeopardy; and
- Civil litigation - the licensee may be held responsible for not adhering to points 1-3, should an unduly intoxicated patron endanger their life or the lives of others. You should be sure of your reasons for refusal of service and these reasons should not be discriminatory (race, sex etc).

A person has the right to take the matter to the Human Rights and Equal Opportunity Commission if they feel they have been subjected to discrimination. Remember, if the patron who just walked in is slurring, it does not automatically mean they are unduly intoxicated. The person may have a disability. Common sense must be applied in each situation. Each state has different criteria for refusal.

8.6.5. Professional Refusal of Service:

Remember, you are complying with the law when you refuse to serve intoxicated or disorderly patrons.

- DO obtain agreement from a supervisor and notify security, if available, before speaking to the patron;
- DON'T call your patron a `drunk' but warn them politely that their behaviour is unacceptable;
- DO be polite and avoid value judgements;
- DO point to poster/signs behind the liquor service to reinforce your decision, e.g. " No More It's the Law";
- DON'T raise your voice - if they raise theirs, lower yours;
- DO report the refusal of service to the supervisor;
- DO explain the reason for refusal or service (e.g. continued bad language, inappropriate behaviour);
- DO offer (if appropriate) non-alcoholic beverages instead, or phone a taxi or a friend to drive them home. It is harder to get angry with someone offering to do something for you;
- DON'T think the matter is over because you have verbally addressed it;
- DON'T put off refusal hoping that the patron will leave after the next drink - act while the patron can still be reasoned with;
- DON'T tell them what to do or how to behave;
- DO make sure that they leave the premises safely and that they don't hang around outside;
- DON'T be persuaded to give them one last drink after you have stated that they have had enough;
- DO enter incidents relating to refusal of service in a log- book, especially those involving threats or aggression; and
- DON'T let the issue go by because the patron has left.

CHAPTER NINETEEN

Unit 9: Food and Wine Harmony

9.1. Food and wine Harmony:

Wine and food matching is the process of pairing food dishes with wine to enhance the dining experience. In many cultures, wine has had a long history of being a staple at the dinner table and in some ways both the winemaking and culinary traditions of a region will have evolved together over the years.

In the restaurant industry, sommeliers are often present to make food pairing recommendations for the guest. The main concept behind pairings is that certain elements (such as texture and flavour) in both food and wine interact with each other, and thus finding the right combination of these elements will make the entire dining experience more enjoyable.

Most food and wine experts believe that the fundamental knowledge of food and wine pairing is to understand the balance between the "weight" of the food and the weight (or body) of the wine. Heavy, robust wines like Cabernet Sauvignon can overwhelm a light, delicate dish like a quiche while light bodied wines like Pinot Grigio would be similarly overwhelmed by a hearty stew.

Beyond weight, flavours and textures can either be contrasted or complemented. From there a food and wine pairing can also take into consideration the sugar, acid, alcohol and tannins of the wine and how they can be accentuated or minimized when paired with certain types of food.

While it is often said that "taste is subjective", there are quantifiable taste characteristics (like bitter, sweet, salty or sour) that can be perceived and measured as low, moderate or high—such as measuring the sweetness of honey or the saltiness of oysters. Flavours, such as butterscotch, char and strawberry, are more personal and can't be quantifiable. Flavours are either perceived to be present or not. The perception of flavours is linked to our sense of smell, while tastes come from the sensory glands of the taste buds.

Though individual sensitivity to the different taste "senses" can vary, hence wine experts will often recommend pairings based on these more objective measurements rather than the more subjective concept of "flavours". In wine there are three basic tastes; bitter, sweet and sour. These three tastes can each be identified with a primary component of the wine-tannins (bitter), residual sugar (sweet) and acidity (sour). A fourth component, 'alcohol', is identified in wine tasting with a perception of "heat" or hotness in the back of the mouth and is the primary factor influencing the body of the wine. The residual heat of the alcohol can be considered in food pairing with some ingredients minimizing the heat of the wine while some will emphasize it.

Acidity:

Acidity is a dominant player in any food and wine pairing due to the pronounced and complex ways that it can heighten the perception of flavours. In wine tasting, acidity is perceived by a mouth watering response by the salivary glands. These mouth watering cans also serve to stimulate the appetite. In wine there are three main acids that have their own associated flavours - Malic (green apples), lactic (milky) and tartaric (bitter). In dishes that are fatty, oily, rich or salty, acidity in wine can "cut" (or standout and contrast) through the heaviness and be a refreshing change of pace on the palate. In cooking, acidity is often used in similar fashions such as a lemon wedges with briny seafood dish such as oysters. The acidity of the lemon juices can make the oysters seem less briny. A wine that is less tart than the dish it is served with will taste thin and weak. A wine that comes across as "too tart" on its own may seem softer when paired with an acidic and tart dish. The complementing "tartness" of the food and wine cancels each other out and allows the other components (fruit of the wine, other flavours of the food) to be more noticeable.

Sweetness:

The sweetness of wines is determined by the amount of residual sugar left in the wine after the fermentation process. Wines can be bone dry (with the sugars fully fermented into alcohol), off-dry (with a hint of sweetness), semi-dry (medium-sweet) and dessert level sweetness (such as the high sugar content in Sauternes and Tokays). Sweet wines often need to be sweeter than the dish they are served with. Vintage brut champagne paired with sweet, wedding cake can make the wine taste tart and weak while the cake will have off flavours. In food pairings, sweetness balances spice and heat. It can serve as a contrast to the heat and alleviate some of the burning sensation caused by peppers and spicy Asian cuisine. It can accentuate the mild sweetness in some foods and can also contrast with salt such as the European custom of pairing salty Stilton cheese with a sweet Port. Sweetness in a wine can balance tartness in food, especially if the food has some sweetness (such as dishes with sweet & sour sauces).

Bitterness:

The astringency associated with wine is usually derived from a wine's tannins. Tannins add a gritty texture and chalky, astringent taste. It can enhance the perception of "body" or weight in the wine. Tannins are normally derived from the skins, seeds, and stems of the grapes themselves (leeched out during the maceration process) or from contact with oak during barrel aging. Tannins react with proteins. When paired with dishes that are high in proteins and fats (such as red meat and hard cheeses), the tannins will bind to the proteins and come across as softer. In the absence of protein from the food, such as some vegetarian dishes, the tannins will react with the proteins on the tongue and sides of the mouth—accentuating the astringency and having a drying effect on the palate. Various cooking methods, such as grilling and blackening can add a bitter "char" component to the dish that will allow it to play well with a tannic wine. While fish oils can make tannic wines taste metallic or off. Astringent tannic wines like Barolo and Cabernet Sauvignon can overwhelm a lot of foods but can be soften by fatty foods with a lot of proteins such as hard cheeses or meats. The dry tannins also serve as a cleansing agent on the palate by binding to the grease and oils left over in the mouth. Spicy and sweet foods can accentuate the dry, bitterness of tannins and make the wine seem to have off flavours.

Alcohol:

Alcohol is the primary factor in dictating a wine's weight and body. Typically the higher the alcohol level, the more weight the wine has. An increase in alcohol content will increase the perception of density and texture. In food and wine pairing, salt and spicy heat will accentuate the alcohol and the perception of "heat" or hotness in the mouth. Conversely, the alcohol can also magnify the heat of spicy food making a highly alcoholic wine paired with a very spicy dish one that will generate a lot of heat for the taster.

9.2. Food & Wine Harmony (International Menu Service):

The following is a guide to partnering Wine and Food:

- White Wine with White Meat
- Red Wine with Red Meat
- Sweet Wine with Sweet Food
- Bitter Wine with Bitter Meat
- Acidic Wine with Salty Food

Aperitif:

- Dry sparkling wine such as dry champagne
- Dry fortified wine such as dry sherry or dry Madeira
- Dry vermouth such as Martine or C inzame
- Aperitif wines such as dubonnet or lillet.

Horsd'oeuvre:

- Dry White Wine such as Chablis or Muscadet
- Dry sparkling wine such as Dry Champagne
- Fry fortified wine such as Dry Sherry or Dry Madeira

Potage:

- Dry fortified wines such as Dry Sherry, Dry Madeira
- Dry fortified wines such as Dry Oloroso, Dry Madeira

Farinaceous:

- Red table wine such as Chianti, Baralo, Sauvignon Blanc

Poisson:

- Dry white wine such as Chablis, Muscadet, Chardonnay.

Entire and Releve:

- Red Table Wine such as Bordeaux, Burgundy, Moselle, Chianti.

Roast:

- Red Table Wine such as Piont Noir, Cabernet Savignon.
- Chardonnay.

Legumes:

- White Wines such as Merlot, Dry Riesling, Chardonnay

Salade:

- Light Dry White Wines such as Samur Brut, Dry Rose and mostly Dry Champagne.

Entremet:

- Champagne goes well with sweet course, Sauternes, Tokay, Muscats Fruit Beer, Colden Ale also go well with sweet course.

Fromage:

- Full bodied white, light Red and Rose such as Rusling, Piont Noir, Burgundy, Cabernet Savignon.

Dessert:

- Sweet Fortified Wines such as Sherry, Port, Marsala
- Sweet White Wine such as Sweet Sauternes.

Cafe:

- Brandy such as Cognac, Armagnac, Liquers, Calvados, Ports.

9.3. Matching wines with Indian menus:

For Spicy Curries and Tomato-Based Sauces:

Examples: Vindaloo, Masala, Jalfrezi, Baingan Bharta:

In these dishes, tomatoes and curry paste are blended together to create a highly spiced tomato gravy. You'll find this sauce profile on many popular dishes including chicken masala, vindaloo lamb and vegetable jalfrezi. The key to pairing wine with this dish is to respect the spice level by matching it with fruity wines that can be served cool or cold and to complement the red tomatoes with a red or rosé wine.

Wine Pairing: Sparkling rosé, still rosé, super fruity light- to medium-bodied reds including Gamay, Pinot Noir, Zweigelt, Garnacha, Carignan or GSM Blends

Cream based Gravy/Sauces:

Examples: Korma, Pasanda, Makhani (Butter Chicken), Tikka Masala, Malai Kofta.

These dishes use heavy cream, half-and-half, yoghurt, or coconut milk to soften rich spices and form a thick sauce. These are great dishes for those new to Indian cuisine because the fats in the cream absorb and diffuse the high level of spice, bringing the focus to the texture in the slow cooked meats. Also, the cream makes it easier to pair these dishes with deeper red wines with medium tannin. Wines that seem to pair well with creamy Indian dishes have subtle brown baking spice flavours and an elegant tart fruitiness.

Wine Pairing ideas: Deep colour rosé wines (Saignée Rosé, Clairet or Tavel), sparkling rosé, Lambrusco and spice-driven medium-bodied red wines including Sangiovese, Zinfandel, Garnacha, Carignan, Cabernet Franc, Barbera and GSM Blends.

Green Gravy based Indian Dishes:

In these dishes, leafy greens are slow cooked with creams, onions, and spices to create a rich herbaceous sauce. Also, you'll find a fresh green chutney made with green coriander (AKA cilantro) that goes on pretty much anything (it's amazing). Although there may not be a wide variety of dishes made with this sauce profile, it's one of the most exciting sauces to pair with wine. White and sparkling wines with a lean green profile will highlight the herbal element in these dishes.

Wine Pairing Ideas: Extra-brut sparkling wine, Sauvignon Blanc, Grüner Veltliner, Vinho Verde, Verdicchio, Silvaner, Albariño, Muscadet, dry or sweet Riesling and dry Chenin Blanc

Note: The best wines to counter-balance the burn of capsicum are wines that have these 3 traits: they're served cold; they have lower alcohol, and some sweetness. It's not surprising then that Riesling is found on most lists in Indian Restaurants

CHAPTER TWENTY

Unit 10: Retail Beverage Outlets

10.1. Coffee Baristas:

In the United States, the term "barista" is used to refer to someone who prepares and serves coffee and coffee drinks. However, the word "barista" comes from Italy, and it translates to bartender. In Italy, baristas are responsible for serving both alcoholic and non-alcoholic beverages, which include coffee and espresso-based drinks.

The coffee industry is experiencing a period of growth as many of the younger generations become interested in not just coffee, but high-quality gourmet coffee that they can only get from a coffee shop. As a result of increased interest in coffee, it's a great time to consider opening a coffee shop or cafe. If you're interested in starting a coffee shop but don't know where to begin, refer to this article because we will detail the most important steps you need to follow to set up your business.

1. Conduct Research
2. Create a Concept
3. Source Your Coffee Beans
4. Write a Coffee Shop Business Plan
5. Get Start-up Loans
6. Cost of Opening a Cafe
7. Finding the Right Location
8. File for Permits and Licenses
9. Design a Layout
10. Order Coffee Shop Equipment
11. Hire and Train Staff
12. Open Your Coffee Shop

10.2. Chai Bars:

(Tea House) Tea is the most consumed beverage in Indian households. There is always a demand for another cup of tea for any average Indian and hence the concept of the small Tea stall on every nook and corner of every city, town or even a village is omnipresent.

The more organised Chai Bars are a relatively new but popularly growing phenomenon in Indian cities. These Chai bars offer a variety of teas and also some options for snacks and tit-bits being strictly non alcoholic joints. The modern Chai bars are clean places and may charge higher on the menu in comparison to the corner tea stall owing to the rentals and cost of services involved and applicable taxes. However, the Chai bars or stalls are very popular in India and always turn out to be a profitable business to any hardworking entrepreneur of even the lowest budget.

10.3. Pubs:

A pub (short for 'public house') is an establishment licensed to serve alcoholic drinks for consumption on the premises.

Bars are essentially places where people can go and enjoy alcoholic drinks. The main purpose of bars is to give you every variety of alcohol you might desire. While it is a specialized business, it also limits the type of customers you could cater to.

Pubs, on the other hand, are the renovated version of the public houses that were found in Europe since medieval times. Even though they too serve alcohol, it is served alongside food. In simple terms, pubs are somewhere between a bar and a restaurant. So, the emphasis on the quality and variety of food is as important as the emphasis on the drinks.

10.4. Juice Bars:

A juice bar is a shop that sells fruit and vegetable juices that are freshly squeezed on the premises. Most juice shops occupy a small footprint because they don't require a full kitchen or a seating area. Kiosks, juice carts, and juice food trucks are all popular models for a juice and smoothie shop. The rising popularity of healthy juices and the low start-up cost make juice shops an appealing business venture. There are many avenues you can take with your juice bar menu. You can keep it simple and stick to fresh cold-pressed juices only. Or you could get creative with different juice combinations and highlight a tropical fruit of the day. Some juice bars include blended smoothies and smoothie bowls. You may also decide to offer a small food menu with healthy salads and sandwiches. Make sure to consider your staffing requirements and the types of equipment you'll need to produce certain menu items.

10.5. Operations in FOH and BOH:

10.5.1. FOH Meaning (Front-of-House):

Front of house, or FOH, is a quick way of referring to the front part of a restaurant and all the staff who works there, outside the kitchen, such as such as waiters or greeters, hosts, bartenders, barbacks, bussers, food runners, floor managers, and cashiers in restaurants who employ them. It is basically the opposite of back-of-house.

The term usually means all the public areas of a restaurant, not only including the dining rooms and bar, the front-door area, which may have a space for waiting, and the restrooms. It can simply be thought of as the part of the restaurant that guests see. Although the abbreviation FOH is used in written form, most people do not use it when speaking, and instead, say "front-of-house."

10.5.2. BOH Meaning (Back-of-House):

Back of house, or BOH, is the part of the restaurant that diners don't see, at least typically. It is the opposite, then, of front-of-house. The BOH includes the kitchen, offices, storage rooms and any other areas hidden from guests. If a restaurant is a show, then the BOH is the back-stage area.

Back-of-house staff includes anyone who works in the kitchen. This includes not only the chef and sous chef, but prep cooks, line cooks, dishwashers, or any other person who works as part of the kitchen crew, and is not involved in front-of-house operations.

Effective Communication Between the Front and Back of House is the Key:

A quite typical problem in restaurants is a lack of communication and animosity between the back-of-house and front-of-house. Often, when things go wrong during busy periods, the FOH blames the BOH, and vice versa. Usually, this comes down to a break-down in the lines of communication. Many restaurants use an expeditor to help with this problem. An expeditor is a liaison between the BOH and FOH and works to make sure the plates get out to the guests properly and quickly and often performs a final quality check. Often, the expeditor is the executive chef or sous chef. Besides an effective expeditor to handle the flow from the kitchen to the dining area, restaurants often hold staff meetings including the BOH and the FOH staff, to ensure that the entire house receives the same communication.

Part C: F&B Control

"F&B Control"

CHAPTER TWENTY-ONE

Unit 1: Cost and Sales Concept

1.1. Introduction:

Cost: Cost is defined as the expense incurred for goods or services when the goods are consumed or the services rendered. In F&B operations, the cost of foods and beverages is incurred when they are consumed, whether sold or thrown away (contamination) or stolen; the cost of labour is incurred when services are rendered, whether the person rendering the services is paid at that point or at a later stage.

Sales: The term sale is defined as revenue resulting from the exchange of products and services and value. In Food & Beverage Industry, sales are exchange of the products and services offered at any of their point of sale like a restaurant, coffee shop, bar etc. for a monitory value.

1.2. Cost Concepts:

1.2.1. Definition of Cost: As we use the term in our discussion of cost control in the food and beverage business, cost is defined as the expense to a foodservice establishment for goods or services when the goods are consumed or the services are rendered. Foods and beverages are considered "consumed" when they have been used, wastefully or otherwise, and are no longer available for the purposes for which they were acquired. Thus, the cost of a piece of meat is incurred when the piece is no longer available for the purpose for which it was purchased, because it has been cooked, served, or thrown away because it has spoiled, or even because it has been stolen.

The cost of labour is incurred when people are on duty, whether or not they are working and whether they are paid at the end of a shift or at some later date. The cost of any item may be expressed in a variety of units: weight, volume, or total value. The cost of meat, for example, can be expressed as a value per piece, per pound, or per individual portion. The cost of liquor can be expressed as a value per bottle, per drink, or per ounce.

1.2.2. Labour costs can be expressed as value per hour (an hourly wage, for example) or value per week (a weekly salary). Costs can be viewed in several different ways, and it will be useful to identify some of them before proceeding.

1.2.3. Material costs: This refers to three principal costs: food costs, beverage costs, and the cost of sundry sales such as cigarettes and tobaccos. Material means the substance from which product is made is known as material. it may be raw or a manufactured state. It can be direct as well as indirect.

All materials which becomes an integral part of the finished good is termed as Direct Material while all material which is used for purposes ancillary to the business is termed as Indirect Material.

Food cost consists of the cost of food consumed, less the cost of staff meals. The formula for the calculation of food cost is therefore:

OS + (P – SM) – CS = FOOD COST

(Where: OS = opening stock of materials; P = cost of purchases; SM = cost of staff meals; CS = closing stock of materials.)

Note: The calculation of beverage cost follows similar lines. We take the opening stock of beverages, add the purchases during the period concerned, and deduct the closing stock of beverages. Whilst in the case of food cost we have to deduct the cost of staff meals, in the case of beverage cost, deduction from the cost of beverages consumed would have to be made in respect of authorized official entertaining and any transfers of beverages to other departments, e.g. the kitchen.

Labour costs for conversion of materials into finished goods, human efforts are required such human effort is called labour. It includes all the remuneration of the employees, both in the form of cash and kind. Thus, in addition to wages, salaries, bonuses, commissions and similar cash payments, labour costs include staff meals, staff accommodation and similar non-cash benefits. Labour can be direct as well as indirect. For example in preparation of Tandoori chicken: salary and wages of kitchen staff will be direct labour cost while salaries of purchase manager, store keeper will be indirect labour cost.

1.2.4. Overhead costs or expenses include indirect material, indirect labour and indirect expenses. Thus all indirect expenses are overheads. These are also of two types: direct and indirect, overhead costs are all costs other than materials and labour costs. Direct overhead expenses or cost may include operating and maintenance cost of machine while rent, rates, taxes, insurance, will come under the indirect overhead costs.

1.2.5. Fixed costs: These are costs which remain fixed irrespective of the volume of sales, for example, rent, rates, insurance, depreciation, and managerial and supervisory salaries.

1.2.6. Semi-fixed costs: These are costs which move in sympathy with, but not in direct proportion to the volume of sales. For example, fuel costs, electricity, telephone, laundry.

1.2.7. Variable costs: These are costs which vary in direct proportion to the sales/output of the establishment. They increase or decrease in the same proportions in which the output increase or decreases. For example, cost of food, beverages and cigarettes and tobaccos.

1.3. Sales Concepts:

The term sale is defined as revenue resulting from the exchange of products and services for value. Food and beverage sales are exchanges of the products and services of a restaurant, bar, or related enterprise for value.

We normally express sales in monetary terms, although there are other possibilities. Actually, there are two basic groups of terms normally used in food and beverage operations to express sales concepts: monetary and nonmonetary.

Sales in Monetary Terms:

1.3.1. Total Sales: A total sale is a term that refers to the total volume of sales expressed in rupees terms. This may be for any given time period, such as a week, a month, or a year.

1.3.2. Total Sale by Category: Examples of total rupees sales by category are total food sales or total beverage sales, referring to the total rupee volume of sales for all items in one category. By extension, we may see such terms as total steak sales or total seafood sales, referring to the total rupee volume of sales for all items in those particular categories.

1.3.3. Total Sales per Server: Total sales per server is the total rupee volume of sales for which a given server has been responsible in a given time period, such as a meal period, a day, or a week. Management sometimes uses these figures to make judgments about the comparative performance of two or more employees. It may be helpful, for example, to identify those servers responsible for the greatest and least rupees sales in a given period.

1.3.4. Total Sales per Seat: Total sales per seat are the total rupees sales for a given time period divided by the number of seats in the restaurant. The normal time period used is one year. This figure is most frequently used by chain operations as a means for comparing sales results of one unit with those of another.

1.3.5. Sales Price: Sales price refers to the amount charged to each customer purchasing one unit of a particular item. The unit may be a single item (e.g., an appetizer or an entré) or an entire meal, depending on the manner in which a restaurant prices its products.

1.3.6. Average Sale: An average sale in business is determined by adding individual sales to determine a total and then dividing that total by the number of individual sales. There are two such averages commonly calculated in food and beverage operations: average check and average sale per server.

Sales in Non-Monetary Terms:

- Total numbers sold, e.g. soups, steaks, and cocktails.
- Total covers.
- Covers-per hour, per day, per server.
- Seat turnover.
- Sales Mix.

1.3.7. Total number sold: refers to the total number of steaks, shrimp cocktails, or any other menu items sold in a given time period. This figure is useful in several ways. For example, foodservice managers use total number sold to identify unpopular menu items in order to eliminate such items from the menu. In addition, historical records of total numbers of specific items sold are useful for forecasting sales. Such forecasts are helpful in making decisions about purchasing and production. Total number of a specific item sold is a figure used to make judgments about quantities in inventory and about sales records, as discussed in later chapters. For example, Figure 1.5 shows that only five orders of roasted duck breast, six orders of loin of pork, and six orders of vegetarian burrito were sold on the day these calculations were made. The purchasing steward would track these items carefully so as not to order too much. Additionally, the manager might consider eliminating these three items from the menu if the number sold does not improve.

1.3.8. Total Covers: Cover is a term used in the industry to describe one diner, regardless of the quantity of food he or she consumes. An individual consuming a continental breakfast in a hotel coffee shop is counted as one cover. So is another individual in the same coffee shop who orders a full breakfast consisting of juice, eggs, bacon, toast, and coffee. These two diners are counted as two covers. **Total covers** refers to the total number of customers served in a given period — an hour, a meal period, a day, a week, or some other period. Foodservice managers are usually particularly interested in these figures, which are compared with figures for similar periods in the past so that judgments can be made about business trends.

1.3.9. Average Covers: An average number of covers is determined by dividing the total number of covers for a given time period by some other number. That number may be the number of hours in a meal period, the number of days the establishment is open per week, or the number of servers on duty during the time period, among many other possibilities.

1.3.10. Seat Turnover: Seat turnover, most often called simply turnover or turns, refers to the number of seats occupied during a given period (or the number of customers served during that period) divided by the number of seats available. For example, if 145 customers are served during one Saturday meal. The restaurant has 72 seats, so seat turnover would be calculated as follows:

Seat turnover = Number of customers served / Number of seats

= 145 / 72

= 2.01

In other words, each seat in the above example was occupied an average of 2.01 times during that Saturday dinner meal. Seat turnover may be calculated for any period, but is most often calculated for a given meal period.

1.3.11. Sales Mix: Sales mix is a term used to describe the relative quantity sold of any menu item as compared with other items in the same category. The relative quantities are normally percentages of total unit sales and always total 100 percent.

1.4. THE COST - TO - SALES RATIO: COST PERCENT

Foodservice managers calculate costs in rupees and compare those costs with sales in rupees. This enables them to discuss the relationship between costs and sales, sometimes described as the cost per rupees of sale, the ratio of costs to sales, or simply as the cost - to - sales ratio.

The industry uses the following basic formula for calculating cost - to - sales ratio.

Formula: Cost / Sales = Cost per rupees of sale

The formula normally results in a decimal answer, and any decimal can be converted to a percentage if one multiplies it by 100 and adds a percent sign (%). This is the same as simply moving the decimal point two places to the right and adding a percent sign. This is the formula used to calculate cost percents ; it is commonly written as

Formula: (Cost / Sales) x 100 = Cost %

This formula can then be extended to show the following relationships:

- (Food cost / Food sales) x 100 = Food cost%
- (Beverage cost / Beverage sales) x 100 = Beverage cost%
- (Labour cost / Total sales) x 100 = Labour cost%

CHAPTER TWENTY-TWO

Unit 2: Control Process

2.1. Introduction:

Food and beverage control can be defined as the guidance and regulations of the cost and revenue for operating catering activities in hotels, restaurants, and other catering establishments. The main purpose of any business is to make profit. Profit not only is earned by sales, but also can be achieved by cost control, and whenever money is saved, money is earned. According to James Keiser, "Control works best when it is used with other management process, such as planning, organizing, directing, and evaluating". According to him, there are two basic approaches:

- **Behaviouristic Approach**
- **Traditional Approach**

The traditional approach has two main aspects. One is directing personnel, or keeping an eye on things or by walking around to see whether he or she can correct what is not right or what is cost control break-downs. The other aspect of traditional approach is, measurement of performance with that desired or deemed attainable. This is the comparison aspect of the management scheme which is usually considered to have four parts:-

- **Establishing Standards or goals:** It can be expressed in different ways, for instance, a budget figure, a percentage figure, and a performance figure, such as meals served per server per hour.
- **Measurement of Performance:** It means measuring performance, and it is usually a quantitative figure, such as amount and percentage figure.
- **Comparison and Analysis:** Once the standard or goal has been established and actual performance is determined, it is possible to compare the two and a manager can find out the variance.

- **Corrective Action:** Once a significant variance is determined, the manager must take corrective action. Such action must involve more observation, personnel changes, and different methods of operation among many others, or perhaps the standard is unrealistic and needs to be changed.

2.2. Control:

Control is a process used by managers to direct, regulate, and restrain the actions of people so that the established goals of an enterprise may be achieved. The objectives of a food & beverage control are as follows:-

2.2.1. Analysis of income and expenditure: The analysis is solely concerned with the income and expenditure related to food & beverage operations. The revenue analysis is usually by each selling outlet, of such aspects as the volume of food and beverage sales, the sales mix, the average spending power of customers at various times of the day, and the number of customers served. The analysis of cost includes departmental food and beverage costs, portion costs and labour costs. The performance of each outlet can then be expressed in terms of the gross profit and net margin and the net profit.

2.2.2. Establishment and maintenance of standards: The basis for the operation of any food and beverage outlet is the establishment of a set of standards which would be particular to an operation. Unless standards are set no employee would know in detail the standards to be achieved nor could the employee's performance be effectively measured by management. The management would have set SOPs (Standard Operational Procedures) which should be readily available to all staff for reference. This can be aided by regularly checking on the standards achieved by observation and analysis and by comments made by customers and when necessary, conducting training courses to re-establish the standards.

2.2.3. Pricing: Pricing is important to determine food menu and beverage list prices in the light of accurate food and beverage costs and other main establishment costs; as the average customer spending power, the prices charged by competitors and the prices that the market will accept.

2.2.4. Prevention of waste: In order to achieve performance standards for an establishment, targets and set for revenue, cost levels and profit margins. To achieve these levels of performance it is necessary to prevent wastage of materials caused by such things as poor preparation, over-production, failure to use standard recipes, etc. This can only be done with an efficient method of control, which covers the complete cycle of food and beverage control, from the basic policies of the organization to the management control after the event.

2.2.5. Prevention of Fraud: It is necessary for a control system to prevent or at least restrict the possible areas of fraud by customers and staff. Typical areas of fraud by Customers are such things as deliberately walking out without paying; unjustifiably claiming that the food or drink that they had partly or totally consumed was unpalatable and indicating that they will not pay for it; disputing the number of drinks served; making payments by stolen cheques or credit cards. Typical areas of fraud by staff are overcharging or undercharging for item served and stealing of food, drink or cash.

2.2.6. Management Information: A system of control has an important task to fulfil in providing accurate up-to-date information for the preparation of periodical reports for management. This information should be sufficient so as to provide a complete analysis of performance for each outlet of an establishment for comparison with set standards previously laid down.

2.3. The Control Process:

The food and beverage control may broadly be envisaged under three phases:-

Phase 1: Planning phase

Phase 2: Operational Phase

Phase 3: Post – Operational Phase (Management Control after the events)

The catering cycle is a model, which represents all the food and beverage activities performed by an organization and provides necessary directives to the owner of the catering establishments to follow the basics of food and beverage operations.

2.3.1. The planning phase of the cost control cycle deals with financial, marketing and catering policies of the establishment. Policies are predetermined guidelines set by senior management according to the goals of the catering establishment to achieve the service excellence, quality control, highest level of profitability, and delighting the guests for repeated business. Financial policies deals with all the decisions to be taken related with the finance such as the budget. The budget has been linked to a road map which gives an accurate route to be followed and serves as a guide to the travellers. The Marketing policy defines the market to be catered for and develops marketing mix to satisfy the needs and wants of the target customers. It outlines the following:-

- Identify the target market the operation is intended to serve.
- Identity the market segment's to be exploited for achieving the desired market share.
- Developing the marketing mix (4 Ps- Product, Price, Place, and Promotion) to satisfy the needs and wants of the target customers.
- Designing the promotion mix (advertising, merchandising, sales promotion, public relations, and direct marketing) to facilitate marketing communication.
- Building the corporate image by meeting customer's expectations.

The Catering policy defines the main objective of operating food and beverage faculties and the methods by which such objectives are to be achieved. It outlines the following:

- **Outlet profile:** - Types of outlet, operating status, hours, décor, ambience, layout plan, covers, service, staffing etc.
- **Clientele Profile:** - Age group, sex, food habits, average spending, frequency of visit, etc.
- **Menu Profile:** - Types of menu, meals, cuisine etc.

2.3.2. The operational phase deals with establishing standards and standard procedures to exercise control in relation to the five main stages of the control cycle:

1. Purchasing
2. Receiving
3. Storing and Issuing
4. Preparing
5. Selling

2.3.3. Post operation management control phase base on comparing and correcting the activities held in operations. Need to observe the measurement of performances, preparation and comparison of various reports and statement, and need to provide information to HODS for further improvement. This phase give chance to take corrective actions on the basis of feedback, further forecasting and future planning.

2.4. Control Systems:

2.4.1. Purchasing: Purchasing can be defined as „a function concerned with the search, selection, purchase, receipt, storage and final use of a commodity in accordance with the catering policy of the establishment". The person employed to purchase foods and beverages for an establishment will be responsible for not only purchasing, but also for the receiving, storage and issuing of all commodities as well as being involved with the purpose for which items are purchased and the final use of them. Coordinating with production departments to standardize commodities and therefore reduce stock levels. Purchasing is not a separate activity. What how and when you buy must always reflect the overall goals of your establishment. Purchase the right product, right quality, right price, right time and from the right source.

2.4.2. Receiving: In large hotels, receiving is a specialized job. While receiving the food or beverage items check delivery note to see if the products delivered agree with it. Inspect products/ raw materials to determine if they are in agreement with the purchase order and specification. List all items received on the daily receiving report. Accept the products by signing the delivery note and returning the copy to the delivery driver. Deliver goods to the correct place.

2.4.3. Storing and Issuing: - The main function of this department is to store and issue food and beverages items that pertain to food and beverages operations of the hotel. Raw material should be stored correctly under the right conditions and temperature. A method of pricing the materials must be decided and adopted for charging the food to the various departments. The cost of items does not remain fixed over a period of time; over a period of one year a stores item may well have several prices. The establishment must decide method of pricing (actual purchase price, simple average weight and weighted average price) as per their convenience.

2.4.4. Preparing: A production system needs to be organized to produce the right quantity of food at correct standards, for the required number of people, on time, making best possible use of staff, equipment and material available. A method of predicting the number of Customers using the catering facilities on a specific day, and also of predicting as accurately as possible what items they will eat and drink. A method of controlling food and beverage costs in advance of the preparation and service stages. It is done by preparing and using standard recipes for all food and beverage items and also by using portion control equipment.

2.4.5. Selling: After the selling price is fixed, the price is verified with the cost price and the reconciliation statement generated. It is necessary to ensure that all items sold have been paid for and that the money is received or credit has been authorized. This is necessary to keep control of the number of covers sold and of the items sold. This may be done through a standard type of waiter's check system. The sales control is done with KOT and BOT for kitchen and bar, respectively, and tailed with the sales.

Post-operational phase of food and beverage control is concerned with three main points:-

- **Food and beverage cost reporting:** Providing accurate and up-to-date data for the preparation of periodical reports on current operations.
- **Measurement of Performance:** Monitoring performance and comparing actual performances with established standards.
- **Corrective Action:** Taking the appropriate action to correct deviations from standards, where necessary. Proper feedback of information to management, future forecasting and future planning whenever required.

2.5. Cost Benefit Ratio:

Cost Volume profit analysis (CVP) is a technique which is used to examine the relationship between the three elements of financial performance, mainly the sales and the cost associated with the volume and the profit. This helps us to analysis and understands how costs respond to various changes in activity and the planning and decision making process. CVP helps to predict the sales in rupees and the volume required to achieve the desired profit based profit based on the known costs. Its main focus is on interaction among the following elements:-

- Price of Products
- Total Fixed Costs
- Volume or level of activity
- Mix of product sold
- Per unit variable costs

2.5.1. Cost/Volume/Profit Equation: In an establishment or an F & B outlet, there is a relationship between sales, cost of sales, cost of labour, cost of overhead, and profit. The relationship can be expressed as follows:-

Sales=Cost of Sales + Cost of Labour + Cost of overhead + Profit

Since the cost of sales is variable cost, cost of labour includes both fixed and variable, and the cost of overhead is fixed, then the equation can be restructured into

Sales = Variable cost + Fixed Cost + Profit

2.5.2. Target Profit Analysis: The CVP Formulas can also used to determine the sales volume needed to achieve a target profit.

Sales = Variable expense + Fixed expense + Profits

2.5.3. Variable Rate: The Variable rate is the ratio of variable cost to the sales in rupees. It is calculated by dividing the variable cost by the sale in rupee and is usually expressed in decimal form.

Variable rate =Variable Cost / Sales

2.5.3. Contribution Rate: When the variable cost is known, the balance would be fixed costs and the profit. As there is an increase in sales, more amounts would be available to meet fixed costs and the profit. Therefore, it can be concluded that if the cost remains constant, there is an increase in sales because of the contribution rate, resulting in increase of profit. The increase is known as contributed rate/percentage/ratio.

Contribution rate is given by the following formulas:-

Contribution Rate (C R) = 1 – Variable Rate (VR)

2.5.4. Break – Even Analysis: Break–even analysis represents the relationship between cost, volume, and profit and is an important exercise in the business it depicts the following:-

1. The Financial state of the business.
2. The profitability of the business at different levels of output.
3. The break-even point (i.e., the point at which neither profit is made nor loss is incurred)
4. The relationship between fixed, semi-fixed and variable costs and the contribution.
5. The margin of safety and the profit-volume ratio.

Break Even = C/(S–V) = units of output at the break-even point

Where,

C -the total capacity costs, that is, the costs of establishing the particular production capacity for an establishment (e.g. this would include rent, rates, insurance, salaries, building and machinery depreciation)

S - Sales price per unit

V - Variable cost per unit

CHAPTER TWENTY-THREE

Unit 3: Control Cycle

3.1. Control Cycle:A continuous cycle process of food purchasing, receiving, storing, issuing, preparation, again storing, serving/selling and accounting is said to be a control cycle in general and in the F&B Service department in particular.

3.2. Purchasing:

Sound purchasing will be reflected in quality, reputation and financial success of a food service operation. Good food and beverage service begins with high quality buying financial success depends upon the profitable sales which in turn depends on wise buying. Purchasing in large for instance consists of specifying a product and placing an order. But the buying of food is a more complex task. Most of the foods service operations are not large and the chef, the manager or the owner does the purchasing. Even in medium sized operations, it is usually the Catering Manager or Ex. Chef who carries out the task of ordering and purchasing. The primary task of purchasing is to obtain the best quality of raw materials, based upon the specifications established by each hotel at the lowest possible price. The objectives are achieved through purchasing are:

a. Procurement of material needed to achieve the desired quality and quantity.
b. Purchase of materials at the most economical price consistent with the desired quality and delivery schedules.
c. Development of dependable source of supply.
d. To study and analyze the market as to the condition of supplies, price trends etc.
e. To maintain complete records of the source of supplies.
f. To advice the management on the effectiveness of buying policies.
g. To develop and maintain an effective buying service.

3.2.1. Standard procedures for Purchasing:

Purchasing policy

a. Corporate
b. Centralized or Decentralized

Purchasing research

a. Markets and Materials
b. Marketing channels
c. Price trends

Product evaluation and assessment

a. Product testing
b. Yield testing

Purchase specifications

a. Food
b. Beverage

Purchasing methods

a. By contract
b. By quotation
c. By cash & carry etc.

Clerical procedures

a. Documentation
b. Information processing

3.2.2. Purchasing Methods:

Within the hospitality industry, there are eight common methods of buying goods and services.

Open Market or Informal buying - This type of buying is done by individual establishments where the buyer invites quotations from the sellers for items according required specifications. The samples are selected on the basis of his samples, prices, delivery schedules and other services. Contract with the supplier is made personally in the market. This type of buying involves for perishables like vegetables, fruits, milk, meat etc.

Formal Buying – involves in large establishments in which central purchasing system has been adopted, like schools, hospitals etc. this type of purchasing needs great deal of competitive bidding and so called as "competitive bid buying". Here sealed quotations are received from individual suppliers and then they are opened. The quotation which has lowest bid and that meets the requirement is accepted.

Negotiated Buying - involves negotiation between the buyer and the supplier regarding prices and quantity. This method is generally used for seasonal items which has limited supply, where both buyer and seller are keen that the product is lifted quickly. This type of buying is also called "mutual agreement buying". This type of buying is adopted mainly for purchasing food items directly from farmers or manufacturers where large quantity of items is to be procured.

Wholesale buying - In this method a contract is signed with a whole seller for purchase of goods at a specific price for a future period, along with quantities required and when.

Blanket Order Purchasing - It is an agreement to provide a specific quantity of listed items for a period of time at an agreed price. The advantage of this type of purchasing is that a variety of items for which frequent deliveries are required can be ordered with one source which may be an agent between the supplier and the buyer. This is the best method of purchasing for those items whose usage rate is not planned accurately.

Contract purchasing - this is also called system contract and is usually used by 5-star hotel chains. The techniques assist the buyer and the seller to improve ordering of materials which are repetitively, with minimal administrative expenses, while still maintaining control. This method is similar to Blanket order except that the arrangement is a long term one and the suppliers are not therefore changed frequently.

Mutual agreement - A mutual agreement with number of regular supplier of goods and services is common. In such an agreement the buyer has no control over the price of the goods and seldom has control over the quality of goods and services. The only plus factor for the buyer is the right to refuse to accept delivered goods and services if the suppliers default in quality, price and services.

Tender - These are the method of buying used by large operations. The purchasing officer compiles detailed formal product specifications, which may or may not include the prices and forwards them to prospective suppliers. The suppliers will tender if they meet the quality. The cheapest tender is not always best tender. This type of buying does not allow the buyer much control over the price of goods; however it does offer the buyer the fairest pricing because of the competitive market forces.

3.2.3. Buying by tenders can be achieved by two methods: -

Fixed tenders- this is a formal contract between the suppliers and the buyer. It is suitable for large quantity of goods and services and specifies price, quality and period of time.

Quotation calling- this method of buying is suitable for fresh products, which is bought in quantities to last for 2-3 days. As for fixed tenders, buyers send formal product specifications to a number of suppliers, but in this case the price is not specified and there are no contracted obligations to buy.

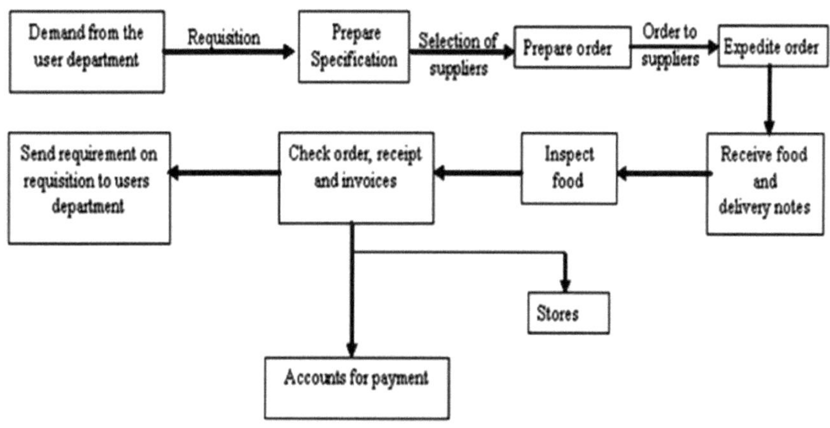

The Purchase Cycle

3.2.4. Standard Purchase Specification: Standard purchase specification (SPS) are concise description of quality, size, weight , or count factor desired for a particular item, Specification buying will give uniformity and consistency to purchasing and receiving, that will aid to maintain a desire food cost and create a standard product.

3.2.4.1. Objectives and advantages of SPS:

a) To establish a suitable buying standard for particular commodity for the hotel.

b) To furnish the supplier in writing in specific term the requirement of the hotel.

c) To help in setting the price of a commodity.

d) To obtain a standard product material for food and beverage department.

e) To obtain a standard product so that measurement of performance of departments can be accurate.

For proper and effective control, purchase specification should be used in all purchasing. It helps in bringing uniformity and consistency in buying, which maintains required cost of product. Each specification is determined by purchase manger, Executive chef, and F & B manager as per the catering policies, menu requirement and price range. The specification format is maintained with F & B service and production, receiving, stores department.

3.3. Receiving:

The receiving process is concerned with the task of monitoring the receipt of all incoming merchandise thoroughly and systematically to ensure that the quantity, quality and price of each item delivered conforms exactly to the order placed.

3.3.1. Duties and Responsibilities of Receiving Officer:

- Receiving of goods by quality and quality.
- Compare with challans /bills/purchase orders.
- Checks for quality, packing, specifications and quality.
- In case of items for maintenance, housekeeping, stewarding, etc. it is checked by quantity.
- In case of perishables these are checked for quality by the Main Kitchen Chef and by the Butchery Chef in case if butchery items only.
- Selling of the scrap also.
- Making daily Receiving report, shortage receipt, scrap report, Gate pass and soft drinks book.

3.3.2. Location of Receiving Department:

Ideally, receiving department should be located near the delivery door, purchase department and stores to minimize the time and effort in movement of goods into appropriate storage areas.

3.3.3. Facilities:

- Motor able road up to the entrance, (8 feet to 10 feet).
- Platform for unloading delivery trucks.
- Ramp to facilitate unloading of other delivery vehicles.

3.3.4. Layout plan:

Ø Well lighted and adequately ventilated receiving area

Ø Interior distribution:

- Receiving clerks' office

- Weighing section
- Washing section
- Packaging section
- Empties outward section

3.3.5. Receiving Equipment:

- Weighing scales: Platform, Counter, and Hanging.
- Hand/Fork-lifts trucks, Movable shelves, Trolleys and Carts for transporting goods.
- Bins, Baskets, Waste bins.
- Tools such as Can opener, Crow bar, Claw hammer, Short bladed knife for opening containers and packages.
- Thermometer for checking temperature of frozen foods.
- Marking & Tagging equipment
- Office equipment: table, file cabinet, calculator, computer, stationery etc.

3.3.6. Receiving schedule:

Receiving department of most of the hotels follow the schedule and basic purpose to make a schedule to control the flow of goods and assure the quality and convenience to suppliers as well as department.

3.3.7. Receiving documents:

Documents from the supplier

- Delivery Notes
- Invoice/Bills
- Statements
- Credit Notes

Documents maintained in the Receiving department

- Goods received book
- Daily receiving report
- Meat tags

Delivery Notes: These are sent with goods supplied as a means of checking that everything ordered has been delivered. The delivery note should also be checked against the duplicate purchase order.

3.3.8. Invoices / Bills:

These are bills from a vendor for goods supplied or services rendered. An invoice should be sent on the day the goods are dispatched or the services are rendered or as soon as possible afterwards. Invoices contain the following information:

Ø The word ***'Invoice'***

Ø Name, address, phone and fax of the firm supplying the goods or services.

Ø Name and address of the firm to whom the goods or services have been supplied.

Ø Date on which the goods or services were supplied.

Ø Particular of goods or services supplied together with prices.

Ø Particulars of discounts, if any and taxes as applicable.

3.3.9. Statements:

These are summaries of all invoices and credit notes sent to clients during the previous accounting period, usually one month. A statement is usually a copy of a client's ledger account and does not contain more information than is necessary to check invoices and credit notes.

3.3.10. Credit Notes:

These are advices to clients, setting out allowances made for goods returned or adjustments made through errors of overcharging on invoices.

Goods Received Book / Daily Receiving Report: This is used to record the details of all the deliveries of goods made by the suppliers.

3.3.11. Receiving procedure:

Quantity inspection:

To ensure that the quantity of the goods delivered is in accordance with quantity listed on the purchase order / invoice. This means that all goods will have to be weighed (for example, fresh fruits, vegetables, meat, etc.) or counted (for example, cases, crates, boxes, sacks, etc.)

Quality inspection:

To ensure that the quality of the goods delivered is in accordance with the quality established in the standard purchase specifications of the establishment.

Price inspection:

To ensure that prices stated on the invoice/delivery note are in accordance with the prices on the purchase order / invoice.

Dispatch to stores/user departments:

The goods, having been checked for quantity, quality, and price must be removed from the receiving area to appropriate stores/user departments. For example, perishable food items to the kitchen and all other food items to the stores.

Clerical procedures:

- Invoice stamping to acknowledge the receipt of supplies.
- Recording invoices on goods received book.
- Raising 'Request for Credit Note' for shortages, breakages, sub-standard items etc.
- Filling out meat tags for expensive food items.
- Forwarding completed paperwork to purchase office.

3.3.12. Beverage Receiving:

The primary goal of receiving control is to ensure that deliveries received conform exactly to orders placed. In practice, this means that beverage deliveries must be compared with beverage orders in regard to quantity, quality, and price. The standards established for receiving are quite simple.

The quantity of an item delivered must equal the quantity ordered. Verifying this normally requires examining bottles to be sure they have been filled and sealed, and then simply counting bottles or cases. It can also involve weighing kegi of beer to confirm the standard of fill or examining containers to confirm that those received conform to the order.

The quality of an item delivered must the same as the quality ordered. For all spirits, wines, and beers, one would check to be certain that the brand delivered was the same as the brand ordered. For wines, verification may also require checking vintages or the bottling dates of wines that are best when young. For beers, it may require checking bottling or canning dates to ascertain freshness.

The price on the invoice for each item delivered should be the same as the price quoted or listed when the order was placed.

3.4. Storing:

After purchasing and receiving beverage products, managers most often must store products until the products are issued to the bar area. Just as purchasing involves more than calling in an order and receiving requires more than putting things in the storeroom, so must the beverage manager be concerned about proper storage and issuing practices. A beverage operation's financial goals are directly affected by storage practices. If products are stored correctly, all of the products that are purchased will be used to generate revenue. However, if products are not properly stored they can be broken, damaged, or stolen. Any of those outcomes will result in increased costs. When products are purchased and paid for but then not used, more products will have to be purchased at additional cost to generate the same amount of revenue. Product quality and cost concerns must be addressed when managers plan storage procedures. If this is not done, all of the efforts to maintain quality and cost standards when products were purchased and received will have been wasted.

Fortunately, the best storage procedures do not require excessive time or costs to implement and maintain. Most beverage products are relatively non-perishable. Unlike perishable food products such as dairy items and produce, most properly stored beverages can be held for long periods of time without this concern. Managers must, however, implement procedures to keep products secure, to maintain quality, and to provide information necessary for accounting systems. Each of these concerns is addressed separately.

3.4.1. Procedures to help reduce the possibility of product theft while it is in storage:

• Access to storage areas should be limited to the fewest possible number of staff members needing this access.

• Keep storage areas locked when possible. In some operations, beverage storage areas are always locked except during times when products are issued.

• Use separate and locked refrigerated storage areas for beverage products. If possible, separate wines that need to be chilled, for example, from other refrigerated products. In some cases, one compartment of a reach-in refrigerator can be used for this purpose. Or alternatively, a lockable shelving unit within a walk-in refrigerator can be used.

• Practice effective inventory control procedures. It is critical that the manager know the amount of each product that is and should be available in storage areas.

• If beverage products must be issued during the shift, a manager or supervisor should be the one to do this, if possible. Not only does this practice encourage effective issuing, but it also helps maintain control over door keys and access to storage areas.

• Storage areas must be effectively designed. Doors and walls must extend to the ceiling; windows are unnecessary. Storage area alarm systems should be considered.

• Use other control practices, if needed. Some operations, for example, keep the most expensive items locked in areas within lockable storage areas. Closed-circuit television systems and motion detectors are also used in some operations.

3.4.2. Retaining the Product Quality:

Beverage products should remain in storage areas for the shortest reasonable amount of time possible. However, it is still necessary to practice effective storage strategies to retain product quality during storage.

Practices that help maintain product quality when beverages are in storage:

• Mark incoming products. Put the date of delivery on cases or bottles of beverage products.

• Rotate beverage products. With the date of entry into storage areas clearly marked on the bottle or case, it becomes possible to ensure that the products in inventory the longest are issued first.

• Keep storage areas clean. Routine cleaning is important; so are regular pest control efforts. Maintain effective lighting so that the results of cleaning programs can be easily inspected.

• Maintain product-specific storage temperatures for beers, wines, and spirits.

3.4.3. Beer Storage:

Beer has the shortest storage life of any alcoholic beverage. Canned and bottled beer may generally be stored at temperatures between 40°F and 70°F (4.5°C and 21°C). However, all but the strongest beers should not be stored for longer than three to four months. Beers with ABVs above 8 percent can be stored and aged for longer time periods. Most beers kept in storage too long will lose their flavour and their aroma. In addition, unpasteurized beer should be refrigerated at all times and all beer should be kept out of direct sunlight. Beer bottles should be stored upright to avoid leakage. Beer cans packaged in cases may be stacked. All bottles and cans should be stored in a way that minimizes the chance for dirt and dust to come into contact with the beer containers. Keg beers should be stored in a manner that allows for easy keg movement and for ease in tapping. Beer storage areas should also allow for easy product rotation and ease of taking inventory.

3.4.4. Wine Storage:

The most important factor in wine storage is even temperature. Temperature fluctuation in wine storage areas should be avoided. There is no single best temperature for storing wines. Rather there are a range of acceptable temperatures that vary based on the length of time the wine is expected to be held in storage. Many wine experts agree that wines are best served at cellar temperature, generally considered to be between 65°F and 70°F (18°C and 21°C). The best temperatures for long-term storage of five or more years for red wines is lower, usually between 55°F and 60°F (13°C and 16°C) For shorter-term red wine storage of less than five years, and for storing white wines, temperatures up to 70°F (21°C) are acceptable. It is not advisable to store any wine in areas where temperatures exceed this level. White wines may be stored under refrigeration temperatures of approximately 41o F (5o C) for several months with no loss of quality.

In addition to proper temperature control, managers must ensure humidity control in wine storage areas. If the humidity level is too high, meaning the air is too damp; molds may grow and damage labels, foil wrappings, and corks. If humidity levels are too low, corks may dry out and cause leakage. Humidity levels between 50 and 70 percent are best for most wines. Air-conditioned storage areas generally can provide proper temperature and humidity control. Sunlight is the enemy of proper wine storage. While most wines are stored in colored glass to minimize the effects of light, care must still be taken to keep wines out of direct sunlight. Bottles of still and sparkling wines should be stored on their sides so that wine is always in full contact with the bottle's cork. This contact with the wine keeps the cork moist and expanded, and prevents it from drying out and causing wine spoilage. Fortified wines and any spirits closed with cork should be stored upright as the higher alcohol content of these products can, over time, damage the corks and cause leakage. Wines and spirits closed with plastic or metal stoppers or screw caps may also be stored upright. Wine products in cases should be stored off the floor to permit air circulation and prevent mold.

3.4.5. Spirits Storage:

In general, spirits may be stored for several years at common dry storage temperatures between 50o F and 70o F (10o C and 21o C). Bottles should be stored upright with their labels facing out for ease of taking inventory. Spirits storage areas should be kept clean and secure.

3.4.6. Other Product Storage:

In addition to dry storage areas for bar supplies such as extra glassware, carbonated beverages, napkins, straws and the like, bars most often will require additional refrigerator and freezer storage areas. Storage for refrigerated items must include adequate space for fruit and vegetables for garnishes, mixers, and dairy products such as milk and cream. Freezer storage is needed for ice creams and sherbets as well as some concentrated drink mixes.

3.5. Issuing:

Issuing is the process of moving products from storage rooms to drink production and service areas. The correct quantity of products must be issued to meet estimated guest demand. This process must be carefully controlled to minimize product misuse and so managers can match issues of items with the amount of revenues they should produce.

Should there be some relationship between the quantity of drinks sold by the operation and the quantity of products removed from storage areas? Of course there should be, and effective issuing practices best ensure that this happens. Some managers allow any employee who needs something from storage to retrieve what is needed at any time. When this tactic is used, every employee is really in charge of issuing. For example, bartenders obtain spirit products, dining-room servers may retrieve wines, and other employees may be permitted to enter storage areas to obtain additional glassware or other items. In each of these cases, the security of products is put at risk. Beverage managers must do all that is practical to control beverage products at the time of issue.

Beverage costs are increased if there is a lack of control in this process. Given the importance of security, it is difficult to justify the open-door policies that exist in some operations. Beverage operations come in all sizes. Large operations may have a full-time receiving and issuing staff member whose duties involve only these two tasks. The vast majority of beverage operations, however, do not employ staff members with only receiving or storing duties. As a result, control at time of product issue in these organizations can become a challenge. In most cases, beverages should be issued from product storage areas on a regular schedule. For example, bars can be stocked at the beginning of the day, end of the day, or between busy shifts. If regularly scheduled stocking of bars takes place, the number of emergency issues during busy bar shifts should be minimized.

3.5.1. Inventory Turnover Rate:

One way to better manage the size of a beverage inventory is to calculate the inventory turnover rate: the number of times each accounting period, typically a month, that the quantity of beverages in inventory must be purchased to generate the beverage revenue for that time period. Inventory turnover rates measure the frequency with which beverages are ordered and sold.

3.5.2. The formula for the inventory turnover rate is:

Cost of goods sold (COGS) / Average amount in inventory = Inventory turnover rate

The cost of goods sold (COGS) is the cost to purchase the beverage products that generated beverage revenue within a specific time period.

CHAPTER TWENTY-FOUR

Unit 4: Menu Engineering & Analysis

<u>4.1. Introduction:</u>

The marketing oriented approach to the evaluation of a menu with regards to its present and future content, design and pricing is termed as menu engineering. The concept of menu engineering requires F&B Managers to adapt themselves to the contribution that menu items make to the total profitability of a menu. The menu engineering highlights the good and the poor performer in a menu, and provides vital information for making the next menu more acceptable and appealing to the customer and also more profitable for the management.

<u>4.2. Menu Engineering:</u>

- Helps to food service operator when to keep menu items and when to take off items from the menu.
- Helps to determine which menu items are over or under priced.
- Helps in designing profitable menu.
- Helps to select the menu items to be repositioned to gain popularity.
- Helps to revise recipe and portion size of the menu item.
- Helps in monitoring menu performance.

The concept of menu engineering requires food and beverage managers to orient themselves to the contribution that menu items make to the total profitability of a menu. It high-lights the good and the poor performers in a menu, and provides vital information for making the next menu more interesting and appealing to the customers, and hopefully more profitable.

<u>Menu engineering is a step-by-step procedure that focuses on the three main elements:-</u>

- Customer demand- the number of customers served.
- Menu mix- on analysis of customer preference for each menu item (Popularity).
- Contribution margin – am analysis of the contribution margin (GP%) for each menu item.

The pre-requisites for using this technique are:-

- The standardization of all recipes (including the presentation), so that the food costs can be accurate.
- The accurate sales analysis of each menu item, daily and by meal period.
- The use of a personal computer, so that simple spreadsheets with standard calculations, may be done accurately and with speed.

4.3. Menu Analysis:

The menu analysis reveals that all menu items can be grouped into any one of the following four categories:-

4.3.1. Stars: Menu items high in menu mix (Popularity) and also high in contribution margin.

- Most popular and profitable items on the menu.
- Can carry a disproportionate share of the burden of margin and profit.

Action:-

- Maintain rigid specification for quality, quantity and presentation.
- Employ high visibility menu locations.
- Determine range of price elasticity.

4.3.2. Plow Horse: Menu items high in menu mix (Popularity) but low in contribution margin.

- These are demand generators.
- Used to attract the price sensitive buyer.

Action:

- Take care in increasing their selling price (Because of consumer / price responsiveness behaviour).
- Lower menu profit positions are appropriate.
- Consider imperceptible portion reductions.
- Shift demand to other, more profitable items.
- Through, merchandising programmes: Menu positioning.

4.3.3. Puzzles: Menu items low in menu mix (Popularity) and high in contribution margin.

- Not popular. Hence slow sellers.

Action:

- Eliminate the item if it is a slow seller.
- Decrease the item selling price.
- Reposition the item on the menu.
- Limit the total no. of Puzzles on a menu.
- Rename the item to influence its popularity.

4.3.4. Dogs: Menu items low in menu mix (popularity) and low in contribution margin.

- Unwanted menu items.
- Unpopular from both consumers and management point of view.

Action:

- Eliminate the items from the menu.
- Consider and adding them with other item.
- Need of special promotion to the menu.

When a restaurant's bottom line starts eroding, F&B Managers tend to:

- Reduce portion size.
- Purchase at lower specification.
- Eliminate complimentary food items.
- Increase menu prices.

- Reduce labour costs.
- Tighten operational controls.

Although these may be popular survival strategies, they have the potential to affect adversely a consumer's perception of value.

A decline in business may result, however a more effective way may be to...

- Develop demand based, recession-proof menus.
- Generate new customer demand (through market segmentation, merchandising, menu design and positioning).
- Increased old customer demand (through, advertising, menu design and customer service).
- Use of assets (enhance employee productivity and customer service).
- Increasing menu-item contribution margin (through improved pricing approaches).

These tend to have a positive effect on perceived value and can lead to a broadened customer base. The key to menu's success is whether or not it produces more customers and more contribution in terms of revenue. Menu engineering is a tool for food service managers with which they can evaluate one menu against another menu. It requires food service managers should know.

a. Each menu item
b. Item cost
c. Selling price
d. Quantity sold over a period of time
e. Each items revenue contribution margin
f. High selling/Low selling item
g. Popularity category

Each menu item is classified and evaluated for both its marketing (Popularity) and pricing (profit) success. By categorizing and classifying menu items through logical and mathematical procedures menu engineering help manager to take the right decisions.

4.3.5. Sequence To Menu Engineering:

Be familiar with: Each dish

- Cost
- Selling Price

Average Number Sold

- Mathematical Calculations
- Analysis
- Categorization & Classification of Items
- Decision Making

CHAPTER TWENTY-FIVE

Unit 5: Controlling Food Sales

5.1. Food Sales Control: Introduction.

The Payment for food may be made in many forms such as cash, foreign currency, credit cards, cheques, traveller's cheques, luncheon vouchers and signed bills. The sales summary report prepared at the end of the day helped produce the total cash and credit sales made on that day. It helped compare sales of each day with that of the same day in the previous week. The sales in F&B are documents by writing it down by the head chef. Through Property Management System (PMS) is used and all orders are typed, the guests can also directly order with the help of a tablet. The order is then sent to the Kitchen this is known as KOT (Kitchen Order Ticket). Whenever there is a sale of a particular dish from an outlet, the same should tally with the number of dishes served from the kitchen. The KOT of a dish should tally with the dish sold for a period of a day.

5.2. The goals of sales control:

When the phrase "controlling food costs" is used, the first thing that comes to mind for many is portion control. It's important, but it's only part of the picture—and not the biggest part. Cost control means controlling the entire Cost Cycle, which starts when you place an order with your suppliers, and ends when you analyze and adjust your operation through comprehensive reporting.

Your point of sale system plays a key role in controlling costs throughout the Cost Cycle. Use it to support your overall process of managing costs at all points along that cycle. That includes placing orders, managing inventory, portioning ingredients, tracking usage and forecasting needs.

The Goals of Sales Control:

- Optimizing the number of sales/customers
- Maximizing profit

- Controlling revenue

5.2.1. Optimizing the Number of Sales/Customer:

To ensure the increase in number of customers or sales the management has to ensure that they are working towards the right direction of reducing the deficit between the promises and delivery. It also needs to be ensured that the superior delivery of F&B is registered positively by the guest so that he becomes a repeat customer and also your indirect marketing mascot.

5.2.2. Maximizing Profits:

Operators can, adopt various merchandising techniques to influence the customer to select one drink (a drink with a greater contribution margin) rather than another.

In food and beverage operations, profit maximization is accomplished by:

- Establishing prices that will maximize gross profit
- Influencing customers' selections
-

5.2.3. Controlling Revenue:

Revenue control consists of those activities established to ensure that each sale to a customer results in appropriate revenue to the operation. There are two basic approaches to recording and controlling food and beverage sales.

- A manual system: Which is commonly used in small and in exclusive type catering units.
- An automated system: Which is commonly used in units with several outlets, in units with a very high volume of business and in up-to-date companies with many units.

5.3. Revenue Control Using Manual Means:

First step to take while establishing sales control-procedures is to ensure that each item ordered and being sold are recorded on a waiter's sales check along with the price of the item. Use numbered checks and control these tightly, recording all cancelled and missing checks. It is more common to find duplicate or triplicate checks being used as a better control method. They provide the kitchen, buffet, or bar with a written record of what has been ordered and issued. The full manual control of a food and beverage operation would be costly, time consuming and data produced would frequently be far too late for meaningful management action to take place. The day-today operational problems of a manual system are many and include such common problems as:

Poor handwriting by the waiting staff resulting in:

- Incorrect order given to the kitchen or dispense bar
- Wrong food being offered to the customer.
- Incorrect prices being charged to the customer.
- Poorly presented bill for the customer, etc.

Human error can produce such mistakes as:

- Incorrect prices charged to items on a bill
- Incorrect additions to a customer's bill
- Incorrect service charge made
- Incorrect government tax (for example VAT) charge made.

The communication between departments such as the restaurant, dispense bar, kitchen and cashiers has to be done physically by the waiting staff going to the various departments. This is not only time consuming but inefficient. Manual systems do not provide any quick management information data, any data produced at best being normally 24-28 hours old, as well as being costly to produce. Manual systems have to be restricted to the bare essentials because of the high cost of labour that would be involved in providing detailed up-to-date information.

5.4. Revenue Control Using Computers:

Pre-check machines are somewhat similar in appearance to a standard cash register and are designed to operate only when a sales check is inserted into the printing table to the side of the machine.

5.4.1 The machine is operated in the following way:

- A waiter has his/ her own machine key.
- A check is inserted into the printing table and the particular keys, depending on the order taken, are pressed giving an item and price record as well as recording the table number, the number of covers and the waiter's reference number.

- A duplicate is printed and issued by the machine which is then issued as the duplicate check to obtain food and/or beverages.
- For each transaction a reference number is given on the sales check and the duplicate.
- All data is recorded on a continuous audit tape that can be removed only by authorized persons at the end of the day when the machine is cleared and total sales taken and compared to actual cash received.

5.4.2. Pre-set Pre-checking System:

This is an up-date on the basic pre-check machine. The keyboard is much larger than the previous machines, and has descriptive keys corresponding to all items on the menu which are pre-set to the current price of each item. A waiter pressing the key for, say one cheeseburger would not only have the item printed out but also the price. A control panel, kept under lock and key, would enable management to change the price of any item if required, very quickly. It is also possible to have a running count kept of each item recorded and at the end of a meal period by depressing each key in turn to get a print out giving a basic analysis of sales made.

5.4.3. Electronic Cash Registers (ECR's):

These are very high speed machines which were developed mainly for operations such as super- markets and were further adapted for use in high volume catering operations. The particular advantages of these machines are that they will:

- Price customers' checks through preset or by price look-ups.
- Print checks, including the printing of previously entered items.
- Have an additional special key-so that the pre-set price can be changed during promotional periods such as a 'happy hour' in a bar.
- Provide an analysis of sales made by type of product and if required by hour (or other similar period) of trading
- Provide an analysis of sales by waiter per hour or per shift period.
- Analyze sales by method of payment for example, cash, cheque, type of credit card, etc.
- Complete automatic tax calculations and cover and service changes.
- Provide some limited stock control.
- Provide waiter check-in and checking out facilities.
- Provide facilities for operator training to take place on the machine without disrupting any information already in the ECR.

5.4.4. Point-of-Sale Control Systems:

At a basic level a point-of-sale control system is no more than a modern ECR with the additional feature of one or several printers at such locations as the kitchen (or sections of the kitchen) or dispense bar. Some systems replace the ECR with a 'server terminal' (also called 'waiter communication' systems), which may be placed at several locations within a restaurant, and is a modification of an ECR in that the cash features are eliminated making the terminal relatively small and inconspicuous.

5.4.5. The objectives for having printers are:

- To provide an instant and separate clear and printed order to kitchen or bar, of what is required and by and for whom.
- To speed up the process of giving the order to the kitchen or bar.
- To aid control, in that items can only be ordered when they have been entered into the ECR or terminal by an identifiable member of the waiting staff and printed.
- To reduced the time taken by the waiter in walking to the kitchen or bar to place an order and, as frequently happens, to check if an order is ready for collection.
- To afford more times, if required, for customer contact.

Printers are at times replaced by VDU screens. Server terminals are part of a computer-based point-of-sale system. These special terminals are linked to other server terminals in the restaurants and bars within one system and, if required to, also interface with other systems so that, for example, the transfer of restaurant and bar charges may be made via the front office computer system. The advantage of a computerized point-of-sale system is that it is capable of processing data as activities occur, which makes it possible to obtain up-to-the minute reports for management who can be better informed and able to take immediate and accurate corrective action if necessary.

This type of point-of-sale control system has been taken one step further with the introduction of hand-held terminals. Electronic Server Pad (ESP), for example, is a palm-size unit which uses radio frequencies to communicate from the guest's table direct to the kitchen and bar preparation areas. The use of such a terminal offers a number of advantages: food and beverage orders are delivered faster and more efficiently to preparation sites; waiters in turn can attend more tables; with a two-way communication service staff can be notified if an item is out of stock; all food and beverage items ordered are immediately charged to the guest's bill, which is accurate and easy to read; finally, operations can reassess their labour utilization and efficiency, certain members of the service staff, for example, can take the simple order, while others can spend more time with customers to increase food and beverage sales.

The ESP is a completely noiseless terminal with orders being entered alphabetically, numerically or by using pre-set codes. When not being used and the unit is closed, its design resembles a conventional order pad, compact and light in weight that can easily be carried around by service staff. It is currently being utilized in a variety of situations, including restaurants.

CHAPTER TWENTY-SIX

Unit 6: Beverage Control

6.1. Beverage Control:

Beverage control refers to control of liquor (including non-alcoholic beverages) during purchasing, receiving, issuing and selling. The control measures used are:-

- Keeping less expensive drinks as house-brands
- Avoiding over buying
- Strict storing and receiving procedures
- Regular physical inventory of stores
- Periodically preparing operational statements
- Control checks and BOT (Beverage Order Ticket/Token)
- Regular bar inventory
- Using standards measures
- Following standard bar recipe cards for cocktails

6.1.1. Reason for extra Control over Beverages:

- Pilferage is common among staff for personal consumption. The lure of alcohol can be compelling for some staff.
- Unauthorized Complimentary drinks are served to customers in the expectation of extra tips.
- Failure to record sales: The staff may not raise a check for the beverage served and pocket the cash.
- Bar Staff have been found to carry their own liquor from outside and serve it in the hotel at higher rates. This eats into the bar sales.
- Inexperienced barmen are often found to over pour or under pour drinks.

- High spillage and breakage is another reason for extra control on beverages.
- The barman may be careless in discarding bottle before emptying.
- Pouring less than the standard measure and selling the excess personally.
- Diluting white spirits such as gin, vodka, and white rum with water. This increase the quantity and allows the barman to pocket sales.
- Claiming „damage by accident" by showing broken empty bottles. The liquor is of course not wasted and is sold without will to pocket cash.
- Over charging guests on number of drinks. This is resorted to if the guest seems drunk.
- Using the same bill for more than one customer. This act in hotel parlay is more commonly called „check playing" and is a a very serious offence. The modus operandi is quite simple. For example, if a table for two orders two beers and leaves without taking the guest copy of the bill, then the same bill for two bears is given to the next customer if the order is the same. The sale of course is not registered.
- Using peg measures of lesser capacity. Short pouring as well as over pouring could be reason for suspecting fraud in a bar.

6.1.2. Beverage Purchasing Control:

The purchasing of beverages aims to purchase the best quality of item at the lower price for a specific purpose. A beverage sale is an important function and a valuable source of income in hotel and restaurant business. An effective purchasing control of beverages is essential. For purchasing of beverages the different sources of supply are as follows:-

Cash and Carry and Retail Outlets: These are many beverages sales units in major towns where purchasing by cash and carry method is prevalent. These establishments offer a limited range of wines, spirits and beers.

Suspended Dept. / Business: The leading beverage companies/ breweries invoice the hotel for its opening cellar stock. The payment is made on subsequent invoice. The first invoice is 'suspended' until the account is closed.

Cellar Stocks and Suspended Debt Accounts: In this method the supplier stocks the cellar free of charges as per its monthly par stock requirements. All opening stock levels are recorded in a cellar ledger. At the end of every month stocktaking is made and all items issued from the cellar are charged to the hotel.

Wholesalers: There are many wholesalers who offer a very wide range of products, a regular delivery service and post-sale service. Many wholesalers offer free printing of wine lists and promotion material for your bar. Large companies offer continuity, competitive prices and regular deliveries.

Wine Shippers: There are some firms who buy beverage in the company of origin and supervise the shipment of it to its destination. They supervised in a particular region and offer a limited in a particular region and offer a limited range of high quality beverages as well as specialist advice.

Direct Buying: This can be done by visiting the wine-growing regions and tasting the wine at vineyards. The various wine growers' consortia and the suppliers hold annual or bi-annual testing where owners and managers can taste the wine and make arrangement of buy at ex-cellar price. Shipping costs, excise duty are paid separately to the supplier.

Auctions: Auctions are useful for buying large quantities or conversely for buying extremely small parcels of fine wine or spirits. They are suitable both for large hotel companies and bars which was to include a small number of fine wines on their lists.

6.1.3. Beverage Receiving Control:

All Stock and equipment of the bar is expensive and if mistakes go unnoticed at the point and time of delivery, and a supplier is paid for items that the bar has not received, this will result in reduced profits. There is also a risk that poor stock control receiving system actually encourages dishonesty, which leads to suspicion amongst employees and the eventual deterioration of workplace relationships. A comprehensive system which includes establishing standards for receiving stock and beverages can counteract these threats and should be adopted and actively operated to the point of delivery for the bar. Access to the main storage areas should be restricted to authorized staff members and not staffed by people with little or no specialized knowledge. All goods received have a monetary value and it is essential to ensure that this value in goods is properly accounted for and received.

Most bars/ cellars make crucial mistakes here by taking short cuts:-

- Take the necessary time to inspect the delivery dockets.
- Check the items on the docket correspond with the items in the order book.

- Any inaccuracies with the delivery must be communicated to the manager in charge for a quick decision.
- Examine the stock for best before dates, breakages or missing seals.
- Note any discrepancies for re-checking purposes, and never sign any delivery dockets until you are fully sure that the order for delivery is intact and correct.
- Carry out „spot checks" during and after the stocks are received to ensure that staff members and delivery personnel are operating in a professional and ethical manner.

6.1.4. Beverage Storing and Issuing Control:

Beverage supplies must be stored until needed, secure against theft and deterioration. Storage process in cellar/bar consists of four main parts which include placing the products in storage, maintaining their quality, safety and security and determining the stock's value. Storage areas must be kept clean, tidy and clear of any litter in the passage ways cellar/Bar adopt a F.I.F.O. (First in First out) system for rotating your stocks, especially perishable foods or beverages with a short shelf life. This means that the oldest stock is always used first and new stocks are stored beneath the old stocks. Remember that stock is money, so ensure that your stock is given the attention and respect it deserves.

Storage of beverage is ideally separated in to five areas:-

- Main Storage area for spirits and red wine (13-16o C).
- A refrigerated area of (10 O C) for storage of white and sparkling wines.
- A cold room for kegs (3-16 O C), with the temperature depending upon the beers stored.
- An area at a temperature of 13OC for storage of bottled beers and soft drinks. A small amount of bottled beverages is sometimes stored in the cold room. This practice ensures that the beverages are cold and ready for immediate service when transferred to the bar service area.
- A totally separate area for empties.

Beverage storage area locked and to issue a single key to one person, but make a second key available in the safe or a secure location to be signed out when the nominated person is away from the bar. In some bars we also decide to install electronic code entry locks, which control the items at which the doors to the storage areas were unlocked and or relocked, or a CCTV (Closed Circuit Television Cameras) in and around the storage areas for additional security and monitoring. The issue of any stock should be recorded on a requisition form, usually from an authorized member of staff, for example Senior Bartender, Bar Manager, informing store keeper or purchasing manager of low levels of items. Using the requisition book depends on the size of the company. A requisition system is a highly structured method for controlling issues and in beverage control a key element in the system.

6.2. Beverage Production Control:

In bar we have to follow beverage production control systems and techniques which help to establish standard procedures for the preparation, size and production method fall all your beverages. If your bar can keep control in this area you will have a significant opportunity to maximize your profits on all your products.

Some of the systems and techniques which will assist you in creating beverage production control are as below:-

- Setting a standard drink size for beers, spirits and wines: Agree a size, but this decision could be set by your local government rules.
- Adopting standard food and cocktail recipes; containing defined, specifically measured ingredients and strict methods of production agreed by management.
- Standard Glassware, Crockery: choosing a standard glass size for your wines, beers, cocktails, coffee and food items.
- Hand held measures, jiggers and optics:- These dispense devices and equipment help to control the exact measurement of alcohol according to your bar or government requirements. Ensure this requirement is not damaged and or been compromised and crucially that the equipment dispenses the correct intended amount.
- Production planning or volume forecasting: It is the forecasting of the volume of sales for an establishment for specified period and the detailing of the volume of sales for each outlet such as a dispense bar, cocktail bar, cash and inclusive function bas, etc.
- Maintain par stock in the establishment. A standard par stock is a predetermined number of bottles of each item and brand used in a particular bar, and the size of the par stock is calculated to be sufficient to meet the demand for a busy day plus a safety factor. The main purpose of a standard par stock is to help determine the average daily

consumption of a bar, to assist with requisitioning, and to promote good control over the stock.

- Automatic beverage dispensing machines-Controlling Standard Portion Sizes is to use automatic beverage dispensing machines. The drink size is pre-set and the drink automatically measured. Each drink can be metered by the selling outlet. This help with inventory control and the calculation of estimated bar revenue.

6.3. Inventory Turnover:

It is the responsibility of the Director of Food and Beverage and the Executive Chef to maintain adherence to established turnover and inventory level goals.

6.3.1 Objectives:

- To establish a standard for food inventory levels.
- To provide guidelines for controlling capital invested in food inventories.
- To detail the methods for calculating and determining turnover

6.3.2. Standard Inventory Control Average:

It is 2.8 times per accounting period or an equivalent of ten days inventory on hand. This is a total average turnover figure for the entire food inventory.

6.2.3. How To Calculate Inventory Control?:

- Food Inventory Turnover Ratio = Consumption / Average Inventory
- Consumption = Beginning Inventory + Purchases – Ending
- Average Inventory = [Beginning Inventory + Ending Inventory] / 2

6.3.4. Beverage Sales Control:

The Objectives of Beverage Sales Control

- Optimizing the number of sales
- Maximizing profit
- Controlling revenue

6.3.5. Optimizing the Number of Sales:

Possible reasons for a customer to decide to patronize bars and restaurants that serve alcoholic beverages:

- Socializing
- Conducting business
- Eating
- Seeking entertainment
- Killing time
- Understanding the real reason of patronizing a bar by a customer can optimize sale.

6.3.6. Maximizing Profits:

Beverage operators can, adopt various merchandising techniques to influence the customer to select one drink (a drink with a greater contribution margin) rather than another.

In beverage operations, profit maximization is accomplished by:

- Establishing drink prices that will maximize gross profit
- Influencing customers' selections

6.3.7. Establishing Drink Prices:

Unlike food sales prices, drink prices are not primarily determined by the costs of ingredients and labour. Beverage ingredient costs and labour costs per dollar sale are both significantly lower than those for food, so they are not as important in establishing sales prices.

This is not to say that labour costs can or should be wholly ignored; in fact, many operators tend to charge more for drinks that require more labour to produce. However, the ingredient and labour costs associated with a particular drink tend to be similar from one operation to another. Other considerations are of greater importance in establishing drink prices. These include overhead costs (occupancy, insurance, licenses, and entertainment, to name a few) and significant market considerations.

Establishments that offer live entertainment must either charge drink prices that are high enough to cover these costs or cover the cost of entertainment in some other way. There are also market considerations that must be taken into account before setting sales prices for drinks. Chief among these is the clientele targeted.

Many operators rely heavily on regular customers—those who patronize an establishment frequently, often because they live or work close by. Such customers tend to be concerned with the prices charged, and operators serving this kind of clientele are usually careful to charge prices their customers consider reasonable and to avoid price increases unless absolutely necessary.

Other market considerations that a beverage operator must take into account in establishing drink prices include average income in the area served, prices charged by the competition, special advantages offered by a specific location (such as the top floor of the city's tallest building), and even a manager's desire to maintain exclusivity through pricing, among others.

No discussion of drink prices can be concluded without a consideration of pricing differences between call brands and pouring brands. Call brands, selected by the customer, are normally considered to be of higher quality. They are typically of higher cost. It is therefore logical that they are given higher sales prices. Pouring brands, selected by the bar operator for the customer who expresses no preference, are commonly of somewhat lower quality, less costly, and are therefore given lower sales prices. In general, the contribution margins of drinks made with pouring brands are likely to be lower than those of drinks made with call brands. Although it is to the operator's advantage for customers to request specific call brands, most customers do not.

6.3.8. Influencing Customer Selections:

As with food products, contribution margins for beverage products vary greatly from one drink to another. For the bar operator, it is obviously desirable to sell more drinks with high contribution margins and fewer drinks with low contribution margins. If a customer is having difficulty deciding which of two drinks to order, it is clearly to the bar operator's advantage for the customer to select the one with the higher contribution margin. In fact, under these circumstances, a bar operator may want the employees to help the customer make a decision in favour of the drink with the higher contribution margin.

Some bar operators attempt to maximize profits by featuring and promoting selected drinks, often drinks specially created for the purpose. These drinks may be given enticing names, be served in unusual ways (in hollowed fruits or with exotic garnishes, for example), or be made from unusual combinations of ingredients.

These special drinks are normally sold for higher-than-average prices, and they normally have higher-than-average contribution margins.

Another technique for influencing customer selections is to produce a carefully designed beverage menu that includes pictures (colour photographs or artists' drawings) of the drinks that management would prefer to sell, along with appropriate descriptive language to entice customers. Customers' orders would not necessarily be restricted to the listed drinks, but the drink menu would

Include only those drinks management prefers to sell.

6.3.9. Controlling Revenue:

Revenue control consists of those activities established to ensure that each sale to a customer results in appropriate revenue to the operation. In beverage operations, the opportunities for revenue control are often somewhat limited. In general, effective control procedures in business are likely to depend on division of work among several employees, but the possibilities for dividing work in this way do not exist in most bars. In many, one employee—the bartender— is responsible for virtually all of the work: taking orders from customers, filling those orders, recording the sales, and collecting cash or obtaining signatures on charge vouchers. This dependence on one individual tends to minimize the possibilities for instituting and maintaining control. In addition, it often sets the stage for the development of a number of control problems.

A common means for determining whether control problems exist in a particular establishment is to assess the work practices of the bartender. Most of those in the following list are considered unacceptable in most well-managed bars because the owners or managers are aware of the kinds of control problems that are likely to develop.

- **Working with the cash drawer open**. This practice makes it possible for dishonest employees to make sales transactions without recording the sales in the register. This is a serious problem if the bartender is held responsible at the end of the shift for only those sales recorded on the register tape.
- **Underringing sales**, either as "No Sale" or as an amount less than the actual sale. Doing so enables an employee to steal the difference between the cash in the register drawer and the sales recorded on the tape.
- **Overcharging customers**, but ringing correct amounts in the register. This too provides a dishonest employee with a source of cash equal to the difference between the amounts collected and amounts recorded in the register.
- **Undercharging customers**. This may be done to accommodate a bartender's personal friends or to increase tips. It may be done in various

ways, such as by using call brands but charging for pouring brands, or by over pouring.

- **Over pouring.** Giving customers more than they pay for, often through failure to measure, typically results in unfavourable cost-to-sales ratios and in reduced profits from operation.
- **Under pouring.** This technique is sometimes adopted by bartenders who selectively over pour. If they over pour for some customers (those who tip well, for example), they may be able to avoid being detected by under pouring for others. One may offset the other. Moreover, the bartender who keeps track of the extent of under pouring may later use the reserved amounts to prepare drinks. These drinks may then be given to friends or sold to customers, with the sales revenue going to the bartender rather than to the bar.
- **Diluting bottle contents.** This practice involves pouring out some of a bottle's contents to reserve for later use and replacing it with an equal amount of water. The liquor poured out and reserved is typically used later to make drinks that are sold to customers. However, the revenue for those drinks goes directly to the bartender's pocket rather than to bar revenue. Bringing one's own bottle into the bar. This practice enables a bartender to become a "silent partner" in the bar operation. The bartender can prepare drinks using his or her own liquor and take the sales revenue without his or her performance being detected through changes in the figures used to monitor bar operations.
- **Charging for drinks not served.** By charging a customer or a group of customers for drinks that were never served, a bartender can then serve equivalent drinks to other customers and steal the sales revenue.
- **Drinking on the job.** In addition to the unprofessional appearance and performance this practice is likely to cause, an employee who is drinking is more likely to make mistakes in pouring, mixing, and recording sales than one who does not drink on the job.

6.4. Beverage Sales Control:

Sales can be defined as the revenue resulting from the exchange of products and services for a value. In the F & B industry, the dishes and drinks served are products and services of both bar and restaurant which are served for value. Sales are broadly divided into monetary and non-monetary. Monetary involves total sales, total sales by category, average sale, average sale per customers and average sale per server.

Non-monetary involves total number sold, cover, total covers, average covers and sales mix. The way to control beverage sales of the establishment, their need of beverage costs by setting a sales value on each bottle item carried in stocks. The revenue value of each bottle is based on the standard size of the drink. The sales value of each drink is called the potential (or standard) sales value. The system requires as a basis for its operation, established standards for a bottle code number system, drink recipes, drink sizes, glassware and par stocks. Whenever the bottle size, drink size or recipe change a new calculation must be made and recorded, as this can affect the price of a drink and should require the price to be reviewed.

The various calculations which have to be made to establish the potential sales values are concerned with:

Full bottle of Spirits: The potential sales value of a full bottle of spirits, etc. which at times may be sold over a bar is equal to the selling price established by management. As little handling is involved in selling a full bottle, its price will usually be lower than when sold by individual glass.

Spirits, etc. sold by the glass: The sales value for a bottle of spirits, wine, etc. which is to be sold by the glass is calculated as in the following example.

Potential sales value for a bottle of whisky:

- Size of bottle750 ml
- Size of straight drink 30 ml
- Selling price per drink Rs.100
- Number of drinks per bottle 25 (As determined by management)
- 25 (Number of drinks) x 100 (selling price per drink) = 2500 (Potential Sales Value)

Soft drink and Mineral water sales: - The potential sales value of soft drinks, etc. depends on the pricing policy of the establishments. For example, it could be:

- A fixed price when sold on its own or when with another drink, for example, gin and tonic water.
- At a lower price when served as part of a mixed drink, for example, a straight 30 ml drink of whisky may cost Rs.100; a split bottle of dry ginger may cost Rs.100; as a mixed drink whisky and dry ginger may be priced at Rs.150 and not Rs.200 as would be the case in fixed pricing.

- The cost of soft drinks is included in the price when selling spirits.
- It should be noted that if a lower or inclusive pricing system is adopted, adjustment must be made when preparing the control sheets so that an accurate potential sales figure is calculated.

Cocktails: If all drinks served to customer were sold as straight drinks or full bottles, it would be simple to calculate the potential sales value. When drinks are sold as cocktails containing two or more high selling price items it often requires an adjustment to be made when preparing the control sheet.

When the sales of mixed drinks on analysis are found to be low, there would be little need to go into great detail calculate the allowances for the various mixed drinks. It is only when the actual money taken in the bars differs from the potential sales value by say more than 2% that detailed analysis of sales and allowances needs to be done. The primary function of most sales system/point-of-sale system is to track sales. A good system will be able to record the following information in hourly, daily, and month-to-date increments as needed: product sales mix, revenue (per shift, sales period, or server), an open check report, and total revenue.

The beverage sales control system you devise to forestall all there little tricks should both reduce opportunity and pinpoint responsibility. You need a system that you can enforce that also leaves a trail behind when it is evaded. Then you must keep after it. Whenever it is evaded. Then you must keep after it. Whenever it is not full proof, you must keep checking up. If your employees know you are policing the system, they are likely to remain honest. Lax enforcement invites pilferage and, sadly, almost seems to condone it.

Here is a suggested system:-

- To start with, use numbered guest checks with your bar's name or logo. Each bartender or server signs out a sequence of numbers for the shift and turns in the unused checks at the end of the shift. You keep the master list and check the used and unused checks. A missing check is a serious breach of work rules that justifies a severe penalty. Make this penalty very clear.

- Direct staff to write all guest checks clearly and in ink. Prohibit alternations unless they are initiated by a responsible person. Drinks should be machine-priced.

- If possible, use a precheck method of registering drinks. In this system, the order is rung up before the drinks are poured. When payment is made, another register or another section of the same register is used to ring up the same sale on the same check but a different record. The totals on the two records should be the same.

- Ring up, total on the register, or add on an adding machine all items on the check before presenting the check to the customer for payment. Do not rely on the server"s mathematics.

- Instruct the server to print the amount received from the customer on the bottom of the check. A box for this purpose is useful.

- Ring up each check individually when paid, and close the register drawer after each transaction.

- File the paid check in an assigned place, even in a locked box.

- Give receipts to customers along with their change.

- Allow only one person at a time to operate case register and to be responsible for cash in the drawer. Train that person thoroughly in the register function in your opening and closing routines.

6.5. Guest Checks and Control:

6.5.1. Bars without Guest Checks:

Many bars, especially small, owner-bartenders require each customer to pay for each drink as it is served; others serve customers more than one drink without requiring payment and somehow remember what each customer has consumed. Cash is collected after each customer has finished his or her last drink.

6.5.2. Bars Using Guest Checks:

A standard procedure is established that requires that all drink orders be recorded on numbered checks. Guest checks are used in a variety of ways. Two of the most common are:

- Pre-check systems
- Automated systems

Pre-check Systems:

A pre-check system incorporates at least one register that enables bartenders to record sales as drinks are served and to accumulate the sales to any one customer on one check.

Automated Systems:

An automated bar is both an electronic sales terminal and a computerized dispensing device for beverages. The dispensing device is controlled by the sales terminal. Bottles are inverted, with flexible tubing connecting the bottles to the dispensing device.

CHAPTER TWENTY-SEVEN

Unit 7: Labour Control

<u>**Labour Cost**</u>: Labour Cost includes the expenses incurred in maintaining the restaurant staff. It also consists of the taxes incurred on the payrolls of the employees.

7.1. Labour Control Considerations:

The cost of labour can be calculated as the basic pay is the fixed salary which an employee receives that is stated on a daily, monthly or annual basis. If the employees are paid on a hourly basis, it is calculated by multiplying the hours worked with the hourly rate for the job. In addition to the basic pay, there are some allowances and fringe benefits; for example, vacation pay, medical insurance, cost of free meals, and sick leave. When an establishment prepares the labour cost objectives, the total employee benefit amount should be included while calculating the cost.

The Labour cost considerations are as follows:

Physical Plan: The layout of an establishment may be the criteria for the presence of more or less employees at the workplace. An efficiently designed establishment my lead to reduction in the number of employees required.

Equipment Used: An establishment which uses a particular type of equipment may help reduce the number of employees and hence reduce labour cost. Automation and usage of computers and software helps in reducing man hours and increases efficiency.

Location: If the establishment is located in a high volume business area as compared to a less volume area, the efficiency of employees is said to be more. Similarly, a restaurant located in a business area will have a higher seat turnover and higher revenue as compared to a restaurant located in the outskirts of a business area.

Unions: Various establishments whose employees are covered by the union contract would have a higher labour cost as compared to an establishment which does not have a union. This happens because higher levels of pay and fringe benefits considerably increase the total labour cost.

Government Legislation: Often, an operation is effected by government legislations; for example, an employee has to pay a minimum rate for the number of hours worked.

Menu: A menu may be determined by the type of market and the number of dishes offered, the Kitchen time required to prepare the dishes, the style of service, and the availability of pre-prepared or convenience food available. A luxury restaurant would require a more skilled staff in the restaurant as well in the front of the house as compared to a fast food outlet.

7.2. Establishing Performance Standards:

7.2.1 Performance Standards:

Performance expectations are the basis for appraising employee performance. Written performance standards let you compare the employee's performance with mutually understood expectations and minimize ambiguity in providing feedback. Having performance standards is not a new concept; standards exist whether or not they are discussed or put in writing. When you observe an employee's performance, you usually make a judgment about whether that performance is acceptable. How do you decide what is acceptable and what is unacceptable performance? The answer to this question is the first step in establishing written standards. From performance standards supervisors can provide specific feedback describing the gap between expected and actual performance.

7.2.2. Effective performance Standards:

- Serve as an objective basis for communicating about performance.
- Enable the employee to differentiate between acceptable and unacceptable results.
- Increase Job satisfaction because employees known when tasks are performed well
- Inform new employees of your expectations about job performance.
- Encourage an open and trusting relationship with employees.

7.2.3. Key Areas of Responsibility:

Write performance standards for each key area of responsibility on the employee's job description. The employee should participate actively in their development. Standards are usually established when an assignment is made, and they should be reviewed if the employee's job description is updated.

7.2.4. Characteristics of performance Standards:

Standards describe the conditions that must exist before the performance can be rated satisfactory.

A performance standard should:-

- Describe the conditions that exist when performance meets expectations.
- Be expressed in terms of quantity, quality, time, cost and effect, manner of performance or method of doing.
- Be measurable, with specific methods of gathering performance data and measuring against standards.

Expressing performance standards on the basis of Quality, Quantity, timelines, Effective use of Resources, effects of effort, manner of performance and methods of performing assignment

7.2.5. Performance Measurement:

Since one of the characteristics of a performance standards is that it can be measured, you should identify how and where evidence about the employee's performance will be gathered. Specifying the performance measurements when the responsibility is assigned will help the employee keep track of his progress, as well as helping you in the future performance discussions.

There are many effective ways to monitor and verify performance, the most common of which are:-

- Direct observation
- Specific work results
- Reports and record, such as attendance, safety, inventory, financial records, etc.
- Commendations or Constructive or Critical Comments received about the employee's work.

7.3. SOP: (Standard Operating Procedures):

- They are the observable behaviours and actions which explain how job is to be done, plus the results that are expected for satisfactory job performance.

- They tell the employee what a good job looks like.
- The purpose of performance standards is to communicate expectations
- Restaurant SOP should include step-by-step instructions for:
- Equipment handling and maintenance
- Safety measures
- Food preparation and handling
- Menu creation
- Guests service standards
- Food presentation
- Food storage
- Health and hygiene regulations
- Take-out and delivery standards
- Front-of-the-house greeting and seating
- Order taking and service
- Billing and final settlement
- Guests complaint management

a. Every restaurant is different and the number of staff you'll need will vary depending on your service, location and the type of restaurant you have. Nevertheless there are some general statistics that can often come in useful.

b. A self-service restaurant: Demands on staff are lower for a self-service restaurant as food isn't being cooked to order and plates aren't being delivered to tables.

c. Typical numbers might be 1 server, per shift, for every 12 tables and 4 back of house staff for every 50 customers across the same time period.

d. Seated but casual dining: Customers expect more in the way of service if they're not helping themselves and you'll need more staff per customers to make sure that you keep up with the logistics of orders and clearing. One server for 5 – 6 tables per shift and 4 back of house staff per 50 tables is a balance that can work quite well.

e. Fine dining: When you're offering fine dining then you need to be far more attentive with more servers out front and more staff in the kitchen. One server for every 3-4 tables per shift and 6-7 back of house staff per

50 customers can be a good ratio.

f. Remember that in addition to the staffs that make the service work you may also need cleaners, a sommelier, a maître d'hotel, a cashier and various different types of chef depending on your establishment. The more high-end the offering, the more people you need to employ to make the whole experience feel effortlessly enjoyable for the customer.

7.4. Standard Staffing Requirements:

There are the organizations in which, employees carry out basic functions of management. They are directly involved in the execution of policies and completion of procedures that are associated with their jobs. They perform all those functions that are necessary to meet the goals. Orders and instructions move from top to bottom. Suggestions, reports and other sets of data move up the organizational ladder. The basic functional executives are involved in their own worlds. They do not interfere in the operations of others. The executives of a line organization do routine tasks, which are defined for them by their bosses. They are less innovative, more mechanical and totally dependent upon the procedures, policies and programmes of the organizations.

In this type of structure, the functional executives of management work according to the rules of the line organization. Scalar chains remain intact. Orders flow from top to bottom and information as well as suggestions flow from bottom to top. In addition, we also have a group of specialist in each functional area. These specialists assist the managers in the tasks related to their functional areas. The routine operations of the firm are supported by the expert suggestions of specialists.

Given chart shows a typical line and staff organization structure. Such specialists may or may not be regular employees of the firm. Latest data indicate that they are hired only for limited periods. So, they act as consultants and not an employee. They are experts who abilities and knowledge levels are unquestionable. Normally, they guide senior managers like GMs and department heads. Their suggestions and strategies are transformed into orders by the senior cadres and passed on to the staff down the line. However, senior managers are not bound to obey staff specialists. They may or not implement the suggestions of these specialists in the line organization. Normally, specialists are not deeply involved with line managers; but there can be expectations to this rule.

In a line organization, line authority gives a superior authority over a subordinate. But in the case of staff structure, there is no authority vested in the expert. According to the scalar principle of organization, if the line of authority from the ultimate management position in an enterprise to every subordinate position is clear, the responsibility for decision making would also be clear. As a consequence, organisational Communication would also be more effective. This discussion also leads us to the fact that a line organization is less complex then a line and staff organisation. In the latter, ego clashes, bureaucrat-tic delay and human problems are common. Output may suffer in many cases of line and staff structure.

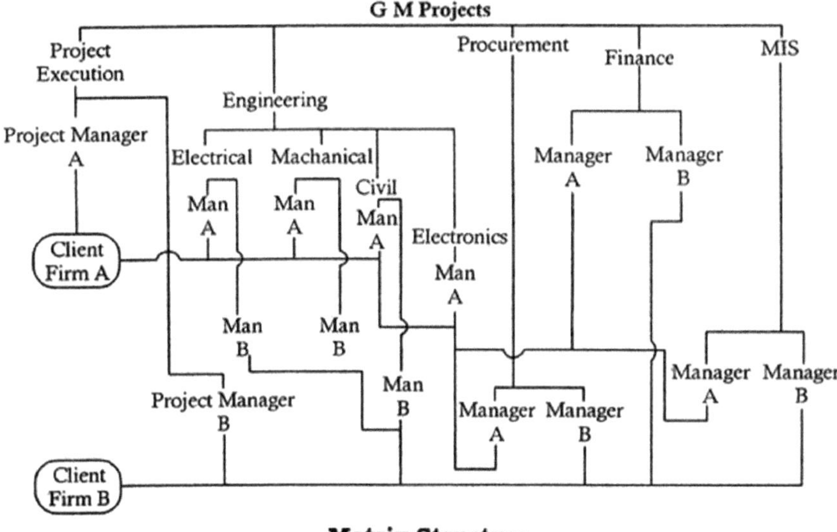

Matrix Structure

7.5. Preparing Job Description:

A job description is a useful, plain-language tool that explains the tasks, duties, function and responsibilities of a position. It details who performs a specific type of work, how that work is to be completed, and the frequency and the purpose of the work as it relates to the organization's mission and goals. Job descriptions are used for a variety of reasons, such as determining salary levels, conducting performance reviews, clarifying missions, establishing titles and pay grades, and creating reasonable accommodation controls, and as a tool for recruiting. Job descriptions are useful in career planning, offering training exercises and establishing legal requirements for compliance purposes. A job description gives an employee a clear and concise resource to be used as a guide for job performance. Likewise, a supervisor can use a job description as a measuring tool to ensure that the employee is meeting job expectations.

Step 1: Perform a Job Analysis:

This process of gathering, examining and interpreting data about the job's tasks will supply accurate information about the job so that an organization can perform efficiently. Performing a job analysis includes the following steps:

- Interviewing employees to find out exactly what tasks are being performed.
- Observing how tasks are performed.
- Having employees fill out questionnaires or worksheets.
- Collecting data on jobs from other resources such as salary surveys and the Occupational Outlook Handbook.

The results should be documented and reviewed by the employee who is currently in the position—and his or her supervisor—for any changes regarding the knowledge, skills, abilities, physical characteristics, environmental factors and credentials/experience of the position:

- **Knowledge**—comprehension of a body of information acquired by experience or study.
- **Skill**—a present, observable competence to perform a learned activity.
- **Ability**—competence to perform an observable behaviour or a behaviour that results in an observable product.
- **Physical characteristics**—the physical attributes an employee must have to perform the job duties with or without a reasonable accommodation.
- **Environmental factors**—working conditions (inside or outside the office).
- **Credentials/experience**—the minimum level of education, experience and certifications acceptable for the position.

Step 2: Establish the Essential Functions:

Once the performance standard for a particular job has been made, essential functions of the position must be defined. This will provide a better avenue for evaluating Americans with Disabilities Act (ADA) accommodation requests. Defining the essential functions encompasses the following steps:

- Ensure that the tasks as part of the job function are truly necessary or a requirement to perform the job.
- Determine the frequency at which the task is performed or how much time is spent performing a task.
- Determine the consequences of not performing the function and whether this would be detrimental to the employer's operation or result in severe consequences.
- Determine if the tasks can be redesigned or performed in another manner.
- Determine if the tasks can be reassigned to another employee.

Once the essential functions are defined, the employer can make a determination as to whether the functions are essential or marginal. The use of the term "essential function" should be part of the job description, and it should explicitly state how an individual is to perform the job. This will provide future guidance as to whether the job can be performed with or without an accommodation.

Step 3: Organize the Data Concisely:

The structure of the job description may vary from company to company; however, all the job descriptions within an organization should be standardized so that they have the same appearance.

The following topics should be included:

- **Job title**—name of the position.
- **Classification**—exempt or non-exempt under the Fair Labour Standards Act (FLSA).
- **Salary grade/level/family/range**—compensation levels, groups or pay ranges into which jobs of the same or similar worth are placed, including minimum and maximum pay bands.
- **Reports to**—title of the position this job reports to.
- **Date**—date when the job description was written or last reviewed.
- **Summary/objective**—summary and overall objectives of the job.
- **Essential functions**—essential functions, including how an individual is to perform them and the frequency with which the tasks are performed;

the tasks must be part of the job function and truly necessary or required to perform the job.

- **Competency**—knowledge, skills and abilities.
- **Supervisory responsibilities**—direct reports, if any, and the level of supervision.
- **Work environment**—the work environment; temperature, noise level, inside or outside, or other factors that will affect the person's working conditions while performing the job.
- **Physical demands**—the physical demands of the job, including bending, sitting, lifting and driving.
- **Position type and expected hours of work**—full time or part time, typical work hours and shifts, days of week, and whether overtime is expected.
- **Travel**—percentage of travel time expected for the position, where the travel occurs, such as locally or in specific countries or states, and whether the travel is overnight.
- **Required education and experience**—education and experience based on requirements that are job-related and consistent with business necessity.
- **Preferred education and experience**—preferred education and experience based on requirements that are job-related and consistent with business necessity.
- **Additional eligibility qualifications**—additional requirements such as certifications, industry-specific experience and the experience working with certain equipment.
- **Affirmative action plan/equal employment opportunity (AAP/EEO) statement**—clause(s) that outlines federal contractor requirements and practices and/or equal employer opportunity statement.
- **Other duties**—disclaimer, see Step 4.

Step 4: Add the Disclaimer:

It is a good idea to add a statement that indicates that the job description is not designed to cover or contain a comprehensive listing of activities, duties or responsibilities that are required of the employee. Duties, responsibilities and activities may change or new ones may be assigned at any time with or without notice.

7.6. Training Staff:

Since one of the characteristics of a performance standards is that it can be measured, you should identify how and where evidence about the employee's performance will be gathered. Specifying the performance measurements when the responsibility is assigned will help the employee keep track of his progress, as well as helping you in the future performance discussions.

There are many effective ways to monitor and verify performance, the most common of which are:-

- Direct observation
- Specific work results
- Reports and record, such as attendance, safety, inventory, financial records, etc.
- Commendations or Constructive or Critical Comments received about the employee's work.

7.7. Corrective Action & Training:

7.7.1. Observation and Feedback:

Once performance objectives and standards are established, you should observe employee's performance and provide feedback. You have a responsibility to recognize and reinforce strong performance by an employee, and identify and encourage improvement where it is needed. You provide informal feedback almost every day. By observing and providing detailed feedback, you play a critical role in the employee's continued success and motivation to meet performance expectations. Coaching is the method of strengthening communication between you and the employee. It helps to shape performance and increase the likelihood that the employee's results will meet your expectations. Coaching sessions provided you and the employee the opportunity to discuss her progress towards meeting mutually- established standards and goals. A coaching session focuses on one or two aspects of performance, rather than the total review that takes place in a performance evaluation.

7.7.2. Effective Training can:

- Strength Communication between you and the employee
- Help the employee to attain performance objectives
- Increase employee motivation and commitment
- Maintain and increase the employee's self esteem

- Provide Support

7.7.3. Key elements of Training/Coaching:

To make your coaching session effective, you must understand the key elements of coaching:-

- Coach when you want to focus attention on any specific aspect to the employee's performance.
- Observe the employee's work and solicit feedback from others.
- When performance is successful, take the time to understand why.
- Advise the employee ahead of time on issue to be discussed.
- Discuss alternative solutions.
- Agree on action to be taken.
- Schedule follow-up meetings to measure results.
- Recognize success and improvements.
- Document key elements of coaching session.

7.7.4. Coaching Behaviours:-

To make the most of coaching the employee, remember to practice these coaching behaviours.

- Focus on behaviour, not personality.
- Ask the employee for help in problem identification and resolution. Use active listening to show you understand.
- Use specific goals and maintain communication.
- Use reinforcement techniques to shape behaviour.

When you conduct a coaching session to improve performance, you may want to use the following format:-

- Describe the issue or problem, referring to specific behaviours.
- Involve the employee in the problem-solving process.
- Discuss Causes of the problem.
- Identify and write down possible solutions.
- Decide on specific actions to be taken by each of you.
- Agree on a follow- up date.
- Document key elements of the session.

7.7.5. Follow-up Discussion:

To conduct a follow-up discussion, consider the following steps:-

- Review the previous discussions.
- Discuss insufficient improvement and ask for a reason why
- Indicate consequences of continued lack of improvement
- Convey your confidence in the employee
- Document your discussion

7.8. Taking Corrective action to address discrepancies between standards and performance:

Controls can be categorized according to the time in which a process or activity occurs. The controls related to time include feedback, proactive, and concurrent controls. Feedback control concerns the past. Proactive control anticipates future implications. Concurrent control concerns the present.

7.8.1. Feedback:

Feedback occurs after an activity or process is completed. It is reactive. For example, feedback control would involve evaluating a team's progress by comparing the production standard to the actual production output. If the standard or goal is met, production continues. If not, adjustments can be made to the process or to the standard.

An example of feedback control is when a sales goal is set, the sales team works to reach that goal for three months, and at the end of the three-month period, managers review the results and determine whether the sales goal was achieved. As part of the process, managers may also implement changes if the goal is not achieved. Three months after the changes are implemented; managers will review the new results to see whether the goal was achieved.

The disadvantage of feedback control is that modifications can be made only after a process has already been completed or an action has taken place. A situation may have ended before managers are aware of any issues. Therefore, feedback control is more suited for processes, behaviours, or events that are repeated over time, rather than those that are not repeated.

7.8.2. Proactive control:

Proactive control, also known as preliminary, preventive, or feed-forward control, involves anticipating trouble, rather than waiting for a poor outcome and reacting afterward. It is about prevention or intervention. An example of proactive control is when an engineer performs tests on the braking system of a prototype vehicle before the vehicle design is moved on to be mass produced.

Proactive control looks forward to problems that could reasonably occur and devises methods to prevent the problems. It cannot control unforeseen and unlikely incidents, such as "acts of God."

7.8.3. Concurrent control:

With concurrent control, monitoring takes place during the process or activity. Concurrent control may be based on standards, rules, codes, and policies.

One example of concurrent control is fleet tracking. Fleet tracking by GPS allows managers to monitor company vehicles. Managers can determine when vehicles reach their destinations and the speed in which they move between destinations. Managers are able to plan more efficient routes and alert drivers to change routes to avoid heavy traffic. It also discourages employees from running personal errands during work hours.

Part D: HYGIENE & SANITATION

“Hygiene & Sanitation”

CHAPTER TWENTY-EIGHT

Unit 1: Food Microbiology

1.1. Food Microbiology:

DEFINITION:

Food Microbiology is the study of microbes (micro-organism)that create, inhibit or /and contaminate food.

Food Microbiology thus deals with:

- Food Spoilage
- Disease causing pathogens
- Beneficial roles of microbes e.g. fermentation, pro-biotics
- Microorganism groups important in food microbiology

1.2 Viruses:

Definition:

Virus, infectious agent of small size and simple composition that can multiply only in living cells of animals, plants, or bacteria. The name is from a Latin word meaning “slimy liquid” or “poison.”

Viruses, especially norovirus and hepatitis A, are an important cause of food borne diseases. Viral contamination of food occurs through contact with infected persons, e.g. food handlers. Food contaminated with viruses can cause dangerous infections in humans ranging from mild diarrhoea to severe hepatitis. Foods that are handled manually and are not processed before consumption are at particular risk of viral contamination.

1.3. Bacteria:

Definition:

- Bacteria are unicellular micro organisms which do not have cell wall and nucleus.
- Bacteria have both beneficial and harmful role in food.

1.4. Beneficial role of Bacteria in Food:

Bacteria are commonly used in the production of variety of dairy products. Bacteria are used to make a wide range of food products. The most important bacteria in food manufacturing are Lactobacillus species, also referred to as lactic bacteria. Bacillus subtilis is used to produce amylase and also used to produce hyaluronic acid, which is useful in the joint-care sector in healthcare.

1.5. Harmful Role of Bacteria in Food:

Bacteria	Inhabitation	Mode of Spread	Illness Caused
Acinetobacter baumannii	Soil Water Fresh Refrigerated Products	Uncooked Contaminated Food	Pneumonia Skin & Wound Infections Meningitis
Bacillus Cereus	Soil Food Milk Meat	Uncooked Cooked Refrigerated food Milk	Diarrheal Illness
Clostridium botulinum	soil and sediments	Improperly Canned food products like meat, poultry	Botulism
Escherichia coli	Different Media and Many Food	Faecal Pollution Food	Food Borne Gastroeneritis Foodborne-illness can be placed into five groups: enteropathogenic (EPEC), enterotoxigenic (ETEC), enteroinvasive (EIEC), enterohemorrhagic (EHEC) and facultatively enteropathogenic (FEEC).
Salmonella (S. typhimurium, S. typhi, S.enteritidis)	Food Finished Food Products	Milk, Meat, Poultry	Leading cause of Food borne illness in humans. Enteric Fever Typhoid Paratyphoid
Staphylococcus aureus	Food	Food	Enterotoxins Gastro intestinal disorders
Shigella	Faeces	Contaminated food	Shigellosis

Harmful Role of Bacteria

1.6. Fungi (Yeast & Molds):

Fungus, plural fungi, any of about 144,000 known species of organisms of the kingdom Fungi, which includes the yeasts, rusts, smuts, mildews, molds, and mushrooms. Fungi are among the most widely distributed organisms on Earth and are of great environmental and medical importance. Many fungi are free-living in soil or water; others form parasitic or symbiotic relationships with plants or animals.

Yeast is single-celled microorganisms that are classified, along with molds and mushrooms, as members of the Kingdom Fungi.

A mold or mould is a fungus that grows in the form of multi-cellular filaments called hyphae.

1.7. Algae:

Algae are a diverse group of aquatic organisms that have the ability to conduct photosynthesis. Certain algae are familiar to most people; for instance, seaweeds (such as kelp or phytoplankton), pond scum or the algal blooms in lakes. Their gelling, thickening and stabilizing properties have led to the development of such products as agar, alginate and carrageenan. Moreover, algae are used in the food industry as food supplements and an addition to functional food.

Algae are also added to meat products, such as pasty, steaks, frankfurters and sausages, as well as to fish, fish products, and oils, to improve their quality. Cereal-based products, such as pasta, flour and bread, are another group of products enriched with algae. Due to their properties algae may also be used for construction of fermented functional food.

Fermented products containing algae are, most of all, dairy products, such as cheese, cream, milk deserts, yoghurt, cottage cheese, and processed cheese. Combination of fermented products offering a high content of lactic acid bacteria with algae possessing biologically active metabolites of natural origin allows not only to compose products with a high content of nutrients, but also to create a brand new segment of fermented food.

1.8. Parasites:

A parasite is an organism that lives on or in a host organism and gets its food from or at the expense of its host. There are three main classes of parasites that can cause disease in humans: protozoa, helminths, and ectoparasites.

Numerous parasites can be transmitted by food including many protozoa and helminth.The most common food-borne parasites are protozoa such as Cryptosporidium spp., Giardia intestinalis, Cyclospora cayetanensis, and Toxoplasma gondii; roundworms such as Trichinella spp.

1.9. Factors affecting the growth of microbes:

The most important factors that affect microbial growth in foods can be categorized as under

(i) Factors related to the food itself, the "intrinsic factors,"

- Nutrient content,

- Water activity,
- Ph value,
- Redox potential, and the presence of antimicrobial substances and mechanical barriers to microbial invasion;

(ii) Factors related to the environment in which the food is stored, the "extrinsic factors,"

- including the temperature of storage,
- the composition of gases and
- relative humidity in the atmosphere surrounding the food;

(iii) Factors related to the microorganisms themselves, the "implicit factors,"

- interactions between the microorganisms contaminating the food and
- between these microorganisms and the food, e.g., their abilities to utilize different nutrient sources, tolerate stresses, and produce promoters or inhibitors of growth of other microorganisms, etc.;

(iv) processing factors, which include treatments such as heating, cooling, and drying that affect the composition of the food and also affect the types and numbers of microorganisms that remain in the food after treatment;

(v) Interaction between the above-described factors can also affect the growth of microorganisms in foods in a complicated way; the combined effects may be additive or synergistic.

1.10. Beneficial role of Microbes:

- Adds variety
- Flavour
- Colour
- Fermentation
- Supplement
- Important component of Food processing industry
- Beer, Wine making

CHAPTER TWENTY-NINE

Unit 2: Food Contamination and Spoilage

2.1. Classification of Food:

2.1.1. Classification-1

Milk and milk products:

1. Milk
2. Cream
3. Kefir
4. Yoghurt
5. Whey
6. Other fermented milk products
7. Cheese
8. Cheese substitutes
9. Ice cream
10. Milk and milk products for dietetic use

Other generic Products:

1. Egg and egg products
2. Meat and meat products
3. Fish, molluscs, reptiles, crustaceans and their products
4. Oils, fats and their products
5. Grains and grain products
6. Pulses, seeds, kernels, nuts and their products
7. Vegetables and vegetable products
8. Fruit and fruit products
9. Sugar, chocolate and related products

10. Beverages (non-milk)
11. Miscellaneous, soups, sauces, snacks and products
12. Products for special nutritional use

2.1.2. Classification 2

1. Bread and rolls
2. Breakfast cereals
3. Flour
4. Pasta
5. Bakery products
6. Rice and other cereal products
7. Sugar
8. Sugar products excluding chocolate
9. Chocolate
10. Vegetable oils
11. Margarine and lipids of mixed origin
12. Butter and animal fats
13. Nuts
14. Pulses
15. Vegetables excluding potatoes
16. Starchy roots or potatoes
17. Fruits
18. Fruit juices
19. Non alcoholic beverages
20. Coffee, tea, cocoa powder
21. Beer
22. Wine
23. Other alcoholic beverages
24. Red meat and meat products
25. Poultry and poultry products
26. Offals
27. Fish and seafood
28. Eggs
29. Milk
30. Cheese
31. Other milk products
32. Miscellaneous foods

33. Products for special nutritional use

2.1.3. Classification of food Based on Perishability:

Some foods have longer shelf life than others. Perishability refers to the quickness with which a food gets spoilt. Foods can be classified into three groups depending on how long they can be kept without any treatment.

Perishable foods can be kept at room temperature for only few hours or 1 or 2 days before spoiling. For example- milk and milk products, meat, fish, poultry, fruits, leafy vegetables and cooked food. These foods keep well under refrigeration at household as well as commercial level. In general, the most perishable foods contain a high level of protein or have moisture and carbohydrates in them. Special methods are used to preserve such foods. The rate of spoilage varies with the temperature, moisture and or dryness of the environment. Storage of perishable foods should be done by keeping following points in mind.

Flesh foods like meat, chicken and fish need to be kept frozen at -60°C in a deep freeze for long term storage. These foods should not be left at room temperature for more than an hour or two. Organ meats tend to spoil faster than muscle meat. Ground meats spoil faster because of high surface area exposed to contamination.

Eggs are best kept in a cool place or in a basket in an airy room refrigerator. Never wash eggs before storing. Store eggs with their pointed end downwards.

Milk in boiled form can be kept at room temperature for 6 to 12 hours during winters. Inside a refrigerator milk can last 3 to 4 days or even more in closed container.

The keeping quality of a vegetable depends upon its nature. Leafy vegetables wilt and deteriorate within minutes of buying unless they are kept wrapped in a damp cloth or inside a plastic bag in the refrigerator wherein they last for more than a day or two.

All other vegetables keep well in a cool place with relatively high humidity in a basket covered with a damp cloth.

Vegetables must be kept in plastic bags to prevent drying by evaporation, if stored in a refrigerator.

Do not wash fruits before storing as they spoil faster.

Remember not to, refrigerate bananas, pineapples, papayas and avocadoes, as these fruits undergo undesirable changes in texture and flavour at refrigerator temperature. Most other fruits keep well, when refrigerated.

Semi -perishable foods can be stored for a couple of weeks or even a month or two without any detectable signs of spoilage. Temperature and humidity of the environment again affects the shelf stability of such foods. Proper handling and storage can result in fairly long storage without spoilage. Examples are all cereal and pulse products like wheat flour, semolina, vermicelli, broken wheat, Bengal gram flour, and some fruits and vegetables like citrus fruits, aonla, apples, pumpkin, roots and tubers, yams, potatoes, onions, garlic etc. Following points should while storing semi-perishable foods.

Processed cereal products develop an off-flavour or are infested by insects very easily if not taken care. Therefore, they should be sieved and cleaned of all such contamination, exposed to the sun for a few hours, allowed to cool and then stored in tightly covered bottles or other containers.

Especially onions and potatoes should be stored in a cool, dry and airy place to prevent them from developing moulds or growing shoots. They are best hung up from the ceiling in a wire or plastic-mesh basket, or kept in mesh containers which permit air circulation.

Nuts become rancid and get infested with insects very easily, therefore, they should be bought in large quantities only when storage space is available.

Fruits like apples, oranges and semi-ripe mangoes do last for a few weeks and should be put in a basket lined and covered with paper to prevent them from drying up. They need a cool environment to last long.

Non- perishable foods will keep for months or years without spoiling unless handled and stored carelessly. Examples of such foods are all preserved food products (canned, dried, pickled etc.), whole cereal, pulse and millet grains, oil seeds, nuts, fats and oils, honey, sugar, jaggery, salt, some spices and essence. Following points should be followed while storing non-perishable foods:

Food should be carefully cleaned i.e. free from gravel, husk and other foreign matter etc. and dried thoroughly in the sun/ drier before storage.

Storage of foods should be done in clean containers with tight-fitting lids. Containers can be made of tin, aluminium, plastic or glass. Clay pots or gunny bags may also used in case of large quantities.

A dry, cool and dark area should be chosen for storage of non-perishable foods.

The perishability of food dictates to a considerable extent the preservation techniques that are used to keep that food in good quality. In case of non-perishable foods, preservation techniques are dedicated to keeping out insects, rodents and other pests and keeping the foods dry to prevent it from becoming moldy. Perishable and semi-perishable foods depend a great deal on the technologies of refrigeration, drying, freezing, canning and the use of chemical preservatives to give shelf stability. These treatments can make such food commodities keep for many months or years if they are performed properly

2.2 Contamination and Cross Contamination:

Microbial Contamination of food can be defined as accidental and/or intended addition of contaminants like bacteria, virus, fungus etc. and/or their toxins & by-products in food causing spoilage of food and diseases in human beings.

2.3. Cross Contamination:

Cross-Contamination in food can be defined as the physical movement or transfer of microbial contaminants from one person, object, or place to another. There are three main types of cross contamination: food-to-food, equipment-to-food, and people-to-food.

2.3.1. Contamination Spoilages of Various Food With The Storing Method:

Spoilages of various foods:

- Many food borne microbes are present in healthy animals (usually in their intestines) raised for food. Meat and poultry carcasses can become contaminated during slaughter by contact with small amounts of intestinal contents.
- Fresh fruits and vegetables can be contaminated if they are washed or irrigated with water that is contaminated with animal manure or human sewages.
- Some types of Salmonella can infect a hen's ovary so that the internal contents of a normal looking egg can be contaminated with Salmonella even before the shell in formed.
- Oysters and other filter feeding shellfish can concentrate Vibrio bacteria that are naturally present in sea water, or other microbes that are present in human sewage dumped into the sea.
- Later in food processing, other food borne microbes can be introduced from infected humans who handle the food, or by cross contamination

from some other raw agricultural products.

- For example, Shigella bacteria, hepatitis A virus and Norwalk virus can be introduced by the unwashed hands of food handlers who are themselves infected.
- In the kitchen, microbes can be transferred from one food to another food by using the same knife, cutting board or other utensil to prepare both without washing the surface or utensil in between.
- A food that is fully cooked can become re-contaminated if it touches other raw foods or drippings from raw foods that might contain pathogens microbes responsible for spoilage.
- The way in which food is handled after it is contaminated can also make a difference in whether or not an outbreak occurs.
- Lightly contaminated food left out overnight can be highly infectious by the next day. Given warm moist conditions and an ample supply of nutrients, a bacterium that reproduces by dividing itself every half hour can produce 17 million progeny in 12 hours.
- If the food is refrigerated promptly, the bacteria multiply at a slower rate. However, Listeria monocytogenes and Yersinia enterocolitica can actually grow at refrigerator temperatures.

2.3.2. Food Storage:

Food preservation aims at preventing the microbial spoilage of food products and the growth of the food borne pathogens. Thus, the two principal goals of food preservation methods are:

(i) Increasing the shelf life of the food and

(ii) Ensuring the safety for human consumption. There are a variety of food preservation methods.

2.3.3. Principles of Food Preservation include the following:

- Prevention or delay of microbial decomposition.
- By keeping microbes out (asepsis).
- By removal of microbes (e.g. filtration).
- By reducing the rate of microbial growth (e.g. by low temperature, drying, anaerobic conditions and chemical inhibitors).
- By killing microbes (e.g. by heat or radiation).
- Prevention or delay of self-decomposition of food
- By inactivation of food enzymes (e.g. blanching).
- By prevention of chemical reactions (e.g. by using antioxidants).

2.3.4. Methods to Prevent Food Spoilage and Contamination:

- Cleaning, washing: Reduces microbial load
- Cold storage (below 8OC): Prevents the growth of most pathogenic bacteria; slows the growth of spoilage microbes.
- Freezing (below – 10OC): Prevents growth of all microbes
- Pasteurizing (60-80OC): Kills most non-sporing bacteria, yeast and molds
- Blanching (95-110OC): Kills surface vegetative bacteria, yeast and molds
- Canning (above 100OC): Commercially sterilizes' food; kills all pathogenic bacteria
- Drying: Stops growth of all microbes when aw<0.60
- Salting: Stops growth of most microbes
- Syruping (sugars): Halts growth when a w < 0.70
- Acidifying: Halts growth of most bacteria (effects depend on acid type)

CHAPTER THIRTY

Unit 3: Sanitary Procedure Followed During Food Handling

3.1. Receiving:

The following are important elements to consider when receiving products in general.

- Never assume that all the food you receive is good enough to eat.
- The receiving dock and related areas should be well lit and kept very tidy. Incorporate this area into a daily cleaning schedule to ensure proper cleanliness.
- Schedule your deliveries to allow adequate time for the proper inspection and receiving of all food products.
- Have all appropriate equipment and containers on hand. Scales, plastic gloves, containers, and thermometers are important pieces to have in easy reach.
- Record the temperatures of the delivery trucks refrigerated and freezer storage. If the temperature is not within an acceptable range, do not accept the shipment (because you are unable to ascertain the length of time that the temperature has been unacceptable).

3.1.1 Receiving of Dry Foods

- Check cartons, bags containers etc.
- Note any damage.
- Check seals on individual packs.
- Check dents and bulging in cans, that denotes spoilage of canned food.

- Check leakage.
- Check date of manufacturing, date of expiry.

3.1.2. Produce

- Check for freshness, ripeness and other signs of quality.

3.1.3. Meat, Poultry and Sea Food

- Check the grades of meat cuts as on invoice.
- Check for quality and freshness of the product.
- Check for leaking vacuum-packed (Cryovac) packages.
- For frozen products check for signs of freezer burn, torn wrappings, partial thawing, or other problems.

3.2. Food Storage:

The proper storage of food is a critical to maintain high standards and reducing the risk of food poisoning. Some foods must be stored in the fridge and eaten within a short span of time. Other foods, such as flour, pulses, canned foods and many others, last much longer and can be stored at room temperature. However, all foods have limits on their storage time. Always follow storage instructions and be aware of manufacturing and expiry dates. Make sure that they always store foods:

- In the right place
- At the right temperature
- For the right time

The following storage guidelines should be followed,

- Avoid cross-contamination,
- store raw foods away from other foods in the fridge,
- Raw meat/poultry should be stored in clean sealed containers on the bottom shelf of the fridge, so it cannot touch or drip onto other food.
- Store foods in separate covered containers.
- Cover dishes and other open containers with foil or film.
- Do not reuse foil or film to wrap other foods.
- Keep food storage areas dry and cool.

- Store root vegetables away from other fruit and vegetables and in a dark place.
- Ensure that all storage cupboards and pantries are pest-free.
- Do not store food on the floor because this can encourage mice, ants and other pests.
- After opening packets of dried foods reseal them tightly or transfer contents to storage jars.
- Ensure that storage containers have tightly fitting lids — always wash and allow them to dry thoroughly after use.
- Do not store food or drinks near cleaning products or other chemicals.
- All food that looks, tastes or smells off or is past its date should be thrown away.
- Cling film is useful for protecting food but it needs to be used correctly.
- Do not use cling film if it could melt into food, such as in the oven or on pots and pans on the hob.
- Cling film can be used in the microwave but should not touch the food.

3.3. Food Preparation:

- As well as being stored correctly, food must be prepared in such as way as to prevent the risk of contamination or the cross-contamination of food or ingredients.
- The following should be followed
- Kitchen staff must ensure good personal hygiene
- All tools, equipment and surfaces that come into contact with food being prepared or served must be kept clean
- Meat should be thoroughly cooked or reheated
- Deep frozen food should be thawed before cooking
- Never reuse utensils with which have been used to prepare raw eggs or meat without first washing them with hot water and detergent
- Never allow juices from raw meat to come into contact with other foods during food preparation
- Use different chopping boards/knives/utensils/equipment/work surfaces wherever possible for raw and cooked and ready to eat foods
- Do not use the same equipment, such as slicers and mincers, for both raw and ready-to-eat food
- Cooked meat should never be placed back on a plate that was used for raw meat and has not been washed

- Fruit, salads and vegetables must be washed thoroughly in clean water
- Those involved in food preparation, cooking and serving must receive adequate supervision, instruction and training in food hygiene.

3.4. Cooking:

- Never touch prepared foods with bare hands
- Always use sanitary cooking/serving utensils
- Check thickest part of the food
- Regulate thickness of foods
- Stir foods in deep pots frequently
- Internal temp higher than 75 °C
- Cook foods to proper internal temperature

IMPORTANT: Normal Cooking Procedures Destroy most pathogens, but not necessarily their spores or toxins.

- While cooking any stuffed preparation, like stuffed chicken or turkey, it as advisable to cook the stuffing and then stuff the bird.
- Food poisoning is more likely to occur from stuffed food, because:

I. More manipulation by hands.
II. Heat transfer is slow, letting bacteria in temperature danger zone for longer time.
III. Temperature at the centre of food may not be adequate, so the staffing may not be cooked to the desirable stage
IV. Always remember when handling left-Over Food:

IF IN DOUBT, THROW IT OUT

- Left –Over Food include:

I. Displayed but not Sold or Eaten during meal time.
II. Food Prepared but not used in cooking Functions.
III. Food Produced in quantities more than that required. Left –Over Food Should be handled carefully, e.g.:

- Stored below 4 °C until required.

- Discard left-over Food refrigerated for more than 3 days from preparation date
- Should not be mixed with fresh food.
- Should be covered and stored in Specific separate areas.
- Reheated before serving only once, with very strict measures.
- You should only reheat Left-over Food once. The more times you cool and reheat food, the more potential there is for food poisoning, bacteria might grow and multiply because the food is cooled too slowly, and might survive because the food isn't reheated properly.
- When you do reheat, make sure that food is reheated thoroughly, so that it is steaming hot all the way through
- For big or catered events, hold reference sample of all foods served for 72 hours.
- Generally, Keep Perishable and frozen food out of temperature danger zone (5°C to 60°C).
- Ill or infected workers not allowed to handle food

CHAPTER THIRTY-ONE

Unit 4: Safe Food Handler

4.1. Safe Food Handler:

Food workers need to be healthy and clean to prepare safe food. The food handler should keep his hands, arms and exposed part very clean. They should wash their hands after touching bare human body and after using the toilet room. Hand, breath, hair, sweat, coughs & sneezes all carry microorganisms. Even food handlers does not feel sick, he or she could still be carrying the microorganisms that can causes illness if they get into the food.

All food handlers should remember the following:

- Personal cleanliness is essential for those responsible for food storage, preparation, cooking &service.
- Food should be handled by hand where there is no alternatives.
- Smocking, spitting, chewing, sneezing over unprotected food is strictly is not allowed.
- Eating & drinking while working cans spread germs from the person's mouth to hands.
- Hand should be clean at all times with short nails & no nail paints.
- Jewellery, watches, pins or other items should not be worn or brought into food handling area.

Personnel should always wash their hands when personal cleanliness may affect food safety, for example:

- At the start of food handling activities
- Immediately after using the toilet,&
- After handling raw food or any contaminated material, where this could result in contamination of other food items, they should avoid ready- to-

eat food.

To understand why employee need good personal hygiene it is vital to consider the following sources of microbial contamination.

Skin:

The skin constantly deposits sweat, oil & dead cells on the outer surface. When this material mixed with dust, dirt, & grease, they form an ideal medium for bacteria to grow. Food handlers rub or scratch the skin & transfer bacteria when they again touch food without washing their hand. Poor skin care & skin disorders can also causes bacterial infections like boils. Straphylococci or other microorganisms are responsible for skin infection.

Hands:

Bacteria may be picked up by the hands when they touch dirty equipment, contaminated food, clothing or part of the body. Food handlers should wash hand frequently & use a hand dip sanitizer after touching these things so that they do not contaminate food.

Food handlers must wash their hands regularly & especially:

- Before starting work
- On returning to work after each break
- After going to the toilet
- On entering the food processing & preparation area
- In between handling of raw & cooked food
- After combing or touching the hair
- After eating ,smoking, coughing or blowing the nose
- After handling waste food & refuse
- After handling cleaning chemicals,&
- After contact with pests or contaminated food.

4.2. Hand Washing:

- Use the hand washing facilities provided by the business.
- Clean their hands thoroughly using soap or other effective means.
- Use warm running water.
- Dry their hands thoroughly on a single use towel or in another way that is not likely to transfer disease-causing organisms onto the hands.

Finger nails

One of the easiest ways to spread bacteria is through dirt under the finger nails. Food handlers should never handle food if their finger nails are dirty. Food handlers should not have long finger nails or artificial finger nails, while working.

Jewellery

Food handlers should not wear jewellery in food processing or food service area. It can fall in the food and can contaminate the food, further it can catch in the machinery, causing a physical & safety hazard.

Hair

Hair is constantly falling out along with dandruff, can causes contamination in food. Scalp carries microorganism like Staphylococci. Food handlers should wear a hairnet or suitable head covering i.e. cap or a scarf which completely encloses the hair. Workers should always wash their hands whenever they scratch their heads.

Eyes

Normally, eyes do not carry bacteria but whenever there is any infection its tendency to rub the eyes and then only there is a possibility of contamination.

Mouth

Mouth carries many bacteria. Food handlers while working should not eat chew gum, tobacco, pan-masala, gutka etc. or blow into glass to polished them. Tasting food with licking finger or an unwashed food is a bad practice.

Smoking is also not allowed in food services establishments. It can causes transition of bacteria from mouth to the food. Smoking leaves an irritating smell in food, spitting also is not allowed in food services areas.

Nose, Throat

Employees who have infection in nose will be suffering from nasal discharges; they should be careful while handling the food, have to wash & disinfected their hands after blowing their nose. Picking &scratching nose is not acceptable. Sore throat is usually caused by microorganisms. The diseases spread if employees' personal is poor.

4.3. First Aid:

According to oxford dictionary, first aid is the medical help that one gives to somebody who is hurt or ill before the doctor arrives. It is mandatory for the establishment that they should have adequate first aid equipment, facilities, and trained personal to provide first aid at the work area. If the injury is serious, the injured person should be treated by a doctor or qualified nurse as soon as possible.

4.3.1. First Aid Equipments:

There should be a first aid box in the work area. First-aid box should be easily identifiable and accessible in the work area. It should be in the charge of a responsible person. A regular replenishment of the first-aid box is necessary so that first-aid may be given in case of requirement.

A first aid box must contain at a least following things:

- A card giving general first-aid guidance
- 20 individually wrapped, sterile, adhesive, waterproof dressings of various sizes
- An antiseptic lotion and antiseptic cream
- 4 X 25 g. cotton wool packets
- 1 dozen safety pins
- 2 triangular bandages
- 2 sterile eye pads, with attachment
- 4 medium-sized sterile un-medicated dressings
- 2 large size sterile un-medicated dressings
- 2 extra large size sterile un-medicated dressings
- Scissors
- A report book to record all injuries.

4.3.2. Common FIRST-AID procedures:

Shock: the signs of shock are faintness, sickness, clammy skin and pale face. Shock should be treated by keeping the person comfortable, lying down and warm. Cover the person with blanket or clothing, but do not apply hot water bottles.

Cuts: All cuts should be washed with the antiseptic lotion and should be covered with waterproof dressing. When there is considerable bleeding it should be stopped as soon as possible. If bleeding persists it may be stopped by bandaging firmly or pressing the artery with the thumbs and immediate medical assistance is necessary.

Nose Bleeding: In case of nose bleeding, sit the person down with the head forward, and loosen clothing round the neck and chest. Warn the person not to blow the nose for several hours. If bleeding persists seek the medical assistance.

Fainting: Fainting may occur after a long period of standing in a hot, badly ventilated area. The signs of an impending faint are whiteness, giddiness and sweating. A faint should be treated by raising the legs slightly above the level of the head and, when the person recovers the consciousness, putting in the fresh air for a while and making sure that the person has not incurred any injury in fainting

Fractures: The best treatment for fracture is to make the affected part immobile before doing anything. Immediately seek the assistance of doctor.

Burns and Scalds: Burn is caused by dry heat source like flame or hot articles whereas scalds are caused by wet heat source like steam or boiling liquids. The burnt part should be placed under running cold water or immerse in cold water till pain ceases. Seek the assistance of doctor if required.

CHAPTER THIRTY-TWO

Unit 5: Hazard Analysis Critical Control Point

5.1. Introduction to HACCP:

HACCP is an abbreviation for Hazard Analysis Critical Control Point system. It is a system which is mandatory for any food establishment from dining to manufacturing units to maintain food safety standards of highest order. For example if a restaurant is HACCP certified follows this system it is regarded as the safest place to dine outside your home.

DEFINITION:

HACCP: It can be defined as a system of identification, evaluation, and control of hazards which are significant for food safety.

HAZARD: A Hazard in HACCP system is defined as a biological, chemical or physical agent in, or condition of food, with the potential to cause an adverse health effect.

CRITICAL CONTROL POINT: Critical Control Point" (CCP) in HACCP system is defined as a step at which control can be applied and is essential to prevent or eliminate a food safety hazard or reduce it to an acceptable level.

5.2. History:

HACCP was developed originally as a microbiological safety system in the early 1960s of the US astronauts as it was very important to serve them safe food in the space. The Pillsbury Company working alongside the National Aeronautics and Space Administration (NASA) of the United States and the US Army Laboratories developed the original system.

5.3. Principles of HACCP:

There are seven principles of HACCP system. These principles determine how to establish, implement and maintain a HACCP plan for a food establishment.

Principle 1-Conduct a hazard analysis:

Identification of hazards in all the steps of production, in the form of a flow chart and then, determining control and preventive measures required at every stage.

Principle 2-Identify/Determine the CCPs:

Developing the points/procedures/operational steps which can be controlled for

- Eliminating the hazards,
- Minimizing the likelihood of occurrence,
- Reducing the hazards to an acceptable level

Principle 3- Establish Critical Limits:

These are target levels and tolerances called as absolute tolerance or safety limit for CCP. These should be in measurable parameters.

Principle 4- Establish a system to monitor control of the CCP by scheduled testing or observation.

Principle 5- Establish the corrective action to be taken when monitoring indicates that a particular CCP is moving out of control.

Principle 6- Establish procedures for verification to confirm that the HACCP system is working effectively.

Principle 7- Establish documentation concerning all procedures and records relating to the application of these principles.

CHAPTER THIRTY-THREE

Unit 6: Food Safety Standards Authority of India (FSSAI)

6.1. Introduction to FSSAI:

FSSAI stands for "FOOD SAFETY AND STANDARDS AUTHORITY OF INDIA". It is an autonomous body established under the Ministry of Health & Family Welfare, Government of India. The FSSAI has been established under the Food Safety and Standards Act, 2006.

The FSSAI is responsible for setting standards for food so that there is one body to deal with and no confusion in the minds of consumers, traders, manufacturers, and investors. Ministry of Health & Family Welfare, Government of India is the Administrative Ministry of Food Safety and Standards Authority of India.

FSSAI is responsible for protecting and promoting public health through the regulation and supervision of food safety. The FSSAI is headed by a non-executive Chairperson, appointed by the Central Government, either holding or has held the position of not below the rank of Secretary to the Government of India. The FSSAI has its headquarters at New Delhi. The authority also has 6 regional offices located in Delhi, Guwahati, Mumbai, Kolkata, Cochin, and Chennai. There are 14 referral laboratories notified by FSSAI, 72 State/UT laboratories located throughout India and 112 laboratories are NABL accredited private laboratories notified by FSSAI.

6.1.1. The FSS Act:

The FSS stands for THE FOOD SAFETY AND STANDARDS ACT (FSS), 2006 is the primary law for the regulation of food products. This act also sets up the formulation and enforcement of food safety standards in India.

The FSS Act took several older acts into one umbrella:

1. Prevention of Food Adulteration Act, 1954
2. Fruit Products Order, 1955
3. Meat Food Products Order, 1973
4. Vegetable Oil Products (Control) Order, 1947
5. Edible Oils Packaging (Regulation) Order 1988
6. Solvent Extracted Oil, De- Oiled Meal and Edible Flour (Control) Order, 1967
7. Milk and Milk Products Order, 1992

Thus the FSS Act is a bucket for all the older laws, rules and regulations for food safety

The following are the statutory powers that the FSS Act, 2006 gives to the Food Safety and Standards Authority of India (FSSAI).

- Framing of regulations to lay down food safety standards
- Laying down guidelines for accreditation of laboratories for food testing
- Providing scientific advice and technical support to the Central Government
- Contributing to the development of international technical standards in food
- Collecting and collating data regarding food consumption, contamination, emerging risks, etc.
- Disseminating information and promoting awareness about food safety and nutrition in India

6.2. Role of FSSAI:

The main aim of FSSAI is to

- Lay down science-based standards for articles on food
- To regulate the manufacture, storage, distribution, import, and sale of food
- To facilitate the safety of food

6.2.1 FUNCTIONS OF FSSAI:

6.2.2. Departments of FSSAI:

1. Import Division
2. International Co-operation

3. Regulatory Compliance Division (RCD)
4. Food Safety Management System (FSMS) Division
5. Risk Assessment and R&D division (RARD)
6. Information Education Communication (IEC) Division
7. Regulation and Codex Division
8. Quality Assurance/ lab Division
9. HR Division
10. Standards Division

Research and Quality assurance:

Research The Research and Development division is responsible for research with the following objectives:

1. Generate new knowledge that would help in continuously updating and upgrading food safety standards which are compatible with international organizations.
2. Carry out evidence based studies for improving or building policies.

Quality Assurance:

1. FSSAI has been mandated to perform various functions related to quality and standards of food.
2. These functions in addition to others include "Laying down procedure and guidelines for notification of the accredited laboratories.

Standards:

Standards framed by FSSAI are prescribed under Food Safety and Standards Regulations, 2011 (Food Product Standards and Food Additives, Packaging and Labelling, Contaminants, Toxins, and Residues).

The FSSAI has prescribed standards for following food products:

- Dairy products and analogues
- Fats, oils and fat emulsions
- Fruits and vegetable products
- Cereal and cereal products
- Meat and meat products
- Fish and fish products
- Sweets & confectionery

- Sweetening agents including honey
- Salt, spices, condiments and related products
- Beverages, (other than dairy and fruits & vegetables based)
- Other food product and ingredients
- Proprietary food
- Irradiation of food

6.3. FSSAI Compliance:

6.3.1. Applicable FSSAI License:

FSSAI issues three types of license based on nature of food business and turnover:

1. Registration: For Turnover less than 12 Lakh
2. State License: For Turnover between 12 Lakh to 20 Crore
3. Central License: For Turnover above 20 Crore

Other criteria like the location of the business, number of retail stores etc. is needed while evaluating the nature of license applicable.

Realizing the necessity to regulate the manufacture, storage, distribution, sale, and import of food products, Government of India consolidated Food Safety and Standards Act (FSSA), 2006. The Act establishes Food Safety and Standards Authority of India (FSSAI) to ensure the availability of safe and wholesome food for human consumption. This national regulatory body provides food regulatory compliance as per the international standards.

Food regulatory compliance in India categorizes food products as:

Standardized products: for which standards have been prescribed and no prior product approval is required.

Non-standardized food products: products which do not have safety parameters defined.

At present FSSAI has standardized 380 food articles in 16 categories. Those food articles that are non-standardized require product approval. It is important to note that traditional foods and their ingredients or additives require product approval. These product approvals are provided by FSSAI under the jurisdiction of various regulations that have been embedded.

The Food Safety and Standards Act (FSSA), 2006 has made it mandatory for all business operators to follow food business compliances. These include licenses and registrations in accordance with the Food Safety and Standards (Licensing and Registration of Food Business) Regulations, 2011.

It further ensures safety, sanitary, and hygiene of food products offered by food business operators to the welfare of customers of the country. It is a compulsion for all food business operators to obtain a license from FSSAI, including entities right from post farming, manufacturing, selling, retailers, labelling, and more.

The preamble of FSSAI act also aims to provide food safety to the consumers. It has developed a checklist to ensure efficiency and transparency in food safety inspections.

6.3.2 List of compliances developed by FSSAI:

- General manufacturing,
- Milk processing units,
- Meat processing units,
- Slaughterhouses,
- Catering,
- Retail,
- Transport, and
- Storage and warehouse units.

These legal compliances are regarding

- The design and facilities provided in the unit,
- control of their operations,
- maintenance and sanitation,
- Personal hygiene,
- Training and complaint handling in these units.

Some Important Points:

- Over the years, increased awareness has been seen regarding the quality of food and its safety. Whether the product is imported or homemade the Food safety and standards authority of India (FSSAI) is monitoring and surveying of food business operators under the provisions of Food Safety and Standards Act (FSSA), 2006. It is important to note here that since the administrative control of FSSA has been assigned to the FSSAI body, it thereby holds to be the single reference point authority. There have been 68 food testing laboratories accredited by FSSAI that have been established under FSSA, 2011 Regulations.

- FSSAI License compliances also include Food Safety and Standards (Food Products Standards and Food Additives) Regulations, 2011. It provides quality compliance such as a sample of any food article has to be sent to the food analyst of a notified laboratory. The referral laboratory will conduct tests and investigate the food samples for the purpose of fixation of food standards for that food item. In order to maintain high standards of accuracy, reliability, credibility, high professional discipline is followed in the laboratories.
- FSSAI compliances have been extended to provide quality food to avoid food adulteration, Contamination of food at any point in time, before it reaches the consumer is a major issue. For this purpose, food business compliances have been issued under Food Safety and Standards (Contaminants, Toxins, and Residues) Regulations, 2011.

Various aspects covered under this are:

- Cross contamination: This includes any substance that has been added unintentionally to the food, as a result of environmental contamination. Cross contamination may occur at the time of manufacture, processing, preparation, treatment, and packaging of the food product.
- Chemical or metal contaminants in the food article beyond the specified limits are considered inappropriate. FSSAI also provides food packaging norms. Packaging and labelling regulations have been provided under the Food Safety and Standards (Packaging and Labelling) Regulations, 2011. Specific regulations have been provided for pre-packaged, proprietary, and other specific products. It claims that the food should be packed in a manner such that its contents remain unchanged until its consumption.

- The particulars of the food product should be provided on the label in Hindi or English language.
- Pre-packaged food should be well presented to avoid providing any false or misleading information about the characters in the food product.
- The labels of the pre-packaged products should be such that, that they cannot get separated from the container.
- Contents of the label must be clear so that the consumer is able to read and understand it while purchasing and using the product.

- In case the container is covered by a wrapper. The wrapper must carry all the necessary information regarding the product and its content.
- Every package of food must carry the name of the food, list of ingredients, nutritional information, declaration of vegetarian and non-vegetarian contents, declaration of food additives, completing details of manufacturer, the quantity of contents in the pack, country of origin in case the good is imported, and instructions for use.

Besides FSSAI, it is also the responsibility of state-level food safety and administration bodies to ensure food quality and safety practices followed in the state. Effective and efficient import, manufacture, sale, and distribution of food articles are important in order to curb sale and consumption of spurious, misbranded, adulterated, and unsafe food products

CHAPTER THIRTY-FOUR

Unit 7: Garbage Disposal

7.1. Garbage Disposal:

Garbage disposal –In the food industry, waste must be disposed off regularly & efficiently to prevent the contamination.

It is classified into three main groups

- Solid waste
- Liquid waste
- Gaseous waste

In solid waste there are two types -

1. Garbage – It is the waste mater result from the preparation, cooking & consumption of food. It includes inedible scraps of food which needs to be disposed off. It includes vegetable & fruits, skin, rotten & spoil food. Bones skin feather etc.
2. Refuse – Any waste material that is not a food item. Example – bottle, cans, bag, napkin, toothpick, tissue paper etc.

Storage of garbage:

It is important to store garbage correctly before it is disposed off. It shouldn't be left overnight near the kitchen area. This area is warmer than the other area & decay is faster here. The ideal storage area is in the yard behind the premises. Garbage should be filled in a bin this bins should be kept in a coolest place. In some hotels there is a garbage collection room where they maintain the proper temperature.

New technology can be used if possible –

- Vermiculture

- Recycling

Liquid waste / sewerage:

Liquid waste includes waste water from sink & drains from the kitchen. Dish washing area, laundry, bathrooms, and other drain from the buildings. It also contains chemical like pesticides, detergents etc. as far as possible sewage should be disposed off in a public sewage system.

Gaseous waste:

It includes smokes &fumes come out from kitchen especially when wood or cool is used. This will pollute the environment so proper layouts of chimney & exhaust fans are required.

Vermiculture :

Vermiculture is a cheap, practical, innovative technology which conserves the hums contain of soil. This is activated with the help of the earthworm Pheritimaolongata. Aerobic bacteria multiply in the gut of the earthworm &decomposed waste like sugars, starch, cellulose &protein into hums &simple forms which can be easily assimilated by plants. The burrowing action of the worm tills the soil ten times deeper than the traditional plough. It increases property & aeration by breaking up the soil.

Vermiculture can be done in garbage bin & or in soil in garden beds were vermicasting can be applied.

Recycling :

This is the reprocessing of waste products so that they can be reused. One way of utilizing the energy from waste food is by using it as feed for pigs and poultry. It should be collected separately, taking care not to mix other refuses like cans, broken glass, etc. Waste food may be used for poultry feed after it is boiled well, shredded, dried and enriched with minerals. Destruction of all pathogens are required, otherwise they may feed their way into the food of animals and ultimately reach the food consumed by humans.

Recycling non-bio degradable waste:

All kinds of glass, plastic, polythene, paper and metal can be regarded. Each of these should be collected in separate containers or bags and sent for recycling. This will reduce the volume of garbage to be disposed off daily and indirectly reduce pollution.

This use of recycled plastics is, however, not permitted in the food industry.

BIOGAS – Is another new technology specially used in agriculture field.

7.3. Municipal Laws and Swachh Abhiyan:

Swachh Bharat Abhiyan or Clean India Mission for a clean and healthy India is to be our nation's gift to Mahatma Gandhi on his 150th birthday, 2nd October 2019. We need to have toilets for all, and manage our waste well. '3R's are Reduce waste (by refusing unnecessary packaging etc), Reuse what we can, and Recycle the rest to reduce the water, energy and pollution from making things from virgin materials.

Understanding waste as per Municipal laws:

Waste is unwanted material discarded by each of us. Most of it can be useful and valuable for others. There are two main kinds of waste discarded. Organic Waste from cooked and uncooked food, fruit and flowers are natural products which decompose quickly and are called 'Wet' waste. Other manmade or manufactured products which are discarded are called "Dry' wastes. These include plastics, rubber, metal, glass, cloth, paper, and packaging. If all these different types of discards are kept unmixed, each of them can be reused or recycled if they are collected and managed separately and not mixed with each other.

Mixed waste = Garbage

Unmixed waste = Useful Resources

'Wet' waste can be converted to organic manure which can make fields more fertile. (Compost standards apply when waste stabilising is followed by sieving and enrichment for sale as compost). Unmixed wet waste can also give biogas for cooking, plus slurry which is also a useful fertilizer. Different methods for processing wet waste are described in detail separately in this guidebook. Garden waste and tree trimmings can be converted to compost or fuel pellets.

'Dry' waste can be reused for different purposes, recycled into new products, or used for energy recovery as described in detail below. Some but not all of it is hand-picked out of dustbins and dump-sites because we throw it out mixed with food waste. Mixed waste needs to be spread on the road before waste-pickers can get what they need to feed their families. Such picking, sorting, baling and recycling is done by 1-2% of every city's population.

If we keep our food waste separate from dry recyclables, all of this can cleanly support all these poorest of the poor, reduce waste volumes needing processing and disposal, and reduce the municipal taxes we pay

for waste transport services.

Some wastes are not easily processed, like e-waste (Electronic waste) which needs special safe recycling. Hazardous waste is bad for the environment if thrown out with general daily waste and needs special safe disposal. So both these need separate collection days, maybe once in 1 to 3 months. Besides separate collection of 'Wet" and 'Dry' waste, 'sani-waste' also needs to be collected separately and managed as per procedure. 'Sani-waste' is domestic sanitary waste like used disposable sanitary napkins, diapers for babies, invalids or old persons, and used bandages or dressings.

Municipal Doorstep Collection Explained:

Doorstep collection of waste is the best way to keep waste off the road, to provide waste pickup services to all and to keep Wet and Dry wastes unmixed. It is most effectively done in pushcarts with four 60-litre bins for wet waste and different large bags for different dry wastes. Four-bin pushcarts have proved very successful in over 70 large and small towns to date. Doorstep collection really means gate-to-gate collection at the main property entrance and not every door in every floor for every family.

For ground-floor dwellings, collection pushcarts move from one entrance to the next one.

For colleges, office complexes, malls, multi-story dwellings, gated communities, the municipal pushcart collection team is not expected to enter private spaces or to climb several floors and knock at every door on every landing.

The Building Society, Apartment Manager or Residents Welfare Association has to provide, from its maintenance budget, cleanliness services and collection of Unmixed Waste within its private areas.

Each apartment should keep two bins and a bag for easy pickup or emptying and return. One bin is for wet waste (food-fruit-flower-leaf) and one or more bags are for dry waste (recyclables without house-dust or garden sweepings).

A second small bin is for sani-waste (used diapers and sanitary napkins and bandages etc).

These three kinds of waste must be separately collected and taken downstairs unmixed to corresponding large bins provided INSIDE the apartment premises, separately for wet waste and sani-waste and bags of dry waste.

A separate sani-waste bin is needed for domestic sanitary waste / saniwaste like used sanitary napkins, baby and adult diapers to be taken separately by the collectors for drop-off at the nearest biomedical waste pickup facility.

These private bins and bags should be kept inside the main gate or side entrance for pushcart pickup, but in a place where passing public cannot throw in any mixed waste.

The private management has to take full responsibility for this and be warned or penalized if waste is mixed. Mixed waste should not be picked up till separated by them on-site.

For small towns with one or two storied houses, daily wet-waste collectors stopping at the gate or street door is compulsory. Pushcart teams need not be discouraged from climbing up to one or more flats to pick it up from upstairs if it does not greatly slow down their normal collection duties. This optional private arrangement is usually in exchange for monthly or festival tips, clothes or snacks.

Collection Targets: Each municipality should fix its own doorstep 5 collection target of 250 - 350 households per team and strictly leave it to the collection teams to use or sell their separated inorganic wastes. Sale proceeds from collected wastes are the team's pocket-money and are not to be factored into or deducted from their salaries. If collection is outsourced, contractors are not to take away dry waste. Allowing the doorstep collectors to benefit from segregation automatically promotes doorstep segregation without municipal effort.

This should be strongly encouraged because that means huge savings at the waste-processing point and less waste to landfills. In many towns, the authorized doorstep collectors allow one or two waste-pickers to follow them around, in exchange for a daily fee or spot sale of recyclables, or sometimes using them as free helpers. Do not discourage this voluntary arrangement unless the waste-pickers complain about it.

Part E: BUSINESS COMMUNICATION

"Business Communication"

CHAPTER THIRTY-FIVE

Unit 1: Introduction to Business Communication

1.1.The main purposes of business communication are:

- To inform
- To request or persuade
- To build goodwill
- To encourage action
- To instruct
- To affirm shared goals

1.2. Definitions of Communication:

Communication is the sum of all the things one person does when he wants to create understanding in the mind of another. It involves a systematic and continuous process of telling, listening and understanding. (Louis A Allen)

Communication can be defined as the process through which two or more persons come to exchange ideas and understanding among themselves. The word Communication describes the process of conveying messages (facts, ideas, attitudes and opinions) from one person to another, so that they are understood. (M.W. Cumming)

Communication is the process whereby speech, signs or actions transmit information from one person to another. This definition is concise and definitive but doesn‘t include all the aspects of communication. There are other definitions, which state that communication involves transmitting information from one party to another. This broader definition doesn‘t require that the receiving party obtain a full understanding of the message. Of course, communication is better when both parties understand... but it can still exist even without that component

Communication is a process of transmitting and receiving verbal and non verbal messages that produce a response. The communication is considered effective when it achieves the desired reaction or response from the receiver, simply stated, communication is a two way process of exchanging ideas or information between human beings.

Communication can be defined as the process through which two or more persons come to exchange ideas and understanding among them. Communication is the understanding, not of the visible but of the invisible and hidden. These hidden and symbolic elements embedded in the culture give meaning to the visible communication process. Equally, if not of more importance is the fact that communication is a personal process that involves the exchange of behaviours.

No matter the type or mechanism of communication, every instance of communication must have a message that is being transferred from sender to receiver. In order for communication to be successful, the sender and receiver must have some signs, words or signals in common with each other so the sent message can be understood. The ideal definition of communication is a 2-way interaction between two parties to transmit information and mutual understanding between themselves. The interchange of information from one party to another is best communicated when a discussion is available so the receiver can ask questions and receive answers to clarify the message.

There are at least three general types of communication goals:

- Self Presentation Goals (who we are and how we want to be perceived),
- Relational Goals (how we develop, maintain, and terminate relationships),
- Instrumental Goals (how we manipulate others, gain compliance, manage interpersonal conflict, use and recognize interpersonal influence strategies (anchoring and contrast effects, reciprocity, commitment, liking, social proof, authority, and scarcity etc.)

1.3. Objectives of Communication:

Communication is the lifeblood of an organization. It is the vehicle that ensures proper performance of organizational functions and achievement of organizational goals. As a separate field of study, business communication has the following objectives:

- **To exchange information**: The main objective of business communication is to exchange information with the internal and external parties. Internal communication occurs within the organization through orders, instructions, suggestions, opinions etc.
- **To develop plans**: Plan is the blueprint of future courses of actions. The plan must be formulated for attaining organizational goals. In order to develop a plan, management requires information. In this regard, the objective of communication is to supply required information to the concerned managers.
- **To implement the plan**: Once a plan is prepared, it is to be implemented. Implementation of a plan requires timely communication with the concerned parties. Thus, communication aims at transmitting a plan throughout the organization for its successful implementation.
- **To facilitate policy formulation**: Policies are guidelines for performing organizational activities. Policies are also termed as standing decisions to recurring problems. Every organization needs to develop a set of policies to guide its operation. Preparing policies also require information from various sources. Therefore, the objective of communication is to collect necessary information for policy formulation.
- **To achieve organizational goal**: Collective efforts of both managers and workers are essential for achieving organizational goals. Communication coordinates and synchronizes the efforts of employees at various levels to achieve the stated goals of the organization.
- **To organize resources**: Various kinds of resources are available in organization such as human resources, material resources, financial resources and so on. In organizing these resources in an effective and efficient way is a key challenge to the managers. Communication is the vehicle to overcome this challenge.
- **To coordinate**: Coordination is a basic management function. It involves linking the various functional departments of large organizations. Without proper and timely coordination, achievement of organizational goals is impossible. Therefore, the objective of communication is to coordinate the functions of various departments for the easy attainment of organizational goals.
- **To direct the subordinates**: The job of a manager is to get the things done by others. In order to get the things done, management needs to lead, direct and control the employees. The performance of these managerial functions depends on effective communication with

subordinates.

- **To motivate employees**: A pre-requisite of employee motivation is the satisfaction of their financial and non-financial needs. Financial needs are fulfilled thorough monetary returns. However, in order to satisfy non-financial needs, management must communicate with employees on a regular basis both formally and informally.
- **To create consciousness**: Employees of an organization must be conscious regarding their duties and responsibilities. Communication supplies necessary information and makes them conscious about their duties and responsibilities.
- **To increase efficiency:** In order to increase employee efficiency, they should be provided with necessary information and guidelines. Communication supplies such information and guidelines for them.
- **To bring dynamism**: Organizations should be dynamic to cope with the internal and external changes. Bringing dynamism requires finding new and better ways of doing things. For this purpose, communication helps to seek new ideas and suggestions from the internal and external parties.
- **To improve labour-management is relationships**: Harmonious relationship between workers and management is a prerequisite for organizational success. In this regard, the objective of communication is to ensure the free and fair flow of information and to create good understanding between them.
- **To increase job satisfactions**: Communication enhances job satisfaction level of employees. It creates a friendly environment where employees can express themselves. As a result, they become more satisfied with their job.
- **To convey employee reaction**: Communication conveys employees' reactions, opinions, suggestions and complaints to their superiors about the plans, policies, programs and strategies of the company.
- **To orient employee**: Communication orients the new employees with the company's policies, rules, regulations, procedures etc.

1.4.. Principles of effective communication:

In order to remove barriers to communication an open door communication policy should be prepared and followed by managers at all levels. The superiors in the organisation must create an atmosphere of confidence and trust in the organisation so that the credibility gap may be narrowed down.

Major efforts in this direction are:

(i) Two-way communication: The organisation's communication policy should provide for a two-way traffic in communication-upwards and downwards. It brings two minds closer and improves understanding between the two parties, the sender and the receiver. A should feedback system should be introduced in the organisation so that distortion in the filtering of damages should be avoided. There should be no communication gap.

(ii) Strengthening Communication Network: The communication network should be strengthened to make communication effective. For this purpose, the procedure of communication should be simplified; layers in downward communication should be reduced to the minimum possible. Decentralisation and delegation of authority should be encouraged to make information communication more efficient, through frequent meetings, conferences and timely dissemination of information to the subordinates.

(iii) Promoting Participative Approach: The management should promote the participate approach in management. The subordinates should be invited to participative in the decision-making process. It should seek cooperation from the subordinate and reduce communication barriers.

(iv) Appropriate Language: In communication certain symbols are used. Such symbols may be in the form of words, pictures and actions. If words are used, the language should be simple and easily comprehensible be avoided. The sender must use the language with which the receiver is familiar. The message should be supported by pictures or action, wherever necessary, to emphasise certain points. The sender must also practise in action what he says to others or expects from others.

(v) Credibility in Communication: One criterion of effective communication is credibility. The subordinates obey the orders of their superior because they have demonstrated through their actions that they are trustworthy. They must practices whatever they say. The superior must also maintain his trustworthiness. If the superior is trusted by the subordinates, communication will be effective.

(vi) Good Listening: A communication must be a good listener too. A good manager gives his subordinates a chance to speak and express their feelings well before him. The manager also gets some useful information for further communication and can also have a better understanding of the subordinates needs, demands etc.

(vii) Selecting on Effective Communication Channel: To be effective, the communication should be sent to the receiver though an effective channel. By effective channel we mean that the message reaches its destination in time, to the right person, and without and distortion, filtering or omission.

1.5. Importance of Good Communication:

Good communication has many advantages for a business:

- Motivates employees – helps them feel part of the business (see below)
- Easier to control and coordinate business activity – prevents different parts of the business going in opposite directions
- Makes successful decision making easier for managers– decisions are based on more complete and accurate information
- Better communication with customers will increase sales
- Improve relationships with suppliers and possibly lead to more reliable delivery
- Improves chances of obtaining finance – e.g. keeping the bank up-to-date about how the business is doing

Communication is to an organisation what the nervous system is to the human body. Effective Communication will lead to the smooth working of any organisation.

The following points illustrate the importance of Communication in Business:

- Smooth Working of a Business Firm
- Basis of Managerial Function
- Maximum Production and Minimum Cost
- Prompt Decision and its Implementation
- Building Human Relations
- Job Satisfaction and Good Morale
- Avoids Illusion
- Contacts with external Parties.

CHAPTER THIRTY-SIX

Unit 2: Types of Communication

2.1. Types of Communication: Communication in an organization carries innumerable kinds of messages which may be difficult to map out; but it may be possible to classify communications in regard to how to transmit, or who communicates to whom, or what kinds of relationships communication develops. Thus communication may be grouped on the following basis:

2.1.1. On the basis of Direction of Communication:

1. Downward Communication
2. Upward Communication
3. Horizontal or Lateral Communication

2.1.2. On the basis of Way of Expression:

1. Oral Communication and
2. Written Communication

2.1.3. On the basis of Organizational Structure:

1. Formal Communication and
2. Informal Communication

On the basis of Direction of Communication:

(i) Downward Communication: Downward communication occurs when information and messages flow down through an organization's formal chain of command or hierarchical structure. In other words, messages and orders start at the upper levels of the organizational hierarchy and move down toward the bottom levels. Responses to downward communications move up along the same path.

(ii) Upward Communication: Communication is a very important part of working in the business environment. Managers must be able to communicate with employees and employees must be able to communicate with managers in order to have a profitable business. Upward communication is the flow of information from front line employees to managers, supervisors, and directors.

(iii) Horizontal or Lateral Communication: Horizontal communication is the transmission of information between people, divisions, departments or units within the same level of organizational hierarchy. You can distinguish it from vertical communication, which is the transmission of information between different levels of the organizational hierarchy. Horizontal communication is often referred to as 'lateral communication.'

On the basis of Way of Expression:

(i) Oral Communication: It occurs through the spoken word. In oral communication, the two parties to communication, the sender and the receiver, exchange their views through speech, either in face-to-face communication between individual and individual, or between an individual and the group, or any mechanical or electrical device, such as a telephone, public address systems etc. meetings, conference, lectures, etc. are some other media of communication.

(ii) Written Communication: The Written Communication refers to the process of conveying a message through the written symbols. In other words, any message exchanged between two or more persons that make use of written words is called as written communication. The written communication is the most common and effective mode of business communication. In any organization, the electronic mails, memos, reports, documents, letters, journals, job descriptions, employee manuals, etc. are some of the commonly used forms of written communication.

On the basis of Organizational Structure:

(i) Formal Communication: The Formal Communication is the exchange of official information that flows along the different levels of the organizational hierarchy and conforms to the prescribed professional rules, policy, standards, processes and regulations of the organization. The formal communication follows a proper predefined channel of communication and is deliberately controlled. It is governed by the chain of command and complies with all the organizational conventional rules.

(ii) Informal Communication: 'Informal Communication' is the communication among the people of an organisation not on the basis of formal relationship in the organisational structure but on the basis of informal relations and understanding. It may overlap routes, levels or positions. Informal communication creates a situation where the different workers communicate with each other, work side by side, hour after hour and day after day irrespective of their formal positions and relationships. It is referred to as the 'grapevine' which indicates informal means of circulating information or gossip. It is direct, spontaneous and flexible. It is personal, unofficial, and mostly verbal.

2.2. Verbal and Non-Verbal communication:

Verbal communication, or communication through words, provides the opportunity for personal contact and two-way flow of information. A large part of our communication, whether at work or outside, is verbal in nature. Verbal communication in turn, may be divided into two areas – oral and written communication. Oral communication may be defined as a process whereby a speaker interacts verbally with one or more listeners, in order to influence the latter's behaviour in some way or the other. Oral communication in a business context can take the form of meetings, presentations, one-to-one meetings, performance reviews and so on.

Written communication is a process whereby a writer interacts verbally with a receiver, in order to influence the latter's behaviour. Written communication at the workplace can take several forms such as letters, memos, circulars, notices, reports and email. We will examine some of these in more detail in later chapters. Non-verbal communication, on the other hand may be defined as communication without words. It refers to any way of conveying meanings without the use of verbal language. The game of dumb charades is a perfect example. Non-verbal communication is generally unintentional, unlike verbal communication. All of us tend to communicate silently and unknowingly send signals and messages by what we do, apart from what we say. Gestures, facial expressions, posture and the way we dress, are all part of non-verbal communication. Non-verbal communication can have a greater impact than verbal communication, since how you say something‖ is sometimes more important than —what you say.

2.2.1. Verbal Communication: We communicate most of our ideas to others through verbal messages, i.e., through spoken or written messages. However, verbal messages have some drawbacks – the message may not be properly worded, or the message may be misunderstood, or interpreted differently from its intended meaning.

- **Avoid Words with Multiple Meanings:** Words sometimes tend to have different meanings in different cultures. Therefore, when communicating verbally, it is important to use words that are precise, unambiguous and have a single accepted meaning.
- **Ensure Clarity through Highly Specific Statements:** Instead of describing an object or idea in general terms or in abstract language, use highly specific language to avoid a variety of interpretations.
- **Avoid overuse of Jargon:** Jargon refers to technical terms or specialized vocabulary. Every profession has its own jargon which only experts in that field can understand. For example, IT experts use terms like —computer architecture‖ which the layperson may not understand. The use of jargon depends on the audience with whom you are communicating. A certain amount of jargon may be permissible when writing a technical report for example, but should be avoided when communicating with a general audience, since the terms may not be understood.
- **Avoid Biased Language and Offensive Words:** Language has the power to arouse negative feelings, if it is not used with care. This can happen when the words used seem to be objective, but actually contain an intentional or unintentional bias.

2.2.2. Non-Verbal Communication: Non-verbal communication can be defined as communication done without speaking or writing. Let us now take a look at some of its characteristics, which distinguish it from verbal communication.

- **Non-verbal Communication Cannot Be Avoided** – While one can avoid verbal communication by refusing to speak or write, it is not possible to do the same with non-verbal communication. That is because non-verbal communication is not always intentional, unlike verbal messages, as pointed out earlier. Sometimes, silence itself may convey a lot of meaning. Example – A speaker making a presentation may find that the audience is not very interactive. Instead he notices people yawning during his presentation. At the end of the session, when he asks for some feedback, there is total silence. The message conveyed in the above example is that the audience is bored with the session. The silence indicates that they have not listened to the session and that the feedback is negative.

- **Non-verbal Communication is Powerful** – Non-verbal communication helps us to form first impressions and make judgments of others. First impressions generally tend to be lasting impressions. Let us say you go for a job interview fifteen minutes late and dressed in informal attire. When asked some questions, you avoid eye contact. This immediately reflects on your attitude and the impression formed of you is that of a person who takes things casually, is insecure and lacks knowledge.
- **Non-verbal Communication is Ambiguous** – While precise words can be used in verbal communication to ensure that that the message is clearly understood, non-verbal communication is not always clear and easy to understand. For example, sitting back in a relaxed posture may be a signal of boredom or fatigue. Similarly, avoiding eye contact with your audience could mean that either you are nervous or guilty of something. Therefore, it is not possible to accurately understand the messages conveyed by non-verbal behaviour.
- **Non-verbal Communication Cannot Express All Messages** – Non-verbal behaviour can only express a person‘s feelings, attitudes, level of interest, liking or dislike for something. Certain messages about ideas or concepts can only be expressed through the spoken or written word. Consider the following, example-A sales manager wanting to report that sales for the current year has exceeded targets, can only do so through a written report or oral presentation. If he is making an oral presentation, his non-verbal behaviour can only indicate how pleased he is about the increase in sales.
- **Non-verbal Communication Varies Across Cultures** – While certain types of non-verbal behaviour are universal, others may be different in different cultures. Examples – There are different rules regarding the appropriateness of the handshake in oriental and western cultures. Generally, in oriental cultures like India, any form of physical contact is not common and is interpreted as being intimate, while it is an accepted thing in western countries. Similarly, a nod of the head means yes in some cultures and no in other cultures.

CHAPTER THIRTY-SEVEN

Unit 3: Essentials of good business letter and types of letters – Official, D.O

3.1 A business letter is usually used when writing from one company to another, or for correspondence between such organizations and their customers, clients and other external parties. The overall style of letter depends on the relationship between the parties concerned. Reasons to write a business letter include: to request direct information or action from another party, to order supplies from a supplier, to identify a mistake that was committed, to reply directly to a request, to apologize for a wrong, or to convey goodwill. A business letter is useful because it produces a permanent written record, is confidential, and formal.

The basics of good writing letters are easy to learn. The following guide provides the phrases that are usually found in any standard business letter. This basic of business letters are important because certain formulas are recognized and handled accordingly. Think of a basic business letter in three steps:

1. **Introduction** - *The reason for writing*

The introduction helps the reader understand in which context the letter should be considered. Possibilities include job interview inquires, business opportunity requests, complaints, and more. Each type of business letter has its own standard phrases.

2. **Details** - *What you would like to accomplish*

The detail section of a business letter is extremely important. This is where you achieve your goals in writing a business letter.

3. **Conclusion / Next Steps** - *What you would like to happen in the future*

Provide a call for future action. This can be a chance to talk in person, a follow-up letter or more. It's important and expected to make it clear what you would like for the next step from the person reading your business letter. The phrases presented in this guide provide a frame and introduction to the content of business letters. At the end of this guide, you will find links to sites that give tips on the difficult part of writing successful business letters - arguing your business objective. By using these standard phrases, you can give a professional tone to your English business letters.

3.2. Business Letter Formats:

E-mail may be the quick and convenient way to relay daily business messages, but the printed business letter is still the preferred way to convey important information. A carefully crafted letter presented on attractive letterhead can be a powerful communication tool. To make sure you are writing the most professional and effective letter possible, use the business letter format and template below and follow these basic business letter-writing.

Ø **Select a professional letterhead design:** Your business letter is a representation of your company, so you want it to look distinctive and immediately communicate "high quality." For a convenient and economical alternative to using traditional pre-printed letterhead, try using our contemporary letterhead and envelope design templates. Simply create a letter within a predesigned colour letterhead template and then print.

Ø **Use a standard business letter format and template:** The most widely used format for business letters is "block style," where the text of the entire letter is justified left. The text is single spaced, except for double spaces between paragraphs. Typically margins are about 1 inch (25.4 mm) on all sides of the document, which the default is setting for most word-processing programs. Business letter format illustrates the specific parts of a business letter:

Ø **Business Letter Template Fields:**

- **Date:** Use month, day, year format, e.g., December 3, 2013 or 3 December 2013
- **Sender's Address:** It is a good idea to include sender's email and url, if available. Don't include this information if it's already incorporated into the letterhead design. This will allow customers to find your small business more quickly.
- **Inside Address:** Use full name. Mr./ Ms. is optional

- **Salutation:** Be sure to use a colon at the end of the name, not a comma as in personal letters
- **Body Text:** State why you are writing. Establish any connection/mutual relationship up front. Outline the solution, providing proof in the way of examples and expert opinions. Group related information into paragraphs
- **Closing "Call to Action":** State what the reader needs to do and what you will do to follow up
- **Signature Block:** Sign your letter in blue or black ink
- **Enclosures:** Use if you have an enclosure
- **Carbon Copy:** Use if you are sending a copy to additional person(s)

Ø **Use a professional tone:** Save casual, chatty language for email - your printed business letter should be friendly but more professional. As Scott Ober suggests in his book Contemporary Business Communication, “The business writer should strive for an overall tone that is confident, courteous, and sincere; that uses emphasis and subordination appropriately; that contains non-discriminatory language; that stresses the "you" attitude; and that is written at an appropriate level of difficulty”. That said, be sure to sound like yourself - you don’t want your letter to read as if a machine wrote it.

Ø **Write clearly:** State your point early in your letter. To avoid any miscommunications, use straightforward, concise language. Skip the industry jargon and instead choose lively, active words to hold your reader’s attention.

Ø **Organize your information logically:** Group related information into separate paragraphs. In a long, information-packed letter, consider organizing information into sections with subheads. You may want to highlight key words to make them "pop" - this technique is possible with most word-processing programs.

Ø **Use bold or Colour Font to Emphasize Words in Text:** It’s easy to put a few words in bold or colour to draw attention to them.

Ø **Be persuasive:**

- Establish a positive relationship with your reader right away. If you have a connection to the reader - you’ve met before or have a mutual colleague, for example - mention it in your introductory paragraph. Whether you think your reader will agree with the point of your letter or not, it is important to find common ground and build your case from there.

- Understand your reader well enough to anticipate how he or she will react when reading your letter. Address his or her needs or wishes, or a specific problem, and then outline your solution. Provide proof in the way of examples and/or expert opinions to back up your point. Make sure to maintain a friendly tone.

Conclude your letter with a "call to action." State clearly what your reader needs to do or believe to achieve the desired solution and then state what you, the writer, intend to do next to follow up.

Ø **Proofread your letter:** All your careful crafting and printing can't cover up spelling or punctuation errors, which leave a lasting negative impression.

3.3. Types of Business Letters:

Letter writing is a prized skill in the world of work. The higher you advance in your career, the more you will need to write letters. Letters are more formal and official than other types of business communication. They offer personal, verifiable authorization. Unlike e-mail, letters often must be routed through channels before they are sent out. Letters are the expected medium through which important documents such as contracts and proposals are sent to readers. There are four basic types of business letters: inquiry letters, special request letters, sales letters, and customer relations letters. Business letters can be further classified as positive, neutral, or negative. Inquiry and special request letters are neutral, sales letters are positive, and customer relations letters can be positive or negative.

Inquiry Letters: An inquiry letter asks for information about a product, service, or procedure. Businesses frequently exchange inquiry letters, and customers frequently send them to businesses. Three basic rules for an effective inquiry letter are to state exactly what information you want, indicate clearly why you must have this information, and specify exactly when you must have it.

Special Request Letters: Special request letters make a special demand, not a routine inquiry. The way you present your request is crucial, since your reader is not obliged to give you anything. When asking for information in a special request letter, state that you are, why you are writing, precisely what information you need, and exactly when you need the information (allow sufficient time). If you are asking for information to include in a report or other document, offer to forward a copy of the finished document as a courtesy. State that you will keep the information confidential, if that is appropriate. Finally, thank the recipient for helping you.

Sales Letters: A sales letter is written to persuade the reader to buy a product, try a service, support a cause, or participate in an activity. No matter what profession you are in, writing sales letters is a valuable skill.

To write an effective sales letter, follow these guidelines:

- Identify and limit your audience.
- Use reader psychology. Appeal to readers' emotions, pocketbook, comfort, and so on by focusing on the right issues.
- Don't boast or be a bore. Don't gush about your company or make elaborate explanations about a product.
- Use words that appeal to readers' senses.
- Be ethical. The "four A's" of sales letters are attention, appeal, application, and action. First, get the reader's attention.
- Next, highlight your product's appeal. Then, show the reader the product's application. Finally, end with a specific request for action.

In the first part of your sales letter, get the reader's attention by asking a question, using a "how to" statement, complimenting the reader, offering a free gift, introducing a comparison, or announcing a change. In the second part, highlight your product's allure by appealing to the reader's intellect, emotions, or both.

Don't lose the momentum you have gained with your introduction by boring the reader with petty details, flat descriptions, elaborate inventories, or trivial boasts. In the third part of your sales letter, supply evidence of the value of what you are selling. Focus on the prospective customer, not on your company. Mention the cost of your product or service, if necessary, by relating it to the benefits to the customer. In the final section, tell readers exactly what you want them to do, and by what time. "Respond and be rewarded" is the basic message of the last section of a sales letter.

Customer Relations Letters: These deals with establishing and maintaining good working relationships. They deliver good news or bad news, acceptances or refusals. If you are writing an acceptance letter, use the direct approach-tell readers the good news up front. If you are writing a refusal letter, do not open the letter with your bad news; be indirect.

- **Follow-up Letters:** A follow-up letter is sent to thank a customer for buying a product or service and to encourage the customer to buy more in the future. As such it is a combination thank-you note and sales letter. Begin with a brief expression of gratitude. Next, discuss the benefits already known to the customer, and stress the company's dedication to its customers. Then extend this discussion into a new or continuing sales area, and end with a specific request for future business.
- **Complaint Letters:** These require delicacy. The right tone will increase your chances of getting what you want. Adopt the "you" attitude. Begin with a detailed description of the product or service you are complaining about. Include the model and serial numbers, size, quantity, and colour. Next, state exactly what is wrong with the product or service. Briefly describe the inconvenience you have experienced. Indicate precisely what you want done (you want your money back, you want a new model, you want an apology, and so on). Finally, ask for prompt handling of your claim.
- **Adjustment Letters:** Adjustment letters respond to complaint letters. For an adjustment letter that tells the customer "Yes," start with your good news. Admit immediately that the complaint was justified. State precisely what you are going to do to correct the problem. Offer an explanation for the inconvenience the customer suffered. End on a friendly, positive note. For adjustment letters that deny a claim, avoid blaming or scolding the customer. Thank the customer for writing. Stress that you understand the complaint. Provide a factual explanation to show customers they're being treated fairly. Give your decision without hedging or apologizing. (Indecision will infuriate customers who believe they have presented a convincing case.) Leave the door open for better and continued business in the future.
- **Refusal of Credit Letters:** Begin on a positive note. Express gratitude for the applicant for wanting to do business with you. Cite appropriate reasons for refusing to grant the customer credit: lack of business experience or prior credit, current unfavourable or unstable financial conditions, and so on. End on a positive note. Encourage the reader to reapply later when his or her circumstances have changed.

CHAPTER THIRTY-EIGHT

Unit 4: Letter Writing

4.1. Circular:

A circular is generally understood as a written communication addressed to a circle of persons and customers. A circular may cover a notice or advertisements, etc., reproduced for distribution. The process of sending circulars is referred to as circularizing. Circulars are a highly effective way to communicate with employees or customers. Many companies use circulars to enforce dress codes and policies or invite employees to meetings or luncheons. Circulars can also be used as an advertising tool. There are a number of benefits to using circulars, but a circular must include certain features to be most effective. Additionally, distribution is important for circulars in business communication.

4.2. Memos:

Memo is a short form for memorandum.

It is derived from a Latin word *memorare* which is later changed to *memorandus* which literally means to provide information. It is used for internal and intra-departmental communication. It provides information by a person or a committee to other people. It is normally used for making communication with one or two persons. Memo is less formal than a letter. The style, tone and format vary from that of the letter. Also when a memo is sent to peers and juniors, it is more informal in style. When a memo is sent to seniors the tone varies and the style tends to be slightly more formal. With the advent of intranet system in organizations, internal communication is made via networking. The advantage is it is instantaneous. Memos are useful for brief notes which need to be put n record. The conversational tone makes it more communicative and interactive, which is a welcome relief from the rigid and formal style of writing.

Correspondence between sections/departments in government offices continues to be through formal notes which invariably end with —Submitted for orders, or —Compliance should be ensured. Though memos are official, the tone and style depends upon the relationship between the sender and the receiver. Conspicuously the pronouns I and You will be used. The obligatory components of a letter – salutation and complimentary close will not be used in a memo. Most of the companies have their own printed formats for memos. Even on a network, there will be standard formats. It will be easier to jot down a few lines on such printed forms and to send across. When compared with letters the format of a memo can have minor variations.

Normally the obligatory component will be the subject. Captions such as urgent or immediate could be added to indicate the nature of the memo. Memos could be used for passing on instructions, information or for making proposals. In government offices, they are used for conveying orders or calling for explanation. Government offices still use colonial style of writing. They are always in third person and passive voice. It is submitted, It has come to the notice of the undersigned, It has been decided, He should therefore explain as to why disciplinary action should not be taken against him etc are the usual expressions.

4.3. Notice:

Notice writing is a formal means of communication. The purpose of notice writing is to bring to notice a certain piece of information to a group of people. They are generally pinned in any common area where the concerned people can read it. It is one of the common methods of communication. It gives important information about something that is about to take place or has taken place. It is usually meant for a wider audience and is put up in a public place for easy accessibility. Notice is a formal, written or a printed announcement for the group of people. It is written in a very precise language avoiding any extra details. Basically, notices are a tool of disseminating information regarding any occasion or issues. They reach a large number of people in less time that is why they are precise and brief in nature.

Format of a Notice

- Name of the Organisation - It refers to the name of the institution of which the person writing a notice is a part of. It is written on the top of the page, it helps the readers identify who issued the notice.

- Title - 'Notice'- This title says" notice', It lets the readers know that they are going to read the notice.
- Date - The date is written on the left corner of the notice after leaving a tile. As the notices are the formal communication, date of issuing a notice is very important. The date should be written in a proper format, which is clear and easily understandable.
- Heading - Heading explains what is the notice about in brief. Heading should reflect the content of the meeting. It is just like a 'subject' of an email, which gives a synopsis or purpose of the communication
- Body - Body of the notice includes the main content for which the notice was issued. The body should contain all the necessary information required in the notice like time of an event, venue of the event and a date and it should be written in a passive voice without the use of first-person.

4.4. U.O. Note: (Un-Official Note):

This form of communication is used within the office. This is mostly used in Secretariat between the secretariat departments. It is also used in Heads of Departments. One way is to send the file to the concerned section for their remarks. The other way is we obtain the information by sending a U.O. Note.

How it should be written?

- The U.O. Note No. is given on the top with date. This is the file number as indicated in the note file and the date of approval of the communication indicated.
- The address entry of the person to whom it is intended is indicated at the left hand side bottom after the body of the U.O. Note as in the case of a Memo & D.O. letter.
- Unlike in the letter, no salutations are used.
- After the words the "subject" is indicated. (Generally the subject will be the same that is noted in the Personal register and the note file)
- Immediately after the subject, Reference is indicated. Here all the references that are required for following the case should be given.
- Body of the U.O. Note in convenient paragraphs comes next.
- Bears no subscription except the designation of the signatory.
- Signed by Designation of the officer approving it.

- Indication of Enclosures at the left end of the body. Purpose to obtain the advice, views, concurrence or comments on a proposal or to seek clarification of rules, instructions this form of communication is addressed to other sections.

Though the name is Un-official note, it is used to obtain information within the organization and it is not something un-official.

4.5. Applications or Cover Letters:

Definition: A letter of application, also known as a cover letter, is a document sent with your resume to provide additional information on your skills and experience. A letter of application typically provides detailed information on why are you are qualified for the job you are applying for. Effective application letters explain the reasons for your interest in the specific organization and identify your most relevant skills or experiences. Your application letter should let the employer know what position you are applying for, why the employer should select you for an interview, and how you will follow-up.

When writing an application letter you should include:

- First Paragraph: Why you are writing - mention the job you are applying for and where you found the listing.
- Middle Paragraph(s): What you have to offer the employer - mention why your skills and experience are a good fit for the job.
- Last Paragraph: Say thank you to the hiring manager for considering you and note how you will follow up.

4.6. Resume:

- It signifies a summary of one's employment, education, and other skills
- It is used in applying for a new position.
- A resume seldom exceeds one side of an A4 sheet, and at the most two sides.
- It does not list out all the education and qualifications, but only highlight specific skills customized to target the job profile in question.
- A resume is usually broken into bullets and written in the first person to appear objective and formal.

A good resume starts with a brief Summary of Qualifications, followed by Areas of Strength or Industry Expertise in keywords, followed by Professional Experience in reverse chronological order. Focus is on the most recent experiences, and prior experiences summarized. The content aims at providing the reader a balance of responsibilities and accomplishments for each position. After Work experience come Professional Affiliations, Computer Skills, and Education.

Types of Resume:

Chronological Resume:

- Lists your work history in reverse chronological order (most recent first).
- A resume format preferred by many employers
- The preferred format for undergraduate to use
- Works best for those who have progressed in titles and have a good work history

Functional resume:

- Centres around skill areas that relate to the position for which you're applying.
- Works well for those with limited education, significant employment gaps, lack of work experience or experience in a different field.
- This format can be used both by recent graduates and career changers.
- If someone likes to use a functional format, must seek assistance from a career adviser for feedback.

Combination resume:

- Combines both detailed work history and skills
- Usually includes a 'skill summary' or 'highlights' near the top.
- Skills section must be kept short, somewhere in four to six bullets.

Mega resume:

- Lists skills, work experience, honours and awards, activities, internship, education, hobbies and interests.
- Includes anything that an employer would want to know.

- Easily customizable, i.e, each resume for each employer; and include only relevant information.

4.7. Invitations:

Written invitations signal to guests that the occasion is special, not just a routine gathering. And replying in kind is a great way to express your gratitude for your host's forethought and hospitality.

***Formal* invitations** are standard for events that call for formal or cocktail dress, such as weddings. Addresses, dates, and times are typically spelled out. A formal invitation card should use third person (e.g., they, their) rather than first (e.g., I, we, my, our) and include the full names of the event's hosts. Letters may use first person, typically *we*, but should still maintain a formal tone. For social invitations, you may follow modified block format and omit the recipient's address.

***Informal* invitations** are appropriate for more casual events, such as a picnic or a baby shower. They are usually written in a conversational tone. Informal invitation cards may be written in first person. When you send an invitation, state the purpose, location, date, and time of the event, and include the host's contact information (address and phone number; email optional) in order for guests to RSVP.

Note: RSVP: Répondez s'il vous plaît; please reply (used at the end of invitations to request a response).

4.8. Greetings:

Greetings are the way we communicate; we convey good wishes and congratulate others. When someone achieves well in their lives, or they have come across something very new. Presently, greeting anyone is very easy and quick through messaging, but the best is the traditional way we follow is writing letters. However, It gives a feeling of affinity to whom you are writing and to the one who is receiving. The greeting letters are welcomed in every field, either official or personal. The only difference is how you write and the tone you use if its formal or informal. The format of style could be the same, but the words you use matter.

Personal Greetings

When to use a person's first name: If you are writing to someone in a professional capacity that you have known personally for many years, it is appropriate to use only their first name.

Professional Greetings

When to use a professional greeting: If you don't know the person well, it is best to use Mr., Ms., or Dr. as an appropriate business letter salutation. If you have any doubts about which greeting you should use, err on the side of caution and use the more formal style of address.

Use a Formal Salutation

Keep it formal: Try to avoid the temptation to begin your professional letter with informal salutations like "Hello," "Greetings," "Hi There," or "Good Morning" if you don't know the name of your contact person. While those informal greetings are fine for casual emails to friends or even for more formal emails you might send to groups of people, in a professional letter you'll need to use a personal salutation with either a first and/or last name ("Dear Mr. Doe") or a job title ("Dear Hiring Manager").

4.9. Apologies:

An Apologize Letter/Sorry Letter, as the name states, is used to apologize to someone for one's mistake. It can also be used to mend broken or troubled relationships between individuals. In the corporate world, an apology letter becomes a permanent record of an event and the consequent response to it, hence, it is important to draft the letter accurately and professionally. Furthermore, there are a few etiquettes to be followed when drafting an apology letter. One of the most important etiquettes is to not get defensive. It is only natural to get defensive and justify your actions, but that does not constitute an apology. Another important aspect of a good apology is to accept responsibility for your actions. Do not try and justify as it will just make the apology seem forced and not genuine. If required, do explain and make the person understand what exactly happened, but do not try to deflect the blame. Lastly, read through the Apologize letter, letter of apology format once again before sending it.

Guidelines for an Effective Apology Letter:

- An apology letter is a formal document, hence, ensure that the tone and language is formal
- Apologize for the event and take responsibility.
- Describe the details of the event if required. However, do not try and justify
- Present a plan or a course of action for the mistake
- Ensure or convince the person that the mistake will not repeat itself in the future
- Proofreading for spelling and grammatical errors before sending it in.

CHAPTER THIRTY-NINE

Unit 5: Communication with Guest and Body Language

5.1. Effective Speaking:

Some speakers are better than the other in getting across their messages, while the others are not that convincing in their oral communication. But according to experts we all can acquire the qualities of a good public speaker with learning and practice.

But before that we have to know what essential qualities churn out an outstanding public speaker.

- **Clear**
- **Relevant**
- **Insightful**
- **Succinct (To the point)**
- **Practiced**
- **Energetic**
- **Respectful**

Clear – If you're even slightly vague in your own mind about your core message, or you don't deliver your message in a logical order, with clear transitions from one point to the next – your audience will be confused. It does take time to work all this through, but it's really important. Content is usually the reason why you and your audience are in the same room and thinking it through well enough beforehand makes all the difference to your reception as a speaker.

Relevant – You need to know your audience, in as much detail as possible. Audiences are sophisticated, and don't appreciate generalities. Tailor what you're going to say by doing as much research you need to beforehand.

You cannot motivate, inspire, inform, or expect your listeners to 'buy in' to your ideas:

- Unless you talk their language.
- If you don't speak at their level of understanding on the subject.
- If you use jargon and words unfamiliar to them.

Insightful – dictionary.reference.com defines the word 'insightful' as —the ability to perceive clearly or deeply; penetration. And Scott Berkun in his great book Confessions of a Public Speaker (O'Reilly 2010) goes so far as to say this: —The problem with most bad presentations I see is not the speaking, the slides, the visuals, or any of the things people obsess about. Instead, it's the lack of thinking.

Succinct – When you're listening to a speaker, no matter how interesting, isn't it true that when they say the magic words —to sum up‖ or —finally‖, you wake up? It just seems to be human nature, and one of the best ways to respect your audience is to be as brief as possible!

Practice – This is absolutely crucial. And it must be done out loud, at least part of the time. Yes, this is tedious, and most people don't do it, which is why it's a characteristic of good speakers.

Energy - Your audience follows your cue: every group who doesn't know you will be cool to start with, we're all metaphorically taking a step back and assessing, in the early moments of hearing a new speaker. But if you show some energy, some life-force, the audience will follow you. You need to set the tone. You can also gain energy from your audience (a topic for another day!).

Respect – Every member of your audience wants to feel respected by you as the speaker. And this applies even more as a speaker if an audience member is rude or difficult. No matter how much you want to retaliate, remember that an audience will feel —as one‖ to some extent, and if you get tetchy with one person, they will potentially all be offended. So even if someone hits your hottest button, continue to be pleasant. That way, you'll gain the respect of the group, and potentially avoid crashing in flames, too!

5.2. Listening and note taking skills:

Good note taking involves effective listening that includes concentrating on, selecting, summarizing, and finally, evaluating what is being said by the lecturer. The key to effective listening is to be an ACTIVE listener.

Suggestions to improve your listening skills:

1. Be prepared. Survey relevant test materials and notes. The more you know, the more interested you will be. Participate in an exchange of ideas rather than a bombardment of unfamiliar ideas and unrelated facts.
2. Acquaint yourself with a lecturer's general lecture method and mannerisms. Pay attention to style, tone inflection of voice, pauses, accentuation of words, and nonverbal cues. Use these as signals for identifying important points.
3. Try not to be affected or distracted by lecturer's mannerisms.

Note taking:

Effective note taking involves extracting and recording the important ideas covered in lecture in a way that will help you to recall them. Good notes provide a valuable means for review and learning, and can increase the probability of doing well on an exam.

Suggestions to Improve your Note taking:

1. Think before writing. Relate what is being said to what you already know or have reviewed. Use your own interests/needs as well as information common to the course to guide your thoughts.
2. Preparing for class is an aid in helping you to become aware of the major concepts and in deciding what to record.
3. Be selective. Listen to everything, but do not try to write it all down. Search for the main ideas and sort out the important sub points and details. Notes should be brief, legible and consistent.
4. Take accurate notes. Use our own words, but don't waste time thinking of synonyms. Lecturer's terms may be simplified later. Use brackets to separate your own ideas from those of the lecturer.
5. Abbreviate words whenever possible, but be consistent.
6. Don't worry about missing a point. Leave spaces and fill what you missed later. Also, leave spaces for expanding and clarifying notes.
7. Record all important facts: dates, names, places, formulas. Copy diagrams and illustrations which will clarify your notes.
8. Draw a single line through mistakes, rather than erase or black out completely. This saves time and energy, and you may find later that the mistakes may have been important to record after all.

9. Integrate lecture notes with text material. This is helpful for clarification and retention of material. If text material is repeated in the lecture, you can make a notation for later referral to the text. Be sure to note supplementary examples or elaborations.
10. Review notes after class. Reread and edit your notes as soon as possible while the information is still fresh in your mind, adding and clarifying in order to increase your understanding. Write a summary (a paragraph or two) or formulate a summary question at the end of your notes to consolidate ideas and to reflect the relationship of facts and ideas with each other and as a whole.

5.3. Body language:

Body language is a form of non-verbal communication. Body language is about using behaviour to communicate. Both people and animals use this form of communication. Part of this behaviour is done subconsciously. It is therefore different from communicating using sign language, for example. Communication using sign language is intentional, body language is not. The forms of behaviour used in body language include body posture, gestures, facial expressions, and eye movements.

Body language may provide clues as to the attitude or state of mind of a person. For example, it may indicate aggression, attentiveness, boredom, a relaxed state, pleasure, amusement and intoxication. Language is significant to communication and relationships. It is relevant to management and leadership in business and also in places where it can be observed by many people. It can also be relevant to some outside of the workplace. It is commonly helpful in dating, mating, in family settings, and parenting. Although body language is non-verbal or non-spoken, it can reveal much about your feelings and meaning to others and how others reveal their feelings toward you. Body language signals happen on both a conscious and unconscious level.

We all subconsciously give away hints as to our true feelings, through our movements and gestures. Some important body gestures are as follows:

1. **Gesture:** Brisk, erect walk. **Meaning:** Confidence
2. **Gesture:** Standing with hands on hips. **Meaning:** Readiness, aggression
3. **Gesture:** Sitting with legs crossed, foot kicking slightly. **Meaning:** Boredom
4. **Gesture:** Sitting, legs apart. **Meaning:** Open, relaxed

5. **Gesture:** Arms crossed on chest. **Meaning:** Defensiveness
6. **Gesture:** Walking with hands in pockets, shoulders hunched **Meaning:** Dejection
7. **Gesture:** Hand to cheek. **Meaning:** Evaluation or thinking
8. **Gesture:** Touching, slightly rubbing nose. **Meaning:** Rejection, doubt or lying
9. **Gesture:** Rubbing the eye. **Meaning:** Doubt or disbelief
10. **Gesture:** Hands clasped behind back. **Meaning:** Anger, frustration, apprehension
11. **Gesture:** Locked Ankles. **Meaning:** Apprehension
12. **Gesture:** Head resting in hand, eyes downcast. **Meaning:** Boredom
13. **Gesture: Rubbing Hands. Meaning:** Anticipation
14. **Gesture:** Sitting with hands clasped behind head, legs crossed. **Meaning:** Confidence, superiority.
15. **Gesture:** Open palms. **Meaning:** Sincerity, openness, innocence
16. **Gesture:** Pinching bridge of nose, eyes closed. **Meaning:** Negative evaluation
17. **Gesture:** Tapping or drumming fingers. **Meaning:** Impatience
18. **Gesture:** Stapling fingers. **Meaning:** Authoritative
19. **Gesture:** Patting/fondling hair. **Meaning:** Lack of self confidence, insecurity
20. **Gesture:** Quickly tilted head. **Meaning:** Interest
21. **Gesture:** Stroking Chin. **Meaning:** Trying to make a decision
22. **Gesture:** Looking down, face turned away. **Meaning:** Disbelief
23. **Gesture:** Biting nails. **Meaning:** Insecurity, nervousness
24. **Gesture:** Pulling or tugging at ear. **Meaning:** Indecision
25. **Gesture:** Prolonged tilted head. **Meaning:** Boredom

CHAPTER FORTY

Unit 6: Speech Improvement

6.1. Pronunciation, Stress, Accent:

(i) Clear Pronunciation: the first important prerequisite of effective oral communication is that words should be pronounced clearly and correctly. Oral messages are often misunderstood because the speaker doesn't talk distinctly. Inability to use the jaws freely, to speak with a limber tongue and limber lips, and to speak slowly often makes for poor oral transmission. If a person tries to talk as fast as he thinks, his words will run to gather and get rammed into one another, so that when he intends asking 'what did you have?' He will succeed only in saying 'wajuhave?'

(ii) Appropriate Word Choice: Words have different meanings for different people. So it is important to be careful in the choice of words. The speaker, while speaking something, knows what he means, so he presumes that his listener also does so, which may be a wrong presumption. In oral communication it is more important to use the terms familiar to the listener rather than the terms that are familiar to the speaker.

(iii) Natural Voice: Some speakers deliberately cultivate an affected style under the impression that it would make them look more sophisticated. Nothing is farther from truth, and nothing impresses so much as the natural way of speech. One of the manuals for office employees in an American firm says, "The most effective speech is that which is correct and at the same time natural and unaffected. Try to tone down an unusual accent and discard all affectations of speech. Try to cultivate a pleasing voice and speak clearly and distinctly."

6.1. Importance of speech in hotels:

Good communication has many advantages for a business: strong communication:

- Motivates employees – helps them feel part of the business (see below).

- Easier to control and coordinate business activity – prevents different parts of the business going in opposite directions.
- Makes successful decision making easier for managers– decisions are based on more complete and accurate information.
- Better communication with customers will increase sales.
- Improve relationships with suppliers and possibly lead to more reliable delivery.

Importance of speech in hospitality Industry: The hospitality industry is a very fast-paced environment that deals with people on a daily basis. Hospitality staffs are not sitting behind a computer sending emails; they are interacting with customers every minute. Customers expect to receive exceptional service when staying at a hotel, visiting a restaurant, or flying on a plane. Without communication, this is not possible.

Communication with Customers:

The first critical part of communication in the hospitality industry is the communication with customers. The hospitality industry is also known as the service industry. In order to provide service to customers, there has to be communication. Customers have to communicate with service staff in order to make reservations for hotels, airlines, and restaurants. The service professionals in the hospitality industry need to be able to speak to customers and provide information.

For example, when checking into a hotel, if there is not clear communication with the customer, then the customer will not know where their room is located or how to get there. This needs to be communicated to them when they check in.

Also, if a customer has an issue, it is vital that the service staff communicate effectively in order to resolve the issue. For example, let's say that you are at a restaurant and your order is incorrect. The server needs to communicate to you that they are going to fix the situation and apologize for the error. If the server is not able to communicate properly in this situation, it could cause bigger issues.

Communication with Co-workers:

In addition to communicating with the customer, the staff and management need to be able to communicate with each other as well. In our example about the restaurant, the situation could have been a communication error that caused the wrong order to be served. It could have been avoided if proper communication was used between the server and the kitchen staff.

Also, managers will find that if proper communication is used between staff and management, they will have a better working atmosphere. If the information is not communicated to the staff, they may become frustrated with their jobs. For example, let's say that a restaurant keeps running out of items on the menu. If the servers are not told about these items, it can become frustrating for them when they are serving tables. This is why it is important for everyone to communicate in order to make it more efficient for both the staff and the customers.

There are two key elements of good communication across the board:

1. Training

The first tip is to make sure the staff is provided with proper training. For example, restaurants need to make sure the staff is trained on the menu so they can communicate with the customers about it. If a customer has a question about a menu item, the staff will not be able to explain it if they have not been trained properly. Hotels need to train their staff on the aspects of the hotel, including the location of rooms, restaurants, pools, and anything else they might need to explain to a customer.

2. Clear and Concise

In the hospitality industry, it is also important to keep communication clear and concise, whether dealing with the customers or the staff. If a restaurant server talks for twenty minutes about the specials, the chances are that the customer will be overwhelmed and forget what was said. If management holds long meetings with detailed information, the staff might not retain all of it. These situations are why it is important to keep communication clear and concise.

6.3. Common phonetic difficulties:

Spelling words in English is challenging work. As a matter of fact, many native speakers of English have problems with spelling correctly. One of the main reasons for this is that many, many English words are NOT spelled as they are spoken. This difference between pronunciation and spelling causes a lot of confusion. The combination "ough" provides an excellent example:

- Tough - *pronounced - tuf (the 'u' sounding as in 'cup')*
- Through - *pronounced - throo*
- Dough - *pronounced - doe (long 'o')*
- Bought - *pronounced - bawt*

Most Important Rules for Avoiding Common Spelling Mistakes

It's enough to make anyone crazy! Here are some of the most common problems when spelling words in English.

Three Syllables Pronounced as Two Syllables

- Aspirin - *pronounced - asprin*
- Different - *pronounced - diffrent*
- Every - *pronounced - evry*

Four Syllables Pronounced as Three Syllables

- Comfortable - *pronounced - comfrtable*
- Temperature - *pronounced - temprature*
- Vegetable - *pronounced - vegtable*

Words That Sound the Same (Homophones)

- two, to, too - *pronounced - too*
- knew, new - *pronounced - niew*
- through, threw - *pronounced - throo*
- not, knot, naught - *pronounced - not*

Same Sounds - Different Spellings

'Eh' as in 'Let'

- let
- bread
- said

'Ai' as in 'I'

- I
- sigh
- buy
- either

The following letters are silent when pronounced.

- **D** - sandwich, Wednesday
- **G** - sign, foreign
- **GH** - daughter, light, right
- **H** - why, honest, hour
- **K** - know, knight, knob
- **L** - should, walk, half
- **P** - cupboard, psychology
- **S** - island
- **T** - whistle, listen, fasten
- **U** - guess, guitar
- **W** - who, write, wrong

Unusual Letter Combinations

- **GH = 'F'**: cough, laugh, enough, rough
- **CH = 'K'**: chemistry, headache, Christmas, stomach
- **EA = 'EH'**: breakfast, head, bread, instead
- **EA = 'EI'**: steak, break
- **EA = 'EE'**: weak, streak
- **OU = 'UH'**: country, double, enough

6.4. Connective drills exercises:

1. Stressing individual words incorrectly:

If you usually speak with native English speakers, this will be the number one reason why they misunderstand you. It's very hard for native English speakers to 'translate' a word spoken as 'caLENdar' to the way they would pronounce it, 'CALendar'.

Non-native English speakers don't have as much of a problem with this, and will probably still understand what you're trying to say.

Quick fix: Listen carefully to the way people around you pronounce their words. If you hear a pronunciation that is different from yours, check the dictionary (even if it's a common word) to be sure that you're stressing it correctly. Some commonly mis-stressed words that we hear (with proper stress in capitals) include: PURchase, COLleague, phoTOGraphy and ecoNOMic.

2. Stressing the wrong words in a sentence:

Remember that you can completely change the meaning of a sentence by stressing different words in that sentence. For example, you could say this sentence in a number of different ways:

"I didn't say we should drive this way."

If you stress **I**, you emphasize that taking that route wasn't your idea. On the other hand, if you stress **drive**, you emphasize the mode of transport.

If you don't pay close attention to the words that you stress, you could end up sending a completely different message than the one you intended.

Quick fix:

Think about placing added emphasis on the word that is most important to your meaning. You can add emphasis by lengthening the word, saying it slightly louder and/or changing the pitch of your voice slightly.

3. Pronouncing certain consonant sounds incorrectly:

If people are misunderstanding you, it could very well be due to you confusing what is called 'voiced' and 'unvoiced' sounds. You might substitute 'p' for 'b' or 't' for 'd', for example. These sounds are so easily confused because their only difference is whether or not you use your voice to produce them. If you aren't careful, you could be making mistakes like saying 'tuck' for 'duck' or 'pay' for 'bay'.

Quick fix:

Pay attention to how you use your voice when you speak. You should be able to feel the vibration of your vocal cords when you make voiced sounds (b, d, g, v, z, r, l, m, n, ng, dge, zh, and voiced th). You can also try to make lists of pairs of words that use the sounds you find challenging and practice repeating those. Record yourself so you can hear whether you're making any progress.

4. Mixing up short and long vowel sounds:

Vowel sounds, like consonant sounds, can also be confused easily. The main problem with vowels happens when you mix up long and short vowel sounds. For example, the long 'ee' sound in 'seat' with the short 'i' sound in 'sit.' If you confuse these sounds, you end up saying completely different words. This can get confusing in conversation and forces people to draw much more from the context of your speech than the speech itself.

Quick fix:

Make practice word lists like the ones you made for the consonant sounds and practice the sounds that are difficult for you.

5. Forgetting to finish your words:

Do you have a tendency to let your word endings drop? We often hear people drop the 'ed' ending off of words in the past tense, for example. This is a dangerous mistake because not only is your pronunciation wrong, but it also sounds like you're making a grammatical mistake. People could judge you based on this type of error.

Quick fix:

Do everything you can to articulate your word endings. One exercise that might help is to move the word ending onto the front of the following word. This will only work if the following word begins with a vowel sound. For example, try saying 'talk tuh lot' instead of 'talked a lot'.

6.5. Introduction to frequently used foreign sounds:

- **Ad nauseam:** From Latin meaning to a sickening degree. "Tom talked ad nauseam about the time he scored the winning run."
- **Bon voyage**: From French meaning has a nice trip. "We all shouted 'bon voyage' as Rosa left for her vacation."
- **Bona fide**: From Latin meaning genuine. "Emma's teacher was a bona fide expert in European history."
- **Carte blanche**: From French meaning unlimited authority. "As the owner of the store, Mr. Williamson had carte blanche regarding what merchandise to sell."
- **Caveat emptor**: From the Latin meaning let the buyer beware. "I learned what caveat emptor meant the hard way when I bought a bike that never seemed to work right."
- **En masse**: From French meaning in a large group. "The fans left the football stadium en masse once the score became 42 to 0."
- **Fait accompli**: From French meaning established fact. "Luis was disappointed, but his losing the election for class president was a fait accompli."
- **Faux pas:** From French meaning a social blunder. "Elizabeth realized too late that not attending Susan's party was a faux pas."

- **Ipso facto**: From Latin meaning by the fact itself. "A teacher, ipso facto, is in charge of his or her class."
- **Modus operandi**: From Latin meaning method of operating. "My modus operandi when studying is to set very specific goals."
- **Persona non grata**: From Latin meaning an unacceptable person. "Sally was a persona non grata in our club because she wouldn't follow the rules."
- **Prima donna**: From Latin meaning a temperamental and conceited person. "Laura wasn't popular with the other girls because they considered her to be a prima donna."
- **Pro bono**: From Latin meaning done or donated without charge. "The lawyer's pro bono work with the homeless gave him a sense of personal satisfaction."
- **Quid pro quo**: From Latin meaning something for something, usually an equal exchange. "Helping Ian with his math was quid pro quo for the time Ian helped me mow the lawn."
- **Status quo**: From Latin meaning the existing condition. "Because he didn't like change, Bert always tried to maintain the status quo."

CHAPTER FORTY-ONE

Unit 7: Electronic modes of Communication

Electronic communication can be defined as, the communication which uses electronic media to transmit the information or message using computers, e-mail, telephone, video calling, FAX machine, etc. This type of communication can be developed by sharing data like images, graphics, sound, pictures, maps, software, and many things. Because of this e-communication, there is a lot of changes have occurred in work areas, society, etc. Thus, people can simply access global communication with no physical movement.

7.1 Use of telephone:

Despite the rapid changes in technology over the years, the importance of telephone communication in business still remains. The advantage of actually speaking to your customers and co-workers in many cases is often more effective, personal, appropriate, and time-saving than written communications such as email and texting.

7.1.2 Reasons why talking with someone on the telephone is still important for your business:

- Talking with Your Customers on the Telephone is Much More Personal
- Tone is Very Important for Effective Communication and Your Tone Can Come through More Clearly on a Telephone
- You Can Get an Immediate Response When You Talk on the Phone
- Leaving a Voice Mail is Usually Easier and Your Message is not limited to a Number of Characters
- Sensitive Issues are Better Handled by a Telephone Call

7.2 Taking telephonic orders:

(Example of Room Service Telephonic Order Taking basic procedure)

- The telephone must be answered within the three (3) first rings.
- Greet Callers Warmly
- Identify your department and introduce yourself by name.
- Announce: "Good morning / Good afternoon / Good evening In Room Dining, (according to the time of the day), this is (name of the order taker), may I assist you Mr./Mrs./Miss" followed by the name of the guest according to the data digitally displayed by the phone system (if available).
- Use good telephone etiquette.
- Do a room enquiry on the POS (Point of Sale) machine and check the billing instructions entered for this guest by the front office team.
- If the guest is on Cash Only list, then politely explain that the guest will have to pay for order when it is delivered.
- If the guest is not on cash list then take the order without discussing the method of payment.
- Pay attention to orders, and know the menu thoroughly.
- Ask questions to find out the guest's choice or preferences for service, such as how he or she would like an item cooked or prepared (eg: medium rare, "on the rocks etc)
- Ask the guest for his or her choice of salad dressings and for any special requests such as fat-free preparation. Etc.
- Write down all information's clearly. Highlight special requests.
- Ask how many guests will be eating and note down the number on the guest check. As this will help the waiter to set the tray/ cart with the appropriate numbers of cutleries and crockery.

7.3 Telephone Etiquette:

The telephone is one of the most important and commonly used tools in business. Multitudes of businesses, companies, and departments use telephones in their work every day; however, most of us don't think of the telephone as a tool, and as a result, accidentally misuse it. The telephone is a link between us and the world outside our business or department. Unfortunately, sometimes we don't pay attention or make a conscious effort to monitor what kind of message we are sending to our callers and the outside world.

Some basic rules of telephone etiquette are. . .

- Speak directly into the mouthpiece of the phone or a headset while talking
- DO NOT eat or chew gum while talking on the telephone
- DO NOT cover the phone with your hand or put it against your chest to avoid the caller hearing you. Chances are, they will still be able to comprehend what you are saying.
- If you are interrupted or must talk to somebody else in your workplace while you are on the phone, simply ask the caller if they can hold and press the HOLD button.
- DO NOT place the handset in the cradle until you've pressed the HOLD button.
- DO NOT lay the receiver on the desk, without placing the caller on hold (the caller will hear everything being discussed in your office).
- Always be courteous.

7.4 Fax:

Fax is nothing but an acronym for facsimile. It is useful for sending letters faster. It also gives authenticity to the communications as it will bear the signature of the sender and is sent on his letter head. However it is necessary to take a photocopy of the message printed on such papers because the print on them fades out in course of time.

7.5 E-mail and protocol:

There are rules for them to manage the messages so the professionalism and politeness are kept.

- Subject: Subject line is very important. Email with no subject can be seen as spam or junk.. Subject is also useful if you want the recipients to read your email first by writing words like [URGENT] as their inbox might be filled with many emails. Please remember that you cannot write subject header with "Hello" or "Hi". Subject line must be relevant with your messages
- Header: Do not forget to change the header to correspond with the subject. By giving a new header, the recipients can find a certain document you sent in their inbox folder without having to check your emails one by one.
- Respect and personal: You have to show respect for example by giving a certain greeting. "Dear Mr. Pandey" is fine. Make sure you write the name of the recipient so it will be more personal.

- Tone: Unlike the face-to-face communication where communication is delivered verbally, exchanging emails need a specific tone so the reader can read the text carefully. Tone is crucial as it helps the reader to correctly understand the text.
- Spelling and grammar: The message you write represents who you are. So make sure you have checked all the spellings and grammar before sending the email.
- Short message: Do not write a long email. Three or four paragraphs are enough with two or three sentences per paragraph.
- Signature: Signature is totally important. Never forget to put your name below the message. You may also need to add contact information like street address, fax and phone. The signature helps you to show your professionalism.
- Quick response: Expecting a quick response is okay, but do not insist to have your email responded like 5 minutes after the sending.

7.6 Responsible social media:

You are 100 percent responsible for everything that appears on your social media accounts, from your status updates and comments to pictures, videos, and links you share. Here are some pointers for staying on top of your personal and professional responsibilities in today's social age.

- You won't agree with everything or everyone you encounter on social media networks, but treat each person with dignity and respect. The Golden Rule of treating others how you want to be treated is a good practice.
- Do not turn to social media as a way to harass, demean, or bully someone else. Sitting in front of a computer screen does not give you license to embarrass, intimidate, or spread hurtful rumours about others.
- Regardless of your privacy settings, keep in mind that anything can possibly be seen by anyone at any time, even by that person that you didn't want to see it. Think before you post!
- Whether you're concerned with maintaining good friendships or future job prospects, be responsible in what you post and how it could affect your reputation. Many employers now check up on job candidates' social media accounts for evidence of bad behaviour.

7.6.1 Social Media Etiquette:

Social media etiquette refers to both the spoken and unspoken set of social conventional rules of personal and business behaviour online. It dictates how people conduct themselves on social media so they remain respectful and respectable.

Bad social media etiquette on your personal account will probably leave you with posts that make your future self cringe. But for businesses, it could affect their brand reputation and can deter customers from returning.

7.6.2 Why is social media etiquette important for business?

With an increasingly vigilant internet population, a single mistake on social media can make or break a business.

Outlining proper social media etiquette in your social media policy will help you:

- **Protect against legal and security issues:** If your industry has stringent privacy and compliance laws, your system will keep you on the right side of the regulations.
- **Protect against privacy risks:** Social media etiquette outlines what's acceptable to share and what isn't. This helps prevent privacy violations for your business and for others.
- **Empower staff:** When your employees know how to share content safely online, they can represent and advocate for your organization, without harming your reputation.
- **Defend your brand:** Social media etiquette ensures that everyone who interacts with your brand on social media will see a respectable, professional business.

Part F: JOB INTERVIEW PREPARATIONS

"Job Interview Preparations"

CHAPTER FORTY-TWO

Unit 1: Preparation for a Job Interview

Through all the different questions, the interviewing officer is silently trying to gauge your personality, how you work and your ability to deal with stress. It will be impossible for someone to tell you exactly what they are looking for, but there are certain aspects you could work on. Most importantly, you need to have a sense of intuition such that you can read between the lines as the interviewing officer posts questions for you and be intelligent in answering them. A judgment call needs to be made every time in order to do well in the process. Most of the aspirant attend the interview without preparing for the PI, you can answer most of the PI questions if you are good speaker and have clarity of thoughts, but most of the aspirants are not able to perform well during personal interview even though they know what kind of questions they are going to face and what importance these questions hold in the complete interview assessment. Below I have picked some important areas from which you could face most of the questions.

Family background

One of the most common and primary questions asked during the interview is the family background of the aspirant. Right from the time a child is interviewed for admission to schools to his or her job interviews, this question continues to be an important one. Why is this so? This is because while we are growing up, the family has the maximum influence on us. According to studies, from birth till the age of seven, a child is influenced by the mother's emotions. For the next seven years, it works on the actions taken up by the father. Thereafter, the personality of the child develops which is again the result of the family and the environment of upbringing. The family background thus speaks volumes about the kind of personality one has.

Mother or the Father?

It is a common theory that girls tend to take the action side of the father while a boy is more inclined to the emotional aspects of the mother. Thus, this tendency to be more like one of the parents than the other could have an impact on the personality you carry. Whether you are emotional in nature or whether you prefer to show your worth with actions is one of the conclusions drawn from it. So, this could be an important question in an interview for observing your behavioural skills.

Independence

Are you independent in your actions? Can you take decisions independently at work? Or do you always need to rely on someone else's judgments in order to perform well? This is one question that the interviewing officer has in mind and expresses it by asking about your daily routines and schedules are like. Independence is an important trait to have and can prove useful for your professional life. During our childhood, we are extremely and completely dependent on our parents of the family for support. This is gradually withdrawn from our lives as we grow up. This removal of support happens at different stages, in different phases. So when the officer repeatedly asks you about your daily life, the kind of work you do and the schedules you follow, this is the question he wants to be answered. Your routines can also speak volumes about your punctuality, how organized you are in your work. So, make sure you answer these questions with care.

Social Circle

The social circle is an underrated part of the interview questions. Often it happens that people don't pay much attention to it and tend to answer it casually. But it has a bigger influence on your life than what you would imagine. The kind of friends you have, the intensity of friendships, how much time you spend with them, how long your friendships last are important points to focus on during the interview. It reflects upon the kind of person you are and how well you can adjust in a social group. Another important query can be what are the things that you look for in a friend before establishing companionship?

Deference

Deference is an important trait to have. This is again something that we learn from our family ambiance or schooling days. If you know how to respect elders and thus cooperate with them, you are in general holding a good personality. Having a sympathetic attitude for everyone, showing empathy to people in need, being generous are some of the qualities that the interviewer is looking forward to in you. The interviewing officer might ask you different questions in order to draw a conclusion about how well you respect others, both peers, and seniors and your ability to work in coordination with others.

Who do you look up to?

Who do you look up to in life? Who is your role model? Who do you want to emulate in your actions in daily life? This is yet another question drawing light on your personality. Having a role model means you admire someone enough to follow them and carve your life around the same virtues, qualities or discipline. Once you have a real-life hero like that, consciously or unconsciously, you are following his or her footsteps. Whether you know it or not, whether you accept it or not, this real-life hero is in your life in different ways. This has two major implications. One is, you will be following a certain type or quality or traits and secondly, you prefer these kinds of qualities over the others. This gives us a lot of information about the kind of personality one has.

Team activities

How often do you take part in team activities in your life outside of work? Do you feel competitive in such cases? Are you able to coordinate with the members of your team? These questions can go a long way in determining your team spirit. Often, participation in group tasks speaks volumes about how well you can adapt to changes in the team, strategies and the likes. Also, how well you react to a win or a loss also determines your personality.

Dealing with failures

Taking the previous concept forward, acceptance of failure is often an important virtue. What happens when you encounter a failure? The first step would be accepting it, getting on with it. Next, you analyze where the work went wrong, regroup with your teammates and ensure that this is not repeated in the future. This is the sequence followed when failure cannot be avoided. The interviewer would want to know how well you are able to abide by this order and whether you can accept blame for your mistakes or not.

Leadership and responsibilities

Next up is an important test of your personality. You have to be very careful while answering questions about leadership. Every company or organization would want to hire a leader, whether the leadership skills are to be used immediately or later in the career. Taking responsibility willingly, managing a team assigned to you, being able to give instructions and follow them when required are some of the values a good leader must have.

Hunger for knowledge

It is one thing to have a very qualified person recruited for a particular job. It is a whole other advantage to have a person who wants to keep learning all the time. Every individual should have a certain level of curiosity and the zeal to keep learning. This indicates that you are able to use your current knowledge to do your work, but also keep adapting in order to expand your knowledge base to improve the quality of work delivered.

Persistent

What would be a better choice for recruitment: A person who tries and gives up on being unsuccessful or a person who is persistent and won't give up till the goal is achieved? The answer is pretty simple. The second kind is the one people want in their teams. It takes a lot of courage, determination, and conviction to keep doing the same thing till the milestone is achieved. Thus, when the interviewer asks you similar questions, ensure that you clearly voice your ideas of being a persistent worker who is ready to work hard in situations of fatigue.

Why do you want to be here?

This is again one of the most popular questions in any interview. Why do you want to work in that particular organization? Most people make the huge mistake of preparing a strategic answer for this question, usually borrowed from someone, in order to impress the interviewer. But, the person sitting opposite to you knows how to read your eyes and your body language. This answer has to be genuine, expressing a clear and honest interest of working there. This could be the deciding question for your selection, so think twice before answering it. While these are some of the guidelines followed for answering the questions shot at you during the interview, there is a bigger trait that is most desirable. One can stress enough on the importance of intuition during an interview. Being able to think independently, take decisions on the spot are important qualities to have. More importantly, how you work spontaneously, having a presence of mind will help you through this selection process and later likewise in your work life. Above all, it is essential to maintain a calm and cool head to have a positive impression on the interviewer.

CHAPTER FORTY-THREE

Unit 2: Introduction to the Hotel and Catering Industry

Restaurants are places where food and drink is available at a cost. These catering establishments are an important link in the food chain. The food chain begins with the procurement of raw material such as meat, fish, eggs, milk, fruits and vegetables from its sources. The raw material is processed and packed in food factories, and beverages are bottled in bottling plants and breweries. They are then stored at the required temperatures in warehouses and cold storages ready for distribution by wholesale vendors, agents and merchants. They, in turn, sell these to eating houses for public consumption as meals and refreshments. Tourism is one of the main foreign exchange earners in India. Foreign guests visiting the country require food (board) and accommodation (lodging). This is provided by the hotel and the catering industry. The hotel and catering industry is made up of hotels and rest houses for lodging and restaurants for dining. This industry is expanding rapidly not only because of foreign tourists but also because of the boost to tourism within the country.

Development of the Hotel and Catering Industry in India

The development of the hotel and catering industry is often attributed to the development of transportation in a country. In Europe, inns and monasteries were the forerunners of the hotels and restaurants of today. Similarly in India, rest-houses called Serais and Dharamshallas were established on highways by kings and emperors of the ancient and medieval periods. These rest houses provided shelter, food and rest to the weary traveller and his beast of burden. However, India has a unique history, where the development of catering can be attributed not only to transportation but also to the legacy left by people belonging to different cultures and ethnic groups who have ruled her since ancient times. The

Mogul rulers brought with them their cuisine from Afghanistan and beyond. Similarly the French and the English brought their cuisine and culinary art from Europe. The art of eating at the table with forks and knives was progressively developed, until recent times when courses or dishes are differentiated by the size of the plate and wines by the shape of the glass. However, our ancient tradition of eating from banana leaves and tails still persists and is highly popular in southern India.

Classification of Catering Establishments:

Hospitality Industry is basically divided into three major categories:

They are: 1. Commercial catering 2. Transport catering 3. Welfare catering

COMMERCIAL CATERING:- Commercial catering involves catering for profit and customer satisfaction. Customer satisfaction cannot be given priority over profit as the existence of a commercial establishment is possible provided the company has enough money to sustain itself and its staff. Conversely customer satisfaction cannot be neglected as the backbone of any business is its customer. For retention of customer it is imperative that the customer has to be satisfied and happy with the services.

The different establishments which come under the category of commercial catering can be broadly categorized into two types.

They are: 1. Residential 2. Non Residential

Residential:- 1. Hotels 2. Motels 3. Resorts 4. Floatels 5. Guest houses 6. Lodges 7. Circuit houses

Non Residential:- These are business premises that provide the facility of only food & beverage but no accommodation.

The establishments which come under this category are: 1. Restaurant 2. Bar 3. Fast food outlets 4. Discotheque 5. Pastry shops 6. Vendors

TRANSPORT CATERING:-

Transport catering refers to catering done in the various modes of transport systems like railways, sea and air etc.

Railway catering: Railway catering in India started in the 19th century and has grown throughout the length and breadth of the subcontinent. People travelling long distances in trains require refreshments and hence canteen and stalls were provided on the large stations. The train would halt for required amount of time to allow passengers to avail of these facilities. The railway hawkers would cater to the economically poorer sections. Later the railway set up railway hotels attached to the railway stations to take care of the need of the people.

Marine catering: Marine catering includes catering for passengers as well as the crew on board. The modern day luxury cruise liners have very high standard and equipped with facilities like, restaurants, ball room, discotheque, casino, swimming pool, golf course, laundry etc. all on board. On luxury liners service reaches the highest standard. Apart from the different meals served in the most professional way social activities like parties, dance etc. are also organized. Events like birthday parties, anniversaries etc. are also celebrated to provide entertainment and create goodwill. The menus served are exclusive and quite elaborate to provide ample amount of choice.

Airline catering: Since no cooking facility is available in the aircraft all prepared food has to be carried before the flight takes off. Because of limitations of space and storage facility the pantries are specifically designed and equipped for holding and reheating the food. Today airline catering has become much more sophisticated and airlines are taking more care to plan more appetizing and varied menu. Civil aviation progressed very rapidly after the Second World War when large war supply air craft were available for disposal. From 1946 onwards commercial airlines started food service. Initially in-flight services were limited and only light meals and dry snacks were being served. This system continued till airlines started to make international journeys. This made it necessary to serve more substantial meals which resulted in the development of flight Kitchens which met the demand.

WELFARE CATERING:-

This type of catering involves catering without the motive of profit. Although loss is not objective either. It is generally done out of compulsion or obligation, or a part of legal requirement or charity.

Welfare catering is carried out basically in three different type of establishments.

They are: 1. Industrial catering 2. Institutional catering 3. Service catering

Culinary History: (Origin of Modern Cookery)

The most important factor in the early development of cooking was the discovery and control of fire. The first cook probably made his discovery by accident. A bit of raw meat probably fell into a fire, and man, realizing it was tastier and easier to chew, became the only animal to cook his food.

The first method of cooking was broiling. An animal or bird was placed on the end of a stick and held over a fire until it was considered sufficiently well done. Later it was discovered that food tasted better when, before cooking, the covering of fur or feathers was removed and the insides of the beast or bird were taken out and replaced with a stuffing of grain and herbs. Man next discovered that food cooks more quickly and evenly on a spit, or metal rod, that conducts heat to the inside. Roasting on a spit was important until 100 years ago. It is still used in outdoor barbecues.

Another major advance in cooking was the use of a heated flat stone for frying and baking. This method was also the earliest way of baking bread. As metals came into use, the flat stone was replaced by a sheet of iron or copper. A later development was the oven, which at first was probably a hole in the ground that was lined with stones and filled with fire. When the fire had burned to ashes, food was put in and covered with large leaves. This method of cooking is still used by some primitive peoples. Early brick or stone ovens were also filled with hot coals, but the coals were raked out before the food was put in. The food cooked while the stones cooled.

Before food could be boiled, it was necessary to have a vessel that could hold boiling liquids. Animal skins, closely woven baskets, soapstone containers, and kettles made of bark served this purpose long before pottery was used. Since these vessels could not be placed over a fire, they were filled with water into which heated stones were dropped.

As various methods of cooking developed, man became interested in controlling his sources of food. At first all food was provided by nature, and it consisted of wild animals, birds, fish, fruit, nuts, and vegetables. The domestication of wild animals began in about 8000 B.C. when man first tamed cattle, sheep, goats, and other animals. The cultivation of grain and other crops began at about the same time, and man was soon able to exert some control over his food supply.

Ancient Cookery

The earliest records of cooking were left by the ancient Egyptians. Wall paintings that date back to 4000 B.C. indicate that the Egyptians were adept at roasting, frying, broiling, and boiling. The Bible contains several references to ancient methods of cooking, and early carvings from Assyria and Babylonia show the use of charcoal in pans, a cooking method still practiced by the Japanese in special braziers, called hibachis.

To the ancient Greeks, food was merely an accompaniment to good conversation and good fellowship. A typical Greek meal consisted of roast meat, bread, wine, fruit, nuts, and a salad served with a tart dressing. In the Roman Empire, cooking began to be considered an art. The Romans brought back food ideas from all over their empire, and simple meals were replaced by elaborate banquets that included such delicacies as snails and dormice. Many chefs specialized in disguising food, and a legendary Roman dinner, described in the 1st century A.D. by the Roman satirist Petronius Arbiter, was climaxed with the appearance of a carved hen sitting on a nest of eggs. Each egg was actually a pastry shell containing a roasted ortolan, a tiny bird.

An indication of the eating habits of Middle Easterners during the 8th century a.d. can be obtained from a section in the Arabian Nights that describes the shopping spree of a lady of Baghdad. The lady's purchases include a large jar of excellent wine, apples, apricots, peaches, lemons, citrons, herbs in vinegar, 25 pounds of boned meat, capers, cucumbers, parsley, walnuts, pistachio nuts, almonds, almond patties, cloves, pepper, nutmegs, and ginger. The boneless meat was probably served in the form of a kabob, which consists of chunks of meat and vegetables broiled on a skewer. Desserts in Baghdad were rich and heavy.

Medieval Cookery

In the medieval world, food prepared in castles, monasteries, and palaces was very different from food eaten by the peasants. The average man had no kitchen, and most of his food was bought from a cook shop. In the great houses, however, there were huge kitchens equipped with all kinds of kettles, saucepans, skewers, and other utensils. Bread was made in tall ovens shaped like beehives, and roasts were carried to the table and served on the spit, each guest carving off his own portion. Dinner included game, a roast, white bread, and custard or a pudding.

Renaissance Cookery

With the beginning of the Renaissance individual cooks began to acquire considerable fame. When Catherine de' Medici left Italy to marry Henry II of France, she brought along her chef.

Under Louis XIV great advances were made in cookery. His second wife, Madame de Maintenon, who was a fine chef, founded a school at Saint-

Cyr, France, for orphaned daughters of French army officers. Girls who won honours in cooking were awarded a blue ribbon, and the term cordon bleu ("blue ribbon") is still the highest compliment a cook can earn. Béchamel, the favourite cook of Louis XIV, had a sauce named for him, and the famous chef Vatel is the hero of a classic story. Vatel supposedly committed suicide when the lobsters ordered for a banquet to be attended by Louis XIV failed to arrive on time.

The rise of the great French restaurants began just before the French Revolution, and in 1789 there were 100 restaurants in Paris alone. One of the great chefs of this period was Marie Antoine Careme, who cooked for Czar Alexander I, Talleyrand, and Baron Rothschild. Another famous chef was Anthelme Brillat-Savarin, who published The Physiology of Taste (La Physiologie du gout, 1825), one of the first books on cookery, as distinguished from cooking.

Rise of Cookbooks

Literature on cooking began with the ancient Greeks, who included a few references to food in their dramas and epic poems. The Romans took greater pains to describe their elegant banquets. During the Middle Ages the training of cooks began with an apprenticeship, as did most other occupations. Boys and girls about nine or ten years old were placed under the supervision of a cook who taught them his methods of cooking. Since few cooks could read, recipes were rarely written down. The first recorded cookbook was printed in Spain in the 14th century. In the 15th century the cooks of King Richard II of England wrote their Forme of Cury, a manual of cooking.

One of the first English cookbooks, The Widow's Treasure, appeared in 1625, and it was soon followed by others. The most famous American cookbook is the Boston Cooking School Cook Book, which was written in 1896 by Fannie Merritt Farmer. This book has been revised several times, and nearly 3 million copies have been printed, making it one of the all-time best sellers.

Since the appearance of the first cookbooks, written recipes have become more and more specific. In the early cookbooks, directions were quite general. They called for such quantities as "the size of a walnut," a "pinch," or a "smidgeon," and the exact measurements were frequently left to the cook's judgment. Because of these vague directions, it was very difficult for anyone to learn to cook. However, it is now possible for an inexperienced cook to produce an appetizing dish by following directions in modern cookbooks.

Modern Cookery

As the sciences of chemistry and physics have progressed, new knowledge has been applied to the preparation and preservation of food. One of the biggest changes came in the middle of the 19th century, when the cast-iron range began to replace the open fireplace. Advances in transportation, refrigeration, freezing, and canning have made it possible to obtain and preserve a wide variety of meats and other foods. Electricity has proved useful not only in kitchen stoves, but also in mixers, waffle irons, rotisseries, blenders, frying pans, and coffee makers.

One of the major advances in modern cookery has been the development of frozen foods. Vegetables, fruit juices, rolls, fish fillets, and entire meals may be purchased frozen in packages. Another relatively recent advance in food preparation is the development of packaged mixes. Using these mixes, even an inexperienced cook can quickly and easily prepare cakes, cookies, brownies, muffins, and other baked goods.

Every day new scientific developments are being applied to cooking. Improvements in kitchens and in cooking utensils are constantly being made. One of the most recent developments is the electronic oven, which cooks by a complicated process of microwaves. In this oven, which produces heat only in the food, not in the container, a cake can be baked in three minutes, and roast beef requires only six minutes of roasting per pound. However, certain foods, such as omelettes and pies, are difficult to cook satisfactorily with microwaves, and there will still be room in the kitchen for the chef to whom cooking is an art.

CHAPTER FORTY-FOUR

Unit 3: Technical Glossary for F&B Service (Important for Job Placements)

Technical Glossary for F&B Service

(Important for Job Placements)

1. **A la Carte** – The menu in which all the items are individually priced and customer select and combined dishes according to their choice
2. **Aboyeur:** The person in a traditional kitchen brigade who controls the hotplate and is responsible for communication between kitchen and waiting staff and who Calls up the orders. Barker.
3. **Aerated Drinks:** Drinks which contain carbon-dioxide either naturally or to which CO2 is introduced to cause aeration.
4. **Agenda:** A list of speakers, presentations and associated timings, given to conference delegates as part of the pre-registration or on-site registration.
5. **Aging**: Wine is aged in bottles and the period of aging may differ from house to house for example Bordeaux and Burgundy wines are aged for 3-4 years while Chablis is aged for 18 months.
6. **Air Conditioning, Comfort.** Use of air conditioning solely for human comfort, as compared with conditioning for industrial processes or manufacturing.

7. **Air Conditioning, Industrial.** Use of air conditioning in industrial plants where the prime objective is enhancement of a manufacturing process rather than human comfort.
8. **Air Conditioning.** The process of altering air supplies to control simultaneously its humidity, temperature, cleanliness, and distribution to meet specific criteria for a space. Air conditioning may either increase or decrease the space temperature.
9. **Alcohol Free Wines:** Alcohol free wines are also known as de-alcoholized wine or non alcoholic wine. These wines start out as real fermented wine, but before it is bottled, it is either filtered or put through a spinning process that removes both the water and the alcohol. Ales (Top fermented beer): Ale is a strong beer that was originally popular in the United Kingdom.
10. **Ales:** are more aromatic and have more pronounced flavour, alcoholic content ranging from 4-5%. Ale is top fermented when the yeast has finished its job, its rises to the top of the liquid rather than settling at the bottom. Ale normally requires less aging than lagar does and can sold within a days after its fermentation is completed. Different types of ales are following:
11. **American Breakfast:** According to Buinessdictionary.com, American breakfast is, A hotel breakfast that includes most or all of the following: two eggs (fried or poached), sliced bacon or sausages, sliced bread or toast with jam/jelly/butter, pancakes with syrup, cornflakes or other cereal, coffee/tea, orange/grapefruit juice‘. Coffee is most preferred beverage in American breakfast.
12. **American Scale**: It is used in United States and in this system 50% alcohol is equal to 100° therefore 100% alcohol is equal to 200° proof.
13. **American Whiskey:** The Americans spell whisky as ‘whiskey’. All American Whiskies are made from cereal (generally, a mixture of various grains of cereals), distilled mostly in patent still at no more than 90% and aged in oak barrels (except for corn whiskey which may not be aged) and bottled at not less than 40% A.B.V. The following are the types of whiskey from the U.S.A
14. **Añejo (Aged):** It is aged for minimum period of one year, but less than three years in government controlled oak casks, which add colour and mellow the spirit.
15. **Annual Operating Budget:** The formal business and financial plan for a business for one year.

16. annual) estimate of an organization's revenue and expenditure; amount of money needed
17. **AOC (Appellation d'OrigineControlée)** : Controlled Designation of Origin, equivalent of AVA (American Viticultural Area) in the States. This classification acts as a consumer guarantee that a wine is of a particular quality and generally of a particular style.
18. **AOP (Appellation d'Origine Protegée)** : the European equivalent of the French AOC.
19. **Armagnac:** Armagnac is the world's second best brandy produced in the Armagnac region of France from the Department of 'Gers', south-east of Bordeaux. The main grape varieties used in production of Armagnac are Saint -Émillion (elsewhere Ugni Blanc), Folle Blanche, Colombard and Baco Blanc.
20. **Aromatized Wine**: Aromatized wine is a fortified wine in which herbs, roots, flowers, barks and other flavouring agents have been steeped in order to change the natural flavours of the wine.
21. **Attendance:** The overall total number of people at an event.
22. **Audio-visual:** Has both a sound and visual component. Typically in the form of images and recorded speech or music.
23. **Auguste Escoffier:** The most famous French chef, known as the emperor of chefs.
24. **Award Ceremony:** An event where the performance of individuals and groups in a company or industry are recognised. It is use to honour and motivate key staff.
25. **Back bar:** it is located behind the front bar leaving adequate space for the bar tenders to work. It holds all kinds of alcoholic beverages in an attractive manner. Few equipments like storage cabinets, bottle cooler, etc are located in the back bar.
26. **Bagasse:** The residue of sugarcane is called a bagasse.
27. **Baize base cloth**: Soft felt cloth usually green in colour used on most dining tables in restaurants and banquets.
28. **Baize:** It is a thick woollen material which is used to cover the wooden table tops to reduce noise and to hold the tableware at its place.
29. **Banquet Service** – It involves serving a meal to a group of people who are celebrating, gathering for a special occasion like conference, meetings etc.
30. **Banquet:** It is a formal meal followed by speeches. However in the hotel industry it means all kinds of function catering.

31. **Bar die:** It is the vertical structure supporting the top of the front bar which separates the customer's side from the bartender's work area.
32. **Bar:** a licensed retail business establishment that serves alcoholic beverages, such as beer, wine, liquor, cocktails, and other non alcoholic beverages along with snacks or full restaurant menu for consumption on premises.
33. **Barley Wine:** Barley wine is style of strong ale of between 8-12% alcohols by volume. This beer is sweet and strong and sold in small bottles or nips.
34. **Beverage Cost:** It refers to the cost of beverages sold.
35. **Bin Card:** It is a storeroom card for each drink with bin number showing stock in hand, maximum stock level, minimum stock level and reorder level of the stock.
36. **Binder**: The binder is the leaf in which the filler is wrapped to form what is known as cigar bunch (Filler and binder together is called "bunch")
37. **Binning:** The wines should be laid down horizontally so that the cork is always in contact with wine and so does not dry out.
38. **Bitter Rot**: Bitter rot is fungal disease of ripens grapes that are active in warm, humid conditions. It is found on damaged tissues and the bitter fruit flavour can be detected in the finished wine.
39. **Black Rot**: Black Rot is a fungal disease which is one of the most economically important diseases of vines in the north eastern U.S, Canada and parts of Europe and South America.
40. **Blanc:** White.
41. **Blanco (White):** It is tequila without aging and it is very clear, without any colour. Some blancos are kept for a little time in wax lined oak or stainless steel containers, which reduce the harshness that is very common with blancos. They are also called plata (Silver).
42. **Blending**: This is an art that requires considerable experience, judgment and sensibility. It is a legitimate, natural and honest way of improving the quality of wine.
43. **Blind receiving:** In this there is no invoice accompanying the delivery of items from the supplier. Invoice is generated at the stores itself while receiving the supplies.
44. **Blush Wine**: It is a new style of rosé wine developed in California. Skins of black grapes are allowed to macerate with the must for a very short period which produces a very light pink colour wine. Red and white grapes are used together.

45. **Bock Beer:** Bock is a strong lager of German origin. Different sub styles exist including Maibock, Doppelbock etc.
46. **Body Language** - Body language refers to any kind of bodily movement or posture, including facial expression, which transmits a message to the observer. In other words it represents the gestures, postures, and facial expressions by which a person manifests various physical, mental, or emotional states and communicates nonverbally with others.
47. **BOT:** Bar Order Ticket
48. **Bottled Cider:** It is a pasteurized and filtered cider bottle with dosages of yeast and sugar to induce secondary fermentation in the bottle. Secondary fermentation can be done in closed tanks or impregnated with carbon dioxide gas. This drink has effervescence and termed as pomagne (produced by Bulmers in the U.K). Bottled ciders are marketed as vintage or special.
49. **Bottling**: Spirit is added to liqueur to bring it to the correct alcoholic strength, if necessary. All liqueurs are given a final filtration to ensure star bright clarity before bottling.
50. **Bottling**: The wine is subsequently bottled in clean and sterilized bottles.
51. **Break-even Point:** It is the level of sales where there is no profit or loss. It is a point where total sales equals total expense or the point where total contribution equals fixed expenses.
52. **Breakfast dishes** includes bread (plain/toasted), egg (boiled, poached, scrambled, omelette, etc.), porridge, cornflakes, fish, meat and poultry and beverages like tea, coffee, milk, hot chocolate and canned/fresh juices of fruits and vegetables.
53. **Breakfast:** According to Oxford Advanced Learners Dictionary, breakfast means –the first meal of the day. It is very important meal of the day.
54. **Briefing:** two way communication between management and staff before an operation
55. **Brigade:** The staff in the dining room or kitchen as an organized team.
56. **British Thermal Unit (Btu):** Quantity of heat required to raise the temperature of 1 lb of water 1_F at or near 39.2_F, which is its temperature of maximum density.
57. **Brunch Buffet:** It consists of both breakfast and lunch menu items. While this leaves caterers with many menu items from which to choose, it‘s better to serve lighter items than more filling ones.
58. **Brut:** Dry.

59. **Budget**: It is a comprehensive plan in writing, stated in monetary terms, that outline the expected financial consequences of management's plans and strategies for accomplishing the organization's mission for the coming period.
60. **Budgetary control**: It refers to any management approach that involves setting some kind of targets, regularly measuring variances between the original targets and actual outcomes, and motivating people to reduce those variances.
61. **Budgeting:** An estimate of revenue or income and expenditure made by a company/ unit /hotel
62. **Buffet:** Meal consisting of a number of dishes set out so that guest can select what they want for themselves.
63. **Butler/valet:** A highly trained member of the staff who takes care of all the needs of a resident guest.
64. **Café complet:** The term _café complet' is widely used in continental Europe and means a continental breakfast with coffee as the beverage. The term **thé complet'** is also used, with tea provided as the beverage.
65. **Café simple or thé simple:** Café simple or thé simple is just a beverage (coffee or tea) with nothing to eat.
66. **Call:** Spirits used when patrons do name— or —call‖—a specific spirit brand in a drink order. (Example: Tanqueray and tonic.) Call bottles tend to be your more popular brands, but are generally not the most expensive.
67. **Calorific Value of Fuel:** The calorific value of a fuel is amount of heat liberated by its complete combustion.
68. **Captain**: A supervisor of service staff in the food and beverage service department.
69. **Carbonated:** A liquid to which CO2 is introduced in order to create a fizz.
70. **Carhops:** Waiters working in the drive- in outlets who takes order and deliver the food to the guest.
71. **Carousel** – It is rotating shelve (usually three) at different heights containing food, where the guest remains standing, taking his choice of meal from the revolving carouse land placing it on his tray
72. **Cash bar:** All the guests pay the bartender for their drinks. In some cases, drink vouchers can be purchased at a centralized location, which makes it easier on the bartenders and controls the collection of money.
73. **Catering:** Providing the service of food & beverage.

74. **Cave:** Wine cellar.
75. **Cellar:** It is a storage space for alcoholic drinks.
76. **Cellaring and Second Pressing:** Once the fermentation is complete the "Running Wine" or "VIN DE GOUTTE" is run off into cask for maturing.
77. **Central Heating or Cooling Plant:** One large heating or cooling unit used to heat or cool many rooms, spaces, or zones or several buildings, as compared to individual room, zone, or building units.
78. **Cépage** : Varietal / Grape.
79. **Chafing dish:** A food warmer used during buffet service.
80. **Chaptalization / Sugaring:** in case of insufficient alcoholic potential of the MUST, cane sugar is added to improve the alcoholic potential. The process of addition of cane sugar to the MUST to improve the alcohol potential is called CHAPTALIZATION, in Germany it is legal.
81. **Château** : Estate. Literally castle, but mostly refers to large country houses.
82. **Cider:** Cider is an alcoholic beverage made from the fermented juice of cider apples. It is also legally permitted to make cider from the mixture of apple juice and pear juice in proportion of 75:25 respectively. Although cider can be made from any variety of apples, certain cultivars are known as Ciders apple, which have perfect sugar, acid and tannin content to produce cider.
83. **Client:** The person or party that hires an event planner and/or various event components required to hold the event.
84. **Coaster:** A small mat Put under a bottle or glass to avoid wet rings on the surface of the table.
85. **Coefficient of Performance:** For machinery and heat pumps, the ratio of the effect produced to the total power of electrical input consumed.
86. **Coffee Shop:** It is a restaurant open round the clock, providing a multi cuisine menu.
87. **Cognac:** It is produce in the Cognac region of France in the department of Charente and Charente-Maritime and considered most famous and prestigious. Brandy produced from grapes grown in the vineyards of the delimited district of Cognac, surrounding the ancient town of Cognac, on the Charente River. Modern delimitation done in 1909, a decree was made to protect Cognac from intimation and accordingly to get Cognac name, the spirit must be made entirely from grapes grown in the delimited region.

88. **Colour rendering index:** A numerical scale from 0 to 100 that indicates how bright a colour appears based on how much light is shining on it.
89. **Combined Settlement Method:** A guest may elect to use more than one settlement method to bring the folio balance to zero.
90. **Comfort Zone:** An area plotted on a psychometric chart to indicate a combination of temperatures and humidifies at which, in controlled tests, more than 50% of the persons were comfortable.
91. **Concept:** The idea for a restaurant, which encompasses menu, theme, décor and other factors that create an image in the minds of customers.
92. **Concert:** A public performance of music (singer(s) and/or instrumentalist(s)) with entertainment purposes. Concerts could have various forms: indoor or outdoor, paid or free, for-profit or fundraising/ cause events.
93. **Condensate:** Liquid formed by the condensation of steam or water vapour.
94. **Condensers:** Special equipment used in air conditioning to liquefy a gas.
95. **Condensing Unit:** A complete refrigerating system in one assembly, including the refrigerant compressor, motor, condenser, receiver, and other necessary accessories.
96. **Conduction, Thermal.** A process in which heat energy is transferred through matter by transmission of kinetic energy from particle to particle, the heat flowing from hot points to cooler ones.
97. **Conference:** discussion about a specific matter, mainly organized by a learned society, and based on a precise agenda. The conference has a didactic goal but can also be the opportunity to exchange knowledge with the participants. It is often organized on the occasion of a congress or a symposium
98. **Consolidated Hotel Budget**: The summary budget for the entire hotel including revenues, expenses, and profit.
99. **Continental Breakfast:** According to Buinessdictionary.com, _A hotel breakfast that may include sliced bread with butter/jam/honey, cheese, meat, croissants, pastries, rolls, fruit juice and various hot beverages.
100. **Contribution Margin Ratio:** It is a contribution margin as a percentage of total sales.
101. **Control Cycle:** A continuous cycle process of food purchasing, receiving, storing, issuing, preparation, again storing, serving/selling and accounting is said to be a control cycle.

102. **Controlling:** Controlling is a process by which the management ensures that the plans and objectives laid down are as per the schedule and the target set would be achievable.
103. **Cooling Effect, Total:** The difference in total heat in an airstream entering and leaving a refrigerant evaporator or cooling coil.
104. **Cooling Tower:** A mechanical device used to cool water by evaporation in the outside air. Towers may be atmospheric or induced- or powered-draft type.
105. **Cooling Unit, Self-Contained:** A complete air-conditioning assembly consisting of a compressor, evaporator, condenser, fan motor, and air filter ready for plugging to an electric power supply.
106. **Cooling, Evaporative:** Cooling effect produced by evaporation of water, the required heat for the process being taken from the air. (This method is widely used in dry climates with low wet-bulb temperatures.)
107. **Cooling, Sensible:** Cooling of a unit volume of air by a reduction in temperature only.
108. **Cooling:** A heat-removal process usually accomplished with air-conditioning equipment.
109. **Coopérative** : A cooperative or more likely, a syndicate of wine growers.
110. **Corking**: The bottles are finally corked and sealed with Spanish wax. Corks are made from bark of tree called „QUERCUS SUBER" and the best corks are produced in Portugal.
111. **Cost:** The amount of expenditure incurred on or attributable to a given thing.
112. **Cost-Volume Profit:** It is the relationship between an organization's revenue, costs and the level of activity presented in a graphic form.
113. **Côte/Coteaux** : Slope of a hill/hillsides.
114. **Cover** - The space required on a table for laying cutlery, crockery, glassware and liner for one person to partake of a meal.
115. **Crémant:** A style of sparkling wine other than Champagne.
116. **Crockery**: Crockery or chinaware is made up of silica, soda ash, & china clay, & dry glazed to give its a fine finish. It is available in different design & colour. It is more heat resistant to glassware. These are available in different types like – bone china, earthenware, stoneware & porcelain.
117. **Cru:** Growth, denotes status of a winery or vineyard.
118. **Crushing/Pressing**: The grapes are crushed or pressed according to the local tradition and custom either by feet or more conveniently by mechanical pressure to extract the juice called "MUST".

119. **Cultural Event:** An event related to and honouring culture in its various forms and aspects and considered as valuable, enriching and enlightening for the society.
120. **Cutlery:** The term cutlery denotes all forms of knives & other cutting equipments. Like – fish knife, butter knife, gateaux slicer, etc.
121. **Cuvéespéciale** : Special blend or batch, AKA —reserve wine‖. Term derived from the French word *"cuve"*, meaning vat or tank. Generally indicates a higher quality wine.
122. **Dark Rum:** It has a strong and pungent flavour. It is aged for a longer duration (six years) in charred oak cask. It gets its dark brown colour from wood, caramel, and/or residual molasses. This rum is extensively used in cookery especially in the preparation of cakes, sweets and ice cream.
123. **Decaffeinated Coffee:** Coffee from which most of the caffeine has been extracted by processing the green beans under steam in vacuum.
124. **Degorgement:** Process of clearing the wine by freezing the segments.
125. **Dehumidification:** In air conditioning, the removal of water vapor from supply air by condensation of water vapor on the cold surface of a cooling coil.
126. **Delegate:** To entrust a task to another person.
127. **Demi sec:** Medium dry.
128. **Design:** In a space plan, the definition of sizes, shapes, styles and decoration of facility and furnishings.
129. **Destalking or removal of stalks:** The stalks are removed from the grapes by a destalking machine. Destalking is necessary if white wine is made but not if red wine is made.
130. **Dhaba:** It is a roadside food stall located at national and state highway specialize in tandoori and Punjab style of cooking.
131. **Dog:** A menu engineering classification of items which are neither profitable nor popular.
132. **Domaine:** Estate.
133. **Doux:** Sweet.
134. **Downward Communication:** Downward communication is the information that is exchanged between a manager and a subordinate in other words from top level to low level.
135. **Draught Cider:** This is usually unfiltered and has a dosage of yeast and sugar to induce fermentation which gives sparkle to the product and termed as cask conditioned cider. It is slightly sweet with sparkle. If it is

complete dry, it is known as scrumpy or farmhouse cider. It is marketed in oak casks or plastic containers.

136. **Dry Wines:** Dry wines produced by grapes with less sugar content and the fermentation is allowed to continue till all the sugar is almost or fully consumed.
137. **Duplicate Method:** in this method the order is taken in two copies. The top copy goes to the supply point, second copy is retained for service and billing purposes.
138. **Duty roaster:** It is a list or plan showing turns of duty or leave in an organization. Having a duty roster not only helps keep your staff organized and minimizes the amount of time spent on hotel chores but also makes a measurable difference in work done by different staff.
139. **Egg to Order:** Egg is one of the most versatile items that are served in breakfast. The egg may be served as hard boiled, poached, scrambled, fried, baked, omelette etc.
140. **English Breakfast:** English breakfast is heavy and includes variety of dishes like fruit juices, stewed fruits, breakfast cereals, egg to order, fish, meat, bread with butter/preserves and beverages like coffee, tea, hot chocolate etc.
141. **Entertainment:** A show or performance designed to amuse and entertain an audience.
142. **Evaporator:** A cooling coil in a refrigeration system in which the refrigerant is evaporated and absorbs heat from the surrounding fluid (airstream).
143. **Event communication:** refers to a non-media communication tool, which can be internal or external, used by companies or institutions with the intention of organizing an event, generally in the form of a trade fair, a congress, an incentive, a gala dinner etc... This event is thought and realized by a specialized agency, comparable to an advertising agency.
144. **Event Manager:** A person in charge of planning, organising, and executing all types and sizes of events.
145. **Event Planner:** A person who coordinates all aspects of professional meetings and events.
146. **Extra Añejo (Extra Aged):** It is aged for a minimum period of three years in oak casks.
147. **Fair:** A public, live event gathering people for a variety of entertainment or commercial activities. It could last from one afternoon to several weeks.

148. **Feedback:** The process of sharing thoughts and observations – can be positive or negative.
149. **Fermentation:** Fermentation is the action of the yeast on the sugar (grape juice) to convert it into alcohol and carbon dioxide. Yeast cells excrete enzymes that convert natural fruit sugars into almost equal quantities of alcohol and carbonic gas.
150. **Filler:** (Shredded Tobacco): The filler is the inner core that forms the body and the shape of cigar.
151. **Filtering:** The wine is then passed through wine filters and filtered several times to produce a clear star-bright wine.
152. **Fine Champagne** – It is the blend of brandies produced from grapes grown in Grande Champagne (minimum 50%) and Petit Champagne areas
153. **Finger bowl:** Small bowl filled with water and perhaps a piece of lemon placed on the table so that guests can clean their finger.
154. **Fining:** This is process of clarifying the young wine during its stay in the cask and is done by adding various fining agents (such as Isinglass, Egg White, Bentinite and Gelatin etc.) to the wine which cause wine to coagulate and settle in the bottom of the cask. After fining the wine is racked once again.
155. **Fixed Cost:** The cost which remains fixed irrespective to quantum of output over a certain capacity of the organization
156. **Flambé:** To pour alcohol over food and set it alights, to enhance visual delight during service.
157. **Flatware:** It consists of all forms of spoons and forks.
158. **Flavoured Rum:** This rum is flavoured with fruits such as orange, lime, apricot, plums, banana, coconut etc.
159. **Flavoured Vodka:** It is flavoured with various spices, herbs, and fruits, e.g. Absolut – Citron, Mandrin, Pepper, Apeach, and Vanilla.
160. **Flowering:** The most critical period of a vine's life is when it flowers. At this stage frost, hail, rain, wind and extreme temperatures could wipe out a crop before the growing season begins in earnest.
161. **Food service:** Food service is an operation in which products/services are created and delivered to the customer almost simultaneously.
162. **Forecasting:** It is an approximation, prediction, or projection of food & beverage sales based on past record and/or information available at the time, with the recognition that other pertinent facts are unclear or unknown.

163. **Formal buying:** In this method quotations are invited from suppliers for items against fixed specification. The request for bids may be made through news papers or any other media. All the quotations are received sealed, and are opened on a said day when it is made final.
164. **Formal Communication Network:** A formal communication network is one which is created by management and described with the help of an organizational chart.
165. **Fortified Wines:** These are the wines which are fortified with spirit like brandy during vinification when fermentation process is going on. If fortification is done in the beginning of fermentation the end product is sweet fortified wine. If fortification is towards the end of fermentation, the resultant wine is dry fortified wine.
166. **Fraud:** It is an act by employees may lead to a reduction in revenue levels and increase in F & B cost percentage.
167. **French toast:** in different versions is popular in many regions, and it has the advantage of being an excellent way to utilize day-old bread. Basic French toast consists of slices of bread dipped in a batter of eggs, milk, a little sugar, and flavourings. French toast is cooked on a griddle like pancakes. Variations may be created by changing the basic ingredients.
168. **Front bar:** This is the portion of the bar where the customers place their order and receive it. This is actually the interaction point of a customer and the bar tender.
169. **Front of House:** The front of house is a term given to the public area of the catering premise or the actual dining room itself. People, who works in this area are called front of house staff including, wait staff, bar staff etc.
170. **Fruit Beers & Flavoured Beers:** Variety of beers with additional flavouring such as honeydew or fruit beers, which have fresh fruits such as raspberry or strawberry introduced during the making process to add flavour.
171. **Fuel:** A fuel is a substance which when once raised to its ignition temperature continues to burn if sufficient oxygen or air is available.
172. **Full Bodied Wine:** These wines have heavy body, texture and higher alcoholic content, rich taste with forceful flavour.
173. **Gangway:** It is the free space available between the chairs and the tables which allows the people to move freely.
174. **Gay Lussac (GL) scale:** It is used in France and in the most of Europe. The absolute is rated as 100; hence proof is equal to the percentage of

alcohol in the spirit. So if whisky has 42% alcohol it is 42° proof GL.

175. **Generic Wines**: Generic wines are those wines which are named after the long established European areas. Many North American and Australian wines are labelled as Claret, Burgundy, Chablis, Graves, Hock and even Champagne.
176. **Glass rail:** It is a 3 inch width rail running along the bar tender's side for keeping the prepared drink glasses.
177. **Glassware:** Glassware is a collective term for various types of glasses which mainly found in bar section. There are various types of glassware of different shapes and sizes, all serving their own purpose. Learning which drinks belong to which glass is beneficiary to both you and your customers.
178. **Goal:** A specific intended result of a strategy; often used interchangeably with Objective.
179. **Gold Rum**: It obtains its colour either while maturing in charred oak casks or from the small quantity of caramel. It is normally aged for three years. It has more flavour than white Rum.
180. **Gold**: It is cask matured to get gold colour. Vodka is matured in the wooden cask to derive olden colour from the wood.
181. **Grading**: After harvesting the grapes are taken to winery where they are graded as per specification. In the winery the rotten & unnecessary grapes are separated from the good ones.
182. **Grand cru:** Great growth. Highest possible classification for a French wine.
183. **Grande Champagne / Grande Fine Champagne**– It is the cognac produced entirely from brandies, made from the grapes grown in Grande Champagne region.
184. **Grappe:** Cluster.
185. **Green Wines**: It is a Portuguese wine comes from vine grown on the granitic soil in the province of Minho. These are acid wines of low alcoholic content, white, rosé and red wines are made.
186. **Grey Rot**: Grey Rot sometimes known as grey mould and one of the most harmful of the fungal diseases that attacks vines. In this form of rot the Botrytis Cinera fungus rapidly spreads throughout the berry flesh and skins breaks down.
187. **Grooming:** Good Grooming is commonly used to refer to a person's appearance. It is made up of personal hygiene, tidy hair, appropriate dressing for an occasion.

188. **Gross profit or kitchen profit**: the excess of sales over the cost of food expressed as a percentage, or in financial terms.
189. **Gueridon:** A Gueridon is a movable service table or trolley on which food may be carved, filleted, flambé or prepared and served to the guest according to his/ her choice.
190. **HACCP**: Hazard Analysis and Critical Control Point (HACCP) is a systematic preventive approach to food safety and pharmaceutical safety that addresses physical, chemical, and biological hazards as a means of prevention rather than finished product inspection.
191. **Harvest Timing**: When to pick is one of the most important decision grower has to make each year.
192. **Harvesting**: The date on which the grapes are picked or gathered varies according to the local customs, climate, region, location but as far as possible a spell of fine dry weather is chosen for harvesting.
193. **Healthy Breakfast:** Breakfast should provide about 20-25% of daily nutritional requirements, and it‘s not just about having any breakfast – it‘s about having a healthy breakfast
194. **Heat Capacity:** Heat energy required to change the temperature of a specific quantity of material
195. **Heat Pump:** A refrigerant system used for heating and cooling purposes.
196. **Heat Transmission Coefficient:** Quantity of heat (usually Btu in the United States) transmitted from one substance to another per unit of time (usually 1 hr) through one unit of surface (usually 1 ft2) of building material per unit of temperature difference (usually 10F).
197. **Heat, Latent:** Heat associated with the change of state (phase) of a substance, for example, from a solid to a liquid (ice to water) or from a liquid to a gas (water to steam vapour).
198. **Heat, Sensible:** Heat associated with a change in temperature of a substance.
199. **Heat, Specific:** Ratio of the thermal capacity of a substance to the thermal capacity of water.
200. **Heat, Total:** Sum of the sensible and latent heat in a substance above an arbitrary datum, usually 320F or 00C.
201. **Hedging:** is a buying procedure. In this items are bought in advance at lower rate in speculation of rise in price in future.
202. **Herbal Tea:** These contain no tea leaf but are made up of flowers, berries, peels, seeds and roots of plant like Camellia, Rosemary, Mint, Lemon Grass, Ginseng, Milfoil, Rose Chip Tea etc.

203. **Hollowware**: The term hollowware is also a collective term for all those utensils whether apart from cutlery or crockery which used to keep or hold dishes/items, for example, water jug, entree dish, portion bowl, butter dish, etc.
204. **Horizontal Communication:** Communication between employees at the same level in their own departments or other departments, to solve problems and to share experiences is called Horizontal Communication.
205. **House Brand:** A brand of liquor a restaurant uses when guests orders cocktails without specifying the use of any particular brand.
206. **House Wines**: Any wine which is not too expensive or too cheap and can be used by any restaurant. No particular brand is branded as house wine.
207. **Humidity, Absolute:** Weight of water vapour per unit volume of a vapour-air mixture.
208. **Humidity, Percent:** Ratio of humidity in a volume of air to the maximum amount of water vapour that the air can hold at a given temperature, expressed as a percentage.
209. **Humidity, Relative (RH):** Ratio of the vapour pressure in a mixture of air and water vapour to the vapour pressure of the air when saturated at the same temperature.
210. **Humidity, Specific (Humidity Ratio):** Ratio of the weight of water vapour, grains, or pounds, per pound of dry air, at a specific temperature.
211. **Humidity:** Water vapour mixed with dry air.
212. **Hygrometer:** A mechanical device used to measure the moisture content of air.
213. **Hygroscopic:** Denoting any material that readily absorbs moisture and retains it.
214. **Hygrostat:** A mechanical device that is sensitive to changes in humidity and used to actuate other mechanical devices when predetermined limits of humidity are reached.
215. **Ice Beer:** The filtration process in beer involves chilling the beer to very low temperature so that ice crystals from in it, crystals are then removed; result is very smooth and strong beer.
216. **IGP (Indication Geographique Protegée)**: the European equivalent of the French VDP.
217. **Incentive Travel / Incentive:** A form of group travel, paid by companies to reward their top performers or customers by sending them on unforgettable trips of a few days' duration. Incentive events are always

'live'/in-person events.

218. **India pale ale (IPA):** Heavily hopped strong pale ale, originally brewed in UK for shipping to British colonies. The modern style is light coloured, hoppy ale.
219. **Indian Breakfast:** India is a country of vast diversity in culture and tradition. Food being part of culture, provides a large variety of dishes in breakfast. It includes dishes like Idli-Sambhar, Vada-Sambhar, Poori-Bhaji, Chole-Bhatoore, Nahari-Kulcha, Stuffed/Plain Paratha with Curd, Poha, Khaman Dhokla with variety pickles and Chutneys.
220. **Industrial Catering:** Preparation and service of food for employees working in factories at subsidized rates.
221. **Informal buying-** In this method, the buyer invites quotations from the suppliers for items according to their specification. The supplies are then selected and then bought.
222. **Informal Communication Network:** In this type of network, information does not flow in a particular direction, as we have seen with formal networks. The information is also not passed on through official channels such as memos, notices or bulletin boards. The information need not be circulated within the organization, but could be passed on outside the work environment, wherever co-workers or colleagues meet socially. Thus, informal networks are based more on friendship, shared personal or career interests.
223. **In-house Breakfast:** In-house breakfast is generally offered by hotel at a fixed price, dishes are laid on buffet and guests are allowed to choose their favourite breakfast dishes from the buffet.
224. **Inn:** A house providing food, beverage and accommodation.
225. **Institutional catering:** These caterers at universities, factories and office blocks provide a wide variety of food and drink to a large number of people on an ongoing basis-usually at the institution itself. The institution usually contracts with a catering company to have this service provided.
226. **Internal Control:** An accounting method, procedure, or system designed to promote efficiency, ensure the implementation of company policies, safeguard assets, and discover and avoid errors or fraud.
227. **Inventory:** It refers to stock of goods.
228. **Invoice:** An invoice is essentially a detailed bill left by vendors and outside suppliers for goods or services rendered to a company.

229. **Irish coffee:** Black coffee, to which Irish Whisky is added, topped with whipped cream.
230. **Isinglass:** Bladder of sturgeon fish used for cleaning of wine.
231. **Job Analysis:** It includes identifying the nature of the Job, prerequisite skills, educational requirements and qualification required for the job.
232. **Job description**: Job descriptionsare written statements that describe the duties, responsibilities, most important contributions and outcomes needed from a position.
233. **Job Satisfaction:** They include the qualities and the qualification required for a particular job and may also include the years of experience.
234. **Job specification**: It contains the information in relation to the qualities sought in a job candidate. Before hiring a catering department employee, a manager generally looks for various qualities like – technical skills, interpersonal skills & conceptual skills.
235. **Joven Abogado**: The word literally means 'young and adulterated'. It is not 100% agave and it is not aged. It is an example of mixto.
236. **Juice:** A liquid extracted from any raw food, usually fruits.
237. **K.O.T.**: Kitchen order Ticket
238. **Keg Cider:** It is pasteurized and filtered cider which is usually carbonated and sweetened and brilliant in appearance.
239. **Labeling**: Labelling is done according to wine.
240. **Labour Cost:** The amount paid to employees.
241. **Lagers (Bottom Fermented Beers):** The name originates from German words "Lagern" means to store. Fermentation takes place at the bottom of the vessel and the beer is stored at low temperatures for up to six months and sometime longer. Different types of ales are following:
242. **Light Bodied Wine**: The term light refers to alcoholic content, texture and weight of wine, light also refers to sensation in mouth. These are not matured in casks rather left in stainless steel or glass vats before bottling. The alcoholic content should be less than 12% for example Mâcon Blanc, Pouilly Fuissé etc.
243. **Light fixture:** The base and writing that connects to an electric power source, and a reflective surface to direct the light of a bulb.
244. **Light:** The wines should be stored in darkness as the light will affect the colour and darken the White Wine
245. **Linen:** It consists of table cloths, napkins, tray cloths, slip cloths, buffet cloths, waiter's cloths and tea cloths used in a food and beverage service

establishment.

246. **Live Event:** 'Live' events or in-person events are events whose attendees are physically present at a certain (physical) location as opposed to online or virtual events.
247. **Low Alcoholic Beers (LABs):** Beer must contain less than 1.2% alcohol by volume.
248. **Main Course:** It is the main dish of the menu.
249. **Master Budget:** It represents the forecasted targets set for the entire organization and combines all income and expenditure estimated for the organization.
250. **Maturing of Wines:** It is said that wine age in bottles and mature in the casks. Maturing takes place naturally by keeping the wine to rest in the wooden casks or barrels for one to more years according to the nature of wine, to develop flavour, aroma and colour.
251. **Maturing:** Natural process of allowing the wine to rest in oak barrels to gain maturity and character.
252. **Maturing:** Natural process of allowing the wine to rest in oak barrels to gain maturity and character.
253. **Mechanical Harvesting**: The advantages of mechanization are reduced labour costs and a quick harvest of the entire crop at optimum ripeness, but the vineyard has to be adapted to the machine chosen and the reception and fermentation facilities must be enlarge to cope with the larger amounts and quicker throughput which is costly.
254. **Medium Bodied Wine**: These are wines which are round, fairly fat with good body, texture, flavour for example Rioja (Spanish), Hermitage (French) etc.
255. **Mélange:** Blend.
256. **Menu Engineering:** It is a term used after considering the marketing of the present and future menu in designing and pricing. The Boston Consulting Group or BCG model is a matrix format to ascertain and analyses the business in the present scenario menu, considering the interest of the organization. It helps chef and F& B managers to plan profitable menu.
257. **Menu Merchandising**: It is the process by which the menu is marketed and may include various forms of presentation, language, theme and type of operation.
258. **Menu Planning**: It is a managerial activity which is marketed between the food production and service personnel having knowledge of various

cuisines, cost of preparing dishes, time for preparing dishes and the clientele.

259. **Menu:** Menu is a selling tool of an establishment which may offer both food and beverages for sale. The menu has all the dishes which are available with the price quoted beside it.
260. **Méthode Traditionnelle:** Traditional method of sparkling winemaking.
261. **Millésime:** Vintage.
262. **Mineral Water:** Usually water from natural springs impregnated with various minerals and gases.
263. **Mini bar:** A small refrigerator placed in hotel rooms from which guest may obtain water bottles, beer, cold drinks and snack which is chargeable.
264. **Mirror Platter:** It is the platter with a mirror finish a base and is normally used for enhanced presentations of salads and cold meats.
265. **Mis en bouteille au château/domaine:** Bottled at the chateau/estate.
266. **Mise en place:** It is also called as "Putting everything in its place or making ready everything" before starting service in restaurant & other food & beverage outlets.
267. **Mis-en-scene:** preparation of the environment in a restaurant.
268. **Mocktails:** A delicate mixture of non-alcoholic beverages possessing all qualities of a cocktail except alcohol.
269. **Monkey bowl:** A small multipurpose bowl used for serving accompaniments
270. **Mousseux** : Generic term for sparkling.
271. **Multiplier effect**: It can also be called as "Multiple effect". In economics, the multiplier effect or spending multiplier is the idea that an initial amount of spending leads to increased consumption spending and so results in an increase in national income greater than the initial amount of spending.
272. **Must :** Unfermented grape juice.
273. **Napery:** Tablecloths and napkins.
274. **Négociant** : A merchant who buys grapes, juice or wine from growers and sells the wines under his own label.
275. **Neutral Vodka**: It is distilled from grain or potato and highly rectified. It is filtered through activated charcoal or quartz sand.
276. **Noble Rot:** A mould which helps to remove moisture from grapes.
277. **Noble Rot**: Noble rot also known as "Pouritture Noble" in French, "Edelfaule" in German, "Muffa" in Italian and sometimes simply

"Botrytis Cineria" (boh-TRY-tiss sin-eh-RAY-ah). The Botrytis is derived from two words of Latin origin i.e. Botrytis – meaning bunch of grapes and Cineria – meaning ashes.

278. **Non Alcoholic Beers (NABs):** Beer must contain less than 0.5% alcohol by volume.
279. **Non-Verbal Communication:** Non-verbal communication can be defined as communication done without speaking or writing. It involves various types of body gestures and postures.
280. **Off-premises catering:** The caterer has a production facility but holds events somewhere else. The caterer transports all required food, beverages, personnel and equipment for event to a location usually choose by the client.
281. **Oolong:** Chinese tea fermented for a short period of time.
282. **Opportunity Cost:** It is the value of the best alternative predetermined in a situation in which a choice has to be made between several mutually exclusive alternatives with limited resources.
283. **Organic Wines**: Organic wines are a wine in which no chemical are added in the soil and good example of organic wines are made by 'Listel' in carmargne region of France.
284. **Organisation Internationale de MétrologieLégale (OIML)**: Most countries follow OIML system. It measures the strength as percentage of volume at 20°C. OIML is same as GL which is most logical of the system.
285. **Organization:** The command, control and feedback relationships among a group of people and information systems. Examples: a private company, a government agency.
286. **Organizing:** Organizing includes allocating resources, allocating duties, and incorporating systems and procedures to meet the requirements or the objectives set in the planning process.
287. **Pantry:** Storeroom, especially for crockery, cutlery etc.
288. **Pasteurization**: This is a process of sterilizing the wine, so that the microorganism it contains is destroyed. The wine in bottles is immersed upright in double boiler with water, heated to temperatures between 180 - 190° F, the immersion is for 1-2 minutes only.
289. **Payroll Analysis:** It is the process by which the salary of the staff is calculated either on a daily or monthly basis and is represented accordingly.
290. **Performance Analysis:** It is the process by which employee performance is monitored after they are trained and briefed about a

particular job.

291. **Perpetual Inventory:** - A perpetual inventory is a system in which the entire inventory is conducted and recorded and any additions or deletions are made to the total inventory as required and then recorded.
292. **Perry:** Perry is an alcoholic beverage made from fermented juice of pears, similar to the way cider is made. In the production of Perry, it is allowed to mix cider apple juice to a maximum of 25%. Perry is carbonated either by tank method or direct impregnation method.
293. **Petite Champagne** –Made entirely from brandies produced from grapes grown in the Petite Champagne region.
294. **Physical Inventory:** - In a physical inventory system, an individual counts each product which is present in the store. After the inventory is taken, the value of the products held in the inventory is also ascertained.
295. **Pilsner:** Clear, pale lagers (originally from Pilsen, Czech Republic hence the name). Morden styles are characterized by a zesty hop taste and bubbly body.
296. **Place setting:** One person's set of flatware, plates and glassware to be arranged on a dining table.
297. **Placemat:** It is a type of mat made up of paper of plastic and is used on tables with a top made of glass, wood, mica or other such finishes which are not covered with a baize cloth.
298. **Planning:** Planning is a process by which various goals and objectives are prepared and framing the steps through which the goals and objectives can be attained.
299. **Porter:** Since this ale was very popular amongst the porters of Dublin and London's Covent garden porters- thus the name. Porter is a dark style of beer developed in London from well hopped beer made from brown malt which contributes bitter taste and darker colour. It has a milder hop flavour, although higher in alcoholic content, it can be as much as 6-7% alcohol by volume.
300. **Pour Cost:** Pour cost is calculated by simply adding up the cost of the product used and dividing it by the cost of the product sold.
301. **Premier cru**: First growth. Denotes land of superior quality, but falls short of a grand cru status.
302. **Premium:** Also known as top-shelf, these items are usually the most expensive and carry a more refined reputation. These bottles are often on display on your back bar or in display cases to pique customer's interest.

303. **Preserves:** Jam, Jelly and Marmalade. Sometimes honey also.
304. **Primary Catering:** Establishments which are primarily concerned with the service of food and beverages.
305. **Propriétaire**: Estate or vineyard owner.
306. **Pruning**: It is important for controlling quantity and quality. If quantity is reduced the quality increases.
307. **Purchase order**- Is a formal written document which states all the specifications required for purchase of items. This order is sent to the supplier for supplying items.
308. **Purchasing:** It is a procurement function concerned with search, selection, purchase, receipt, storage and final use of commodity in accordance with the catering policy of the establishment.
309. **Puzzle:** A menu engineering classification of items that are particularly profitable but not very popular with the guest.
310. **Racking**: Draining the clear wine off its LEES or sediments into another vat or cask is known as Racking. In modern vinification, racking is usually conducted several times throughout the maturation period in vat or cask to make a „Clear Wine", the wine gradually throws off less and less of a deposit.
311. **Raisin**: Dried Grape.
312. **Receiving:** Process of examining shipments to determine if they should be accepted or refused.
313. **Récoltant**: Grape grower. May also refer to the person harvesting the grapes.
314. **Récolte**: Harvest (may also refers to vintage).
315. **Rectified Sprit:** A pure sprit e.g. Vodka, gin.
316. **Red Wine**: Red wine is always made from red grapes. The skins are retained in the must during all or part of fermentation to extract the pigment from grapes giving the wine red colour.
317. **Reduced Alcohol Beer:** Reduced alcohol beer is beer with little or no alcohol content. Most low alcohol beers are lagers but there are some low alcohol ales. Low alcohol beer is also known as light beer, non alcoholic beer or near-beer etc. In the U.S.A, beverages containing less than 0.5% alcohol by volume are legally called non-alcoholic beer may be legally sold to minors in many American states. In United Kingdom there are two different categories apply:
318. **Refrigeration or Cold Stabilization**: The young wine is pumped into a refrigeration unit to stabilize the wine.

319. **Registration Fee:** Cost of attending a conference. Fees can vary according to the time of registration, level of participation and also membership type.
320. **Remwage:** Process of cleaning the wine by freezing wine bottles in wooden racks at an angle.
321. **Reposado (Rested/Aged)** : It is aged in oak casks for a period of two months to one year. The same cask used for maturing Bourbon whiskey may be used for aging tequila. This process mellows the tequila and adds colour to the some extent.
322. **Risk Purchase:** If supplier fails, the item is purchased from other agencies & the difference in cost is recovered from the first supplier.
323. **Rosé Wine:** Rose wine is made from red grapes, never a mixture of red and white grapes, as is commonly thought. The skins are kept in must for only a short time (12-36 Hours) to impart the light pink colour.
324. **Rouge:** Red.
325. **Sake:** Sake is national drink of Japan. Sake is an alcoholic beverage made by fermenting rice that has been polished to remove the bran. It is brewed and fermented drink made from rice in Japan.
326. **Salad Bar:** It is self – service concept in which each guest is given the opportunity to prepare his or her own salad from an attractive array of fresh vegetables and fruit that have been cleaned and sliced.
327. **Salver:** Tray, usually, round and made of silver, on which drinks etc are presented.
328. **Scheduling:** It is the time frame in which employees report to work, and perform and complete their work.
329. **Secondary Caterings:** The provision of food and beverage is a part of another business.
330. **Seminar:** most of the time organized by a private company with the intention of training and exchanging on a specific topic, the seminar gathers, without imposed regularity, professionals that may be members of this company.
331. **Service area:** Service areas are platform or place where foods are kept after final cooking, so that steward come & receive the prepared food & serve to the guest.
332. **Service of Cigars:** Cigar should be offered in their own boxes to allow the guest to choose his own. The type of cigar will be printed on box. The guest having chosen the cigar he/she wishes, the server should offer to remove the band. A cigar cutter should be used to cut the cigar. The

server should then offer to light the cigar of guests. (Cigar should be offered at the end of meal with coffee)

333. **Serviette:** It is a type of cloth which is used by the stewards during service.
334. **SGN (Sélection de Grains Nobles)**: Selection of noble berries. Refers to wines made from grapes affected by noble rot, or botrytized. SGN wines are sweet dessert wines with rich, concentrated flavours. Some of the finest botrytized wines are literally picked berry by berry in successive "*tries*" (French for selections).
335. **Side Board:** furniture central to an operation at a station.
336. **Sikes Scale**: It is used in Britain and the commonwealth countries. Bartholomew sykes introduced a hydrometer which calculated that 57.1% of alcohol is equivalent to 100° proof. So 100% alcohol is equal to 175° proof.
337. **Silverware:** A term used for cutlery made up of silver or plated silver.
338. **Smoking Cigars**: There is an art involved in smoking a cigar, it should never be inhaled. The end with joins the mouth is "V" shaped or straight cut with care and never bitten off. The paper band must be removed before smoking a cigar. The cigar is then lit evenly all sides with a match and never with a lighter, which may taint it with aroma of spirit. The butt end is bitter due to the accumulation of oil and tannin, therefore cigar is never smoked to the end.
339. **Sommeliers:** This is the person to handle the ordering and serving of wine. They must be thoroughly knowledgeable about their own wine lists and competent in helping guest to select wine appropriate to the food they order.
340. **Soup tureen**: Deep Covered dish from which soup is served at the table using a ladle.
341. **Sparkling Wine**: These are sparkling in appearance due to presence of CO2 gas and thus give off bubbles of gas. The best known is "champagne", it is produced by a complicated process. Sparkling wine is one where natural gas from fermentation is retained in the bottle or one where the wine has been artificially impregnated with gas.
342. **Specialty restaurant:** A fine dining out let in which service is both formal and stylish.
343. **Spiced Rum**: it is dark in colour, flavoured, and coloured with spices and caramel. Inexpensive white rum may be coloured with liberal caramel.

344. **Squash:** Edible fruit of the gourd family, divided into two categories – (1) summer (2) winter.
345. **Stakeholder:** An individual or group with an interest in the success of an organization in delivering intended results and maintaining the viability of the organization's products and services. Stakeholders influence programs, products, and services
346. **Standard Buffet:** Platters or chafing dishes of food are placed on centralized tables and guest serves themselves.
347. **Standard Cost:** This is the cost of a product worked out for a standard portion.
348. **Standard Recipe**: A standard of recipe is prepared by every establishment so that each chef/bartenders prepares the dish/drink with the same ingredients..
349. **Standard yield-** Standard Yield of a particular food item may be defined as usable part of that particular food product after initial preparation, or the edible part of the product after preparation and cooking.
350. **Stateroom:** A private cabin on a passenger ship.
351. **Station**: A set of four or five table in a restaurant.
352. **Still wine:** Wine which lacks carbonation.
353. **Stopover/transfer:** when a group of passengers stay for more than 24 hours at the same place, we use the word stopover. If the passenger does not leave the airport or stays less than 24 hours in the country, we use the word transfer.
354. **Stout:** Stout has high hop content and a strong malt taste. The malt used for stout is also first roasted, which gives this beer its very dark colour. Has a smooth malty flavour and creamy consistency. One of the best known stouts is Guinness of Ireland.
355. **Suggestive Selling:** A sales technique used by servers to increase guest satisfaction and sales by encouraging guests to order extras like appetizers, cocktails, mocktails, desserts etc.
356. **Sulphuring**: It is frequently necessary to add SO2↑ fairly early in the fermentation process to prevent the air from oxidizing the must and converting the alcohol into vinegar.
357. **Supérieur**: Wine with higher (superior) alcohol content as a result of being made fromriper grapes.
358. **Sweet Wine**: Sweet wine produced by grapes having high sugar content, as in these wines even after fermentation a lot of sugar is still left, which is not consumed by yeast, the sugar left renders a very sweet wine.

359. **Table d hote** - It is a restricted menu, offering small number of course with limited choice of food in each course, fix selling price and dishes being ready at a set time.
360. **Table d'hote Menu:** Table d'hote menu is a restricted menu, offering a small number of courses (three of four) a limited choice within each course, fixed selling price and all the dishes being ready at a set time.
361. **Tableware:** A term used for all pieces of flatware, cutlery and hollowware.
362. **Tender**- This type of formal buying method. In this sealed structural documents invited by organization from respective sellers for a fixed type of item and according to fixed specification.
363. **Trappist:** Beer brewed in Trappist monasteries, usually under the supervision of monks. It is a kind of strong beer with 6-12% alcohol by volume; six Belgian breweries produce this beer, which is complex and unpasteurized.
364. **Traveller's Cheques:** These are issued by reputed banks to avoid the risk of carrying cash.
365. **Triplicate Method:** in this method the order is taken in three copies. The top copy goes to the supply point, second copy is sent to the cashier for billing; third copy is retained by the server as a means of reference during service.
366. **Ullage:** It is the space between the cork and the top of the wine. It is also referred as weeping wine.
367. **Under bar:** This is the area inside the bar counter, under the front bar, which holds the essential equipments and liquor supplies required for making drinks.
368. **Upward Communication:** It is non directive in nature. Effective upward communication is possible only when organizations empower their employees and allow them to participate freely in decision making. Through this type of communication employees can communicate information to their superiors freely and can voice their opinion.
369. **Variable Cost:** The cost which tends to vary indirect proportion to change in the volume of output or turnover.
370. **Varietal Wines**: These are the wines of North America, which are labelled after the main grapes variety in the bottle. Single grape variety is used for making wine, best known examples are:
371. **Venue Manager:** The person in charge of a location or event space.
372. **Venue:** A place to hold your event.

373. **Verbal Communication:** Communication done through spoken words is called verbal communication

374. **Vertical communication:** Vertical communication occurs between various hierarchies. It may be upward or downward. For example manager to employee, general manager to managers, foreman to machine operator, head of the department to cashiers, etc.

375. **Vibration:** The wines should be permitted to sleep peacefully without agitation. The bottles should be completely still. There should be no vibrations of the floor.

376. **Vine Training**: The manner in which a vine is trained will guide the size, shape and height of the plant towards reaping maximum benefits from the local conditions of aspects and climate. Vines can be trained high to avoid ground frost or low to hug any heat that may be reflected by stony soils at night.

377. **Vinification:** The process which converts grapes into wine.

378. **Vintage Wines**: The French word "vintage" means harvest, although any wine is a vintage wine as any year can be vintage year. However some year's climate is so good that the government in France declares it as vintage year for particular region.

379. **Vintage:** Year when the grapes density is constant, hence quality of wine is superior to wine from other year.

380. **Viticulture Sprays:** The use of sprays was once confined to protecting the vine against pests and diseases and for controlling weeds but now they have addition uses. Some sprays deliberately induce two disorder called Millerandage and Coulure to reduce the yield and increase quality.

381. **Waffles and pancakes:** Waffles and pancakes, also called *griddle cakes* and *hot cakes*, are made from pourable batters. Pancakes are made on a griddle, while waffles are made on a special tool called a *waffle iron*.

382. **Waiter's friend:** Tool that is a combination of bottle opener and corkscrew.

383. **Weighing**: The grapes are weighed to determine the quantity required for fermentation.

384. **Welcome Signage:** A sign that introduces or welcomes visitors to the venue / event.

385. **Well:** Spirits used when patrons don't name a spirit brand in a drink order. (Example: Gin and tonic). Your well bottles are often the best deal for both the bar and the customer.

386. **White and Light Rum**: It has very little flavour and is colourless. Its colourless and flavourless feature has made this variety perfect ingredient for cocktails. Most of the white rums come from Puerto Rico.
387. **White Wine**: White wine is made from white grapes, in rare cases also made from red grapes.
388. **Wine:** An alcoholic beverage made from partial or complete fermentation of grape juice.
389. **Work flow**. A workflow consists of a sequence of connected steps. It is a depiction of a sequence of operations, declared as work of a person, a group of persons, an organization of staff, or one or more simple or complex mechanisms.
390. **Workshop:** workshops generally have more hands-on and group activities. The sessions are quite interactive and require individuals to participate.
391. **Wrapper**: Wrapper or outer covering of cigar consists of a ribbon leaf rolled spirally around the cigar bunch. Wrapper leaf must be strong, elastic and silky in texture and of even colour and it must possess good flavour and burning properties. It is most expensive leaf used in cigars.
392. **Yield management**. Yield management is the practice of maximizing profits from the sale of perishable items like food, hotel rooms / airline seats, by controlling price and inventory and differentiating product & service.
393. **Zero-based Budgeting:** It involves budgeting from the beginning without any reference to historical data.

CHAPTER FORTY-FIVE

Unit 4: Career in Food and Beverage Industry

Preparing for a career:

Persons involved in this industry also need to have knowledge about planning and establishing the physical facility for food preparation and service. Some of the personal skills essential to succeed in the food service industry are: An interest in food and regular update of trends in national and international cuisines. Ability to have a good focus on quality, production, sanitation and food cost controls. Ability to establish, maintain and enforce consistently high performance standards. Good communication and interaction skills (Ability to communicate effectively, both verbally and in writing, to an array of diverse internal and external clients). Good organising abilities with an eye for detail. Pleasant, cheerful and energetic personality. Good command over English, other preferred languages especially foreign languages. Ability to be on your feet for long hours.

Scope:

Within this one vast industry, there are different kinds of jobs requiring different kinds of skills. Some who have the appropriate training may work in a palatial '7'-star establishment, with a luxurious atmosphere and come into contact with famous and important people of many nationalities. It is an international industry, providing opportunities for trained persons to be able to work abroad for some or throughout their careers. There is demand for well-trained experienced professionals who can participate in opening hotels and other catering establishments in different countries. Other opportunities to work in this field are in the catering units providing food to cruise ships, airlines and the railways. Large private hospitals also have catering managers in their kitchens, cafeterias and hostels. Most departments in the catering industry are complicated specialisations requiring a great deal of work, dedication, practice and mastery. These are basic qualities that must be possessed by any young person who wants to embark on a career.

Careers in the Catering and Food Service Industry:

In this industry, a person can work in various positions such as Food Service Supervisor, Cafetaria Manager, Catering Manager, Production Manager, Purchase Manager and Food Service Director /Asst Food Service Director. Placement can be obtained in independent restaurants, corporate restaurants, franchised restaurants, managed services in educational institutions, health care industry, e.g., hospitals, industrial canteens, catering services in travel related transport systems such as air (flight kitchens), trains, cruise lines (ship).

Persons who are interested in cooking, who have good culinary skills, with additional and specialised training can work as Executive Chef, Sous Chef, Chef Tournant, Station Chef. Besides this, there are vast opportunities to take up catering independently. One can set up independent restaurants, corporate restaurants, franchised restaurants.

Also, one can undertake managed services for education, healthcare, business and industry (catering meals at work places), catering in amusement parks, catering in national, state, and regional parks, catering for adventure/eco–tourism, catering for theme parties, product launches, banquets, official functions, etc., preparing and supplying special, nutritionally modified meals/health foods that are low in Calories, fat, and cholesterol, high in fiber and nutrition, breakfast foods that are healthier. Media, particularly television, has stimulated interest in cooking and the different food patterns of various cultures. In fact, the scope of the food service industry is unlimited.

About The Author

Dr Anshumali Pandey, PhD, Author.

Dr. Anshumali Pandey, is a renowned & reliable name in the field of Education, Hospitality, Tourism and Tribal Food. He is a Teacher and Chef by profession, and also an Author, a Business Auditor, and an avid culinary traveller to the Indian Sub continental hinterlands. Dr. Anshumali Pandey is a Hospitality Educator (PhD) who specialises in Higher Education, Office Administration, Pay roll, HR, Labour Laws, Audit, and Procurement & Tender Process. He is an Author with 36 Publications consisting of 21 Books.

The books written by Dr Anshumali Pandey are essentially a banquet arising from an experience of over 25 years of Professional life and have boiled down to crisp and accurate writing on his favourite subjects. Hospitality Sector champion requires to be a specialist in many fields and

Dr Pandey is one of them. His knowledge is evident from the spectrum of subjects which he has chosen for his books so far, which ranges from being a specialist chef, to Master of Human resources, to Education and to love for children, and topped with Spirituality.

Books written by the Author are: – (Available on Amazon, Flipkart, etc.)

1. Theory of Indian Cookery
2. Beauty and Irony of Silvassa Tourism
3. A Short Indian Food Story
4. Be Your Own Guide to Indian Cuisine
5. Cookery Fundamentals
6. History of Indian Food
7. The Great Indian Story Book for Children
8. Personal Budget: Easy Work Book
9. Online Classes Log Book
10. Dictionary Making Work Book for School Children
11. The Lazy Bed
12. Hindu Dharm (In Hindi Language)
13. Where is my coffee?
14. Your First Job is Never your Last (Volume 1)
15. You are Almost There (Quick Fix Resume and Interview Hacks)
16. Working for the Enemy? - A lesson in Career Management
17. Public Speaking for the Young
18. A Date With Coffee
19. How to be The Best Hotel Front Office Employee
20. Diploma in Food Production, The complete Syllabus
21. **Diploma in F&B Service, The Complete Syllabus**

This book "Diploma in F&B Service, The Complete Syllabus" is written with an aim to help the Students, the Teachers, and all those would be chefs and managers who could not get a formal education in the field of Commercial Food, Service and Catering.

Connect with me: anshumali.pandey@gmail.com
https://notionpress.com/author/337004

Please scan this QR code to connect securely with the Author and Books.

Printed by Libri Plureos GmbH in Hamburg,
Germany